# THE INSTITUTIONALIZATION OF ISLAM IN SOUTHERN SENEGAL

## AFRICAN PERSPECTIVES

Kelly Askew, Laura Fair, and Pamila Gupta
Series Editors

*The Institutionalization of Islam in Southern Senegal: Intermarriage, Qur'anic Education, and Jihād*
Aly Dramé

*The Education Alibi: Tracing Education's Entanglements across Contemporary Africa*
Elizabeth Cooper, Erdmute Alber, and Wandia Njoya, Editors

*The Homeowner Ideology: Economic (F)Utility of Real Property Rights in Four African Cities*
Singumbe Muyeba

*Typologies of Humor in African Literatures*
Adwoa A. Opoku-Agyemang

*Between HIV Prevention and LGBTI Rights: The Political Economy of Queer Activism in Ghana*
Ellie Gore

*Protest Arts, Gender, and Social Change: Fiction, Popular Songs, and the Media in Hausa Society across Borders*
Ousseina D. Alidou

*The Imaginative Vision of Abdilatif Abdalla's* Voice of Agony
Abdilatif Abdalla, edited by Annmarie Drury

*Congo Style: From Belgian Art Nouveau to African Independence*
Ruth Sacks

*Lagos Never Spoils: Nollywood and Nigerian City Life*
Connor Ryan

*Continuous Pasts: Frictions of Memory in Postcolonial Africa*
Sakiru Adebayo

A complete list of titles in the series can be found at www.press.umich.edu

# The Institutionalization of Islam in Southern Senegal

## *Intermarriage, Qur'anic Education, and Jihād*

Aly Dramé

University of Michigan Press
Ann Arbor

Published in the United States of America by the
University of Michigan Press
First published July 2025

A CIP catalog record for this book is available from the British Library.

*Library of Congress Cataloging-in-Publication data has been applied for.*

ISBN 978-0-472-07750-2 (hardcover : alk. paper)
ISBN 978-0-472-05750-4 (paper : alk. paper)
ISBN 978-0-472-90515-7 (open access ebook)

DOI: https://doi.org/10.3998/mpub.11535757

Authorized Representative: Easy Access System Europe, Mustamäe tee 50, 10621 Tallinn, Estonia, gpsr.requests@easproject.com

The University of Michigan Press's open access publishing program is made possible thanks to additional funding from the University of Michigan Office of the Provost and the generous support of contributing libraries.

*I dedicate this book to the memories of my brother Ibrahima Djiby Dramé (1955–2014); James F. Searing (1953–2014), my outstanding academic advisor at the University of Illinois at Chicago; and El Hadji Manding Dramé (1941–2017) who generously hosted me in Karantaba. May God Bless Their Souls!*

## CONTENTS



Digital materials related to this title can be found on the Fulcrum platform via the following citable URL: https://doi.org/10.3998/mpub.11535757

# FIGURES AND TABLES

# NOTE ON ORTHOGRAPHY

I have written this book by relying on different languages and cultures, given the ethnic heterogeneity that has characterized the Casamance at large for many centuries. In travelers' accounts, general publications, and archival documents many terms, such as ethnonyms, hydronyms, and patronyms, are written differently. The spelling of the ethnonym Bainounk, for instance, obeys no orthographic conventions in European written sources. Most travelers to Senegambia heard this name and spelled it in specific ways based on local sounds and accents (Banyun, Bayum, Bagnoun, Banhum, Bainounk, or Banyuk). To facilitate the reading, I have transcribed most of the words used in the book, following the official system now in use in contemporary Senegal (Diola, not Jola; Sédhiou, not Seju; and Diéli, not Jeli, for example). In addition, whenever necessary, I have doubled the vowels to respect the elongated pronunciation. This rule does not apply to foreign terms in Arabic and other languages as well as sources cited throughout the book, with few exceptions.

# ACKNOWLEDGMENTS

The research, writing, and production of this book would have been impossible without the considerable aid and support I received from innumerous people; I will never be able to pay the debt of gratitude I owe them. To all these individuals, including those whose names I have not mentioned only because of space constraints, I say *dieureudieuf* and *alabarkaa*, or thank you in Wolof and Mandingo, respectively!

It was my good fortune to have Dr. James F. Searing as my academic advisor at the University of Illinois at Chicago (UIC). During those years Jim tirelessly went above and beyond the call of duty to accommodate me in ways I will never forget for the remainder of my life. This included welcoming my wife and I to his family vacation home in Nova Scotia, Canada, where we spent a wonderful time with his wife Trish and his two sons, Alexander and Keith. Jim and I became great friends until the very last moment of his life, and his sudden death in 2014 was a painstaking experience for me. I also thank Professors Kirk H. Hoppy, James Sack, Lynett Jackson, Lansiné Kaba who passed away in 2023, and all the instructors and administrators who contributed to my education at UIC.

I would also like to thank the Casamançais who warmly welcomed me to their towns and villages and shared their best historical recollections with me. This extensive list of people includes imams, village chiefs, elected officials and family mothers, in addition to my relatives, old colleagues, former students, and joking partners. My special thanks to my hardworking fieldwork assistants, Alioune Badara Sarr, Abdoulaye Cissé and Ibrahima Mané in Sédhiou, as well as the high school students who sacrificed their Easter break (Fêtes de Pâcques) to help me conduct oral interviews across the Middle Casamance.

Since 2006 my colleagues at Dominican University have consistently been supportive of me. I thank particularly Liesl Orenic, Rosalind Hayes, Peter Taylor, Douglas Keberlein-Gutiérrez, John Menet, John Jenks, Samina Hadi-Tabassum, Jeniffer Morrissey, Sister Marcella Hermesdorf, Richard

Calabrese, and Deans Jeff Carlson and Chad Rodman of the Rosary College of Arts and Sciences. Robert Launay, Omar Guéye, Papa Seydina Ndiaye, Assan Sarr, John Glover, Joy Gehner, El Hadji Samba Diallo, Mara Liechtman, and Siacka Dramé were among a good number of friends and colleagues who inspired me through their constructive criticisms and suggestions.

Throughout my undergraduate and graduate studies at Université Cheikh Anta Diop in Dakar many professors like Mohamed Mbodji, Joseph Ki-Zerbo, Mamadou Diouf, Boubacar Barry, Mamadou Fall, Abdoulaye Bathily, and Iba Der Thiam were a powerful source of inspiration for me. Most notably, I cannot remember to this day how many times I have benefitted from professor Diouf's aid and encouragements since the early 1980s in our common hometown of Rufisque. I thank these scholars for their professionalism and commitment to taking good care of their students.

Many thanks to professors Rudolph Ware, Derek Peterson, and Kelly Askew for their impeccable collaboration during my Mellon Sawyer Foundation fellowship at the University of Michigan in Ann Arbor. Thanks also to the entire staff at the University of Michigan Press, including Dr. Ellen Bauerle, Marcella Landri, Marcia Labrenz, Sarah Berg, Professor Askew, Mary K. Hashman, Delilah McCrea, and Jamie Jones, for their time and consideration. I have a wide range of friends, colleagues, and relatives between Senegal, Europe, and America who have constantly helped me carry out my dreams and visions in multiple ways; I owe them a large debt of gratitude.

My special thanks to my extended Johnson family in Chicago for their outpouring love and support: mother Marjorie, Vanessa, one of the best educators in Illinois, and Michael senior and his family. Finally, I don't know how many times my wife, Valerie, had to wake up in the middle of the night to help me resolve extremely complex computer issues. I cannot find the right words to express my deepest gratitude to Val, whose love, patience, understanding, and support paved the way for the completion of this book. May all these special people find throughout these pages the expression of my heartfelt gratitude!

# Introduction

This book investigates the institutionalization of Islam in the Casamance region of Senegal from the first half of the seventeenth century, when the original Mandinka Muslim settlements began to mushroom, to the second half of the nineteenth century, when the region was included in the French colonial empire. It is about how new spaces were negotiated, acquired, and incorporated into the Islamic world or Dar-al-Islam by early Muslim clerics who immigrated to this region. I have noticed some lingering, interconnected gaps in historical studies of the Islamization paradigms in Senegambia. The common thread that weaves these gaps together is a propensity to concentrate on the populations of northern Senegambia in the period since the mid-nineteenth century.

The early Mandinka settlements of the Middle Casamance are among the oldest Muslim townships, with the oldest mosques and Qur'anic schools in Senegambia, but historians have neglected to fully consider their contributions to the expansion of Islam in this region. This book seeks to correct this lacuna by emphasizing the pioneering role of Karantaba in this process. Fodé Héraba Dramé, a cleric who hailed from Mali, founded this township on the south bank of the Casamance River by the 1630s. This happened centuries before the establishment of many famous Islamic centers of northern Senegambia. As we shall see in chapter 2, Karantaba's name alone is a powerful indication of what has been its religious orientation since its creation. This long-term perspective will help us better reframe the debates about the development of Islam in Senegambia.[1]

Within the past forty years Senegambia has occupied a crucial place as one of the two main sources of paradigms of Islamization in West Africa. The first, Sufism (*tassawuf*, Arabic), is the mystical branch of Islam. This term etymologically emanates from the rudimentary woolen cloth (*suf*, Arabic)

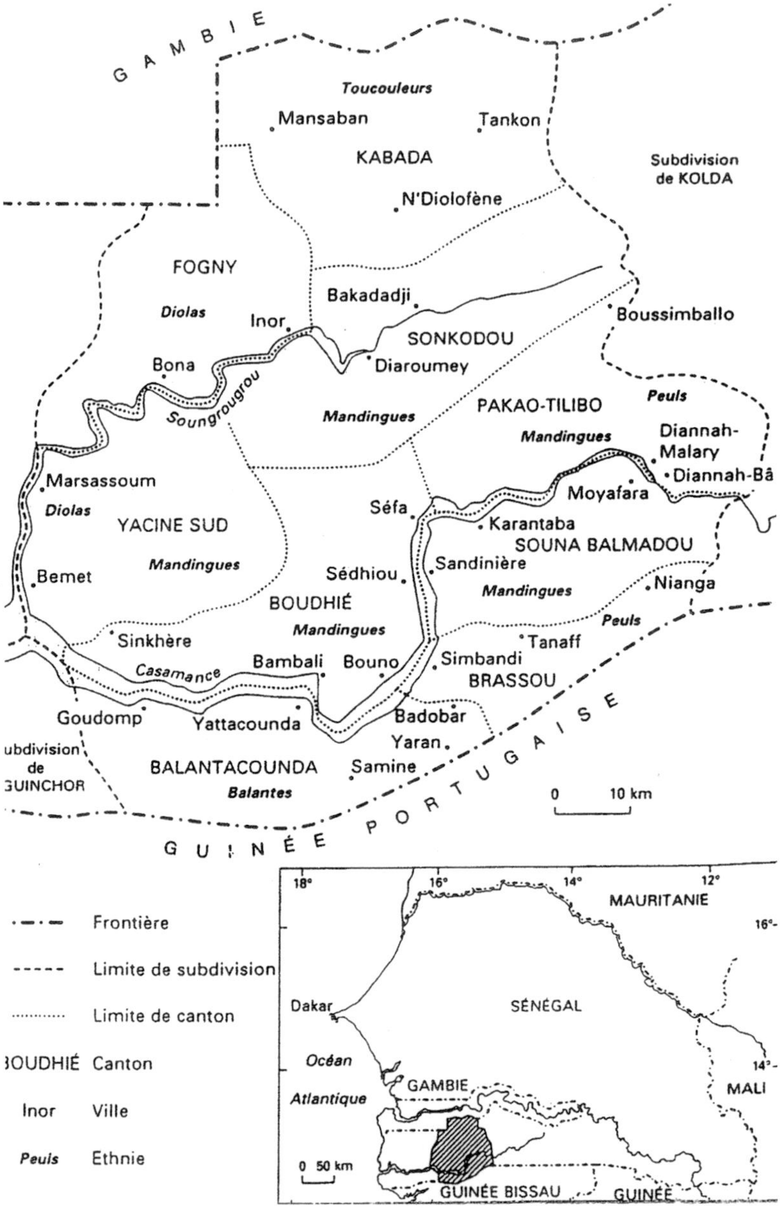


Figure 1. Map of Colonial Seju with its nine cantons. Until 1909 Seju (Sédhiou ) served as the capital of French colonial Casamance. This map shows the different local communities that were part of colonial Seju at this time, including the old Islamic center of Karantaba, located on the south bank of the Casamance River. Courtesy of the Archives of the Republic of Senegal, 2G/50–105.

worn by early Muslims as a symbol of modesty. It is difficult to pinpoint when Sufism exactly began, but during the time of the Umayyad Caliphate (661–850 CE) theologians like Hasan al-Basri urged Muslims to exercise more humility in practicing Islam.[2] Devout preachers took Sufism to the next level, organizing their congregations more pragmatically between the twelfth and the fourteenth centuries. Among the most famous were Abu Hamid al-Ghazzali (1058–1111), Abdul Qadir al-Gilani (1078–1166), Ibn al-Arabi (1165–1240) and Jalal al-Diñ Rumi (1207–73). In the following centuries, Sufism kept looming large until it became a standard practice, which explains the plethora of Sufi orders (*turuq*, sing *tariqa*) that are scattered around the world today.[3]

Based on Sufi teachings, the leaders of of these orders (*cheikh* or *shaykh*) are saints who can perform innumerous miracles thanks to their God-given, hidden knowledge (*batin*) and blessing (*baraka*).[4] They can subsequently transform into genuine Muslims those who approach, watch, imitate and venerate them not exclusively during their lives but also after their deaths. In this master-disciple relationship, the disciples must scrupulously obey their masters, a prerequisite for meriting their *baraka* on earth and thereafter. As the Qur'an stipulates, people who believe in God must fear God and seek a spiritual guide (*wasila*) who will lead them to God.[5] Sufi devotional practices encompass the acquisition of divine knowledge via education and worship (*marifat*); the search for the most perfect chemistry with God (*ihsan*); the remembrance of God by meditatively reciting God's numerous names (*zikr*); the daily performance of special litanies (*wird*); the holding of public festivals honoring saints' accomplishments and making pious visits to their burial grounds (*ziara*); and the commemoration of the Prophet's birthday (*mawlud*).[6]

From the Middle East Sufism little by little established foothold in sub-Saharan Africa in the past several centuries, but its practice as a mass movement in regions like West Africa still deserves more scholarly scrutiny.[7] The oldest Sufi order in Senegambia specifically is the Khadiriyya, founded in the twelfth century by Al-Gilani. Kounta clerics like Sidy al-Moukhtar and their disciples were among the most active propagators of this order across the broader Senegambia particularly since the second part of the eighteenth century.[8] The others were either created or popularized while European colonial rule was slowly developing its tentacles in West Africa during the second half of the nineteenth century, like the Mouridiyya by Cheikh Amadou Bamba and the Tidjaniyya by Cheikhou Oumar Tall followed by El Hadji Malick Sy. These orders have become increasingly popular since the deaths of their founders or propagators in the first part of the twentieth century.[9] Thanks to the cumulative experiences of these dedicated clerics, the vast majority of Senegambian Muslims belong to these brotherhoods today.[10]

The second paradigm falls in the category of the clerics' wars (*la guerre des marabouts*, French), a wave of Islamic reform movements that erupted in West Africa during the eighteenth and nineteenth centuries. The Moorish marabout Nasir al-Din set the tone for Islamic reform through military jihãd in Senegambia and surrounding areas in the 1690s; he died while confronting some Mauritanian warrior groups a few years later, putting a damper on his political ambitions.[11] Al-din's death did not prevent other Islamic movements from extending their reach in the next centuries, with the eruption of revolutions called "holy wars."[12] For the most part, these were sparked by a burning desire to end the intense economic exploitation of African peasant communities by the ruling classes and their associates; abuses directly or indirectly associated with the slave trade; and efforts to replace religious syncretism with a puritan brand of Islam.

Some jihãds resulted from the determination to overthrow preexisting governments (usually monarchies or dynastic states) and then replace them with new Muslim governments. Others culminated in new political structures in the form of Islamized monarchies, more decentralized systems of rule by clerics, or a mixture of both. In the Wolof states and in Haussaland, for instance, jihãd leaders planned to dismantle the old political apparatus, blaming its representatives for intolerable actions like enslaving their fellow Muslims. Certain jihãds led to the formation of theocratic states, as in Fouta Diallon in 1725, Fouta Tooro in 1776, and Sokoto in 1814.[13] One scholar made a similar categorization by distinguishing two "Islamization paradigms" in Africa: the peaceful one championed by El Hadji Salim Souwaré and the military one led by Nasir Al-Din.[14] In the Casamance and other areas in Senegambia, Muslim leaders from different generations, doctrinal affiliations, and ethnic backgrounds participated in these movements.[15]

A third Islamization paradigm preconizing another way of being Muslim through the implementation of a more puritan model of Islam is currently taking shape in the empirical literature. The roots of this alternative model partly go back at least to the time of the Hanbali theologian Ahmad Ibn Taymiyya, who probably lived between the thirteenth and fourteenth centuries. As a Sufi master himself, Taymiyya probably did not indiscriminately criticize the entire Sufi leadership of his time. His criticisms were most likely directed at those who seized their position of authority in furtherance of their own agenda, to the detriment of the real teachings of Islam.[16]

Muhammad Ibn Abd al-Wahhab (1703–92 C.E), who spearheaded an anti-Sufi movement geared toward reforming Islam in Arabia, was inspired by Taymiyya's worldview. From Al-Wahhab's perspective, the Qur'an, the prophetic tradition (*sunna*), and the Prophet's sayings and deeds (*ahadith*) are the only authentic sources of Islamic knowledge; and the Prophet and his Four Orthodox Caliphs (*al-khulafa' al-raashidoon*) understood the raison d'être of these sources better than any other individuals. This means Muslims must fulfill their religious duties by exclusively imitating the lifestyles of the original ancestors (*salafs*).[17] Thus, Al-Wahhab denounced many important Sufi rituals as useless innovations (*bida*) or expressions of polytheism (*shirk*), including the celebration of the Prophet's birthday.[18] Within the past two centuries, other clerics like Rashid Rida, Jamal al-Afghani, and Muhammad Abduh followed al-Wahhab's lead.[19]

Since between the 1960s and '70s particularly Salafism has slowly expanded from the Middle East to other parts of the Islamic world, including Muslim-majority countries in Africa. But in Senegal, this movement began much earlier thanks to efforts by some men who sojourned in the greater Middle East, like El Hadji Mahmoud Bâ and Cheikh Touré. After finishing his graduate studies in Saudi Arabia and performing the hajj in Mecca, the former returned home to be a Qur'anic teacher in Fouta Tooro in the 1940s.[20] The latter, who came from the village school of Fass-Touré in the region of Thiés, created the Union Culturelle Musulmane (UCM) in the early 1950s after his studies in Egypt. This theoretically aimed at freeing Senegalese Muslims from French colonial rule and any other type of oppression.[21]

The following decades witnessed the appearance of new Islamic groups like the Harakat al-falah (HAF) movement, the Jama'atou ibadou rahmane (JIR), and the Association of Muslim Students of Dakar (AMSD).[22] Senegalese popular memory often lumps together the members of these groups by categorizing all of them as "*ibadou*" or "*arabisants*." In truth, they differ in a number of ways, including their denominations, modus operandi, and foreign affiliation.[23] One common denominator consists of implicitly or explicitly dismissing the preexisting Sufi groups (*l'islam confrérique*), calling them too obsolete and too hermetic to ideas of modernization.[24] Because of it, these new groups celebrate Islamic holidays, perform the daily prayers, educate their children, teach Islam and the Arabic language, run their mosques, and dress publicly in specific ways.[25] Many groups get material and financial support from Salafi organizations from the oil-rich countries of the Middle East: the distribution of Qur'anic manuscripts, the building of mosques, libraries, and schools, and scholarships for study abroad programs, for example.[26]

There were times when the *ibadou* were stereotyped in various ways, including avoiding them in public or referring to them in pejorative terms, and these Senegalese still embody this essentialism. However, with the passage of time, many others have come to tolerate the *ibadou* by dint of seeing their own relatives, classmates, friends, neighbors, and colleagues embrace this religious lifestyle.[27] Today their membership transcends age, gender, ethnic, economic, and professional backgrounds; and it is nearly impossible to go any public place across Senegal now without noticing the presence of the *ibadou*.[28]

These reform groups have undeniably grown in importance numerically, while recruiting many new members from *l'islam confrérique*, which means every ground gained by one denomination may become a ground lost by the other.[29] But so far these breakthroughs have not prevented *l'islam confrérique* from remaining the dominant form of religious affiliation in Senegambia. Nonetheless, as one expert warns, it is not impossible to see the formation of a theocratic state in Senegal someday, despite its old tradition of secularism.[30] As one self-identified Salafi student put it, within a few decades from now, Islam in Senegal will be dominated by a battle of legitimacy between Salafi and Sufi organizations, and those who can provide "the best road map to Heaven" will probably control the future of millions of Muslims.[31]

The premise of this book is not to deny the vitality of these Islamization paradigms in the wider Senegambia. Meanwhile, the book argues that centuries before the mass movements represented by militant Islam and Sufi organizations in the eighteenth and nineteenth centuries, some Muslim clerics had sowed the seeds of Islam through peaceful means in the Casamance. Scholars have documented the role of immigration, interethnic marriages, and landlord-stranger interactions in reshaping the course of West African history since the arrival of Portuguese mariners in the mid-fifteenth century.[32] But this literature has neglected the missionary work accomplished by Muslim clerics in the Bainounk chiefdoms that existed in the Middle Casamance since the precolonial period.

Most significantly, the book calls attention to what I call the Karantaba landlord paradigm that has previously been overshadowed by the Sufi and jihād ones in the historical literature of Senegambia. These old client-patron interactions were based on a double tradition of intermarriage. The first was interfaith marriages between local Bainounk women and Muslim clerics who immigrated to the Middle Casamance and demonstrated their professional skills. These marriage ties helped Muslims get land concessions that became the foundation of the Dar al-Islam in this region. The second was the moment when Muslims switched roles by becoming progressively landlords for other immigrants to their new homelands. Muslims took this opportunity to consolidate the foundation of their new homelands, initiating another tradition based on interlineage marriages among themselves.[33] I argue that these repeated processes of interfaith marriages, Muslim intermarriages, Islamic education, and later military jihâd provided the vehicles for the institutionalization of Islam in the Middle Casamance and surrounding areas.

At the center of Karantaba's history was a triptych: a tree (*taabo*) serving as a spiritual guiding light; a moment of mystical illumination; and a cleric dedicated to serving God, in this case Fodé Héraba Dramé who migrated from Daramane (Daramané), a clerical township situated in the region of Kayes, in southwestern Mali.[34] Like many of his contemporary clerics, he was affiliated with the Khadiriyya before leaving his homeland. I describe him as another representative of the pacifist tradition in West African Islam, or of "the jihãd without the sword," like El Hadji Salim Souwaré, the patron saint of the Diakhanké clerical network.[35] Contrary to the distinguished title of shaykh (*cheikh,* Senegal) carried by some emblematic figures of West African Islam, the *fodé* at the beginning of Fodé Héraba's name constitutes the highest badge of honor among Mandinka Muslims in Senegambia.[36] He was among clerics who created a "tariqa-way without a tariqa brotherhood in that he incorporated some core dimensions of Sufism in his Islamic model, but not most of the frameworks that have historically shaped Sufi orders in Africa.[37]

The largest ethnic groups in the Casamance as a whole are the Diola in the Lower Casamance, the Foula in the Upper Casamance, and the Balante and Mandinka in the Middle Casamance. Most Balante and Diola groups did not begin embracing Islam in increasing numbers until the late nineteenth century and the first half of the twentieth century. This happened centuries after the Mandinka Muslim townships created in the Middle Casamance.[38] Muslims gradually popularized their culture and religion among their non-Muslim neighbors. The correlation between the landlord paradigm and the formation of Dar al-Islam in this region is a refrain in oral traditions used in this book.

It is worth mentioning that the concept of "Mandinkization "generally refers to the ethnic encounter that results in the gradual adoption of core Mandinka beliefs and practices by other populations: life-cycle celebrations, farming techniques, gender role expectations, land ownership, conversion to Islam, and clothing, to mention but a few. Some Diola groups in the Lower Casamance and coastal Gambia are good examples for understanding this process of Mandinkization.[39] In the Middle Casamance as well many Balante groups converted to Islam with the false assumption that this gesture must imperatively be accompanied by the automatic adoption of their Mandinka converters' traditions and customs.[40] According to Balante elders, this Mandinkization, whether accomplished through voluntary or involuntary imitation, contributed to the slow disappearance of key aspects of their ancestral heritage.[41]

However, some Diola and Balante groups have successfully restricted Mandinkization by managing to maintain important dimensions of their cultural heritage.[42] Others took this ethnic resistance a step further through innovative ways that helped them end Mandinkization by the close of the nineteenth century.[43] These same observations are hardly applicable to the Bainounk who underwent a more profound, long-lasting process of Mandinkization than any other populations across the Casamance. The book will show how the landlord paradigm was the lifeblood of this process, giving it strength and vitality, as more and more Muslim immigrants resettled in the Bainounk country.[44]

## THE MIDDLE CASAMANCE: A GENERAL OVERVIEW

This overview will help us better comprehend the Middle Casamance, the physical setting of this study. Senegambia is one of the three geographic entities that form Atlantic Africa, alongside West Central Africa and the Niger River region. Senegambia roughly encompasses the territories stretching from the Senegal River in the north to the southern rivers region in the south, and from the Atlantic Ocean in the west to the Senegal-Mali border in the east. The Gambia River splits Senegambia in two major zones: northern Senegambia is the largest and most populous zone, whereas southern Senegambia (including the Casamance) is the smallest but most ethnically and linguistically diverse one.[45] The Casamance corresponds to the southwestern part of Senegal and covers about one-seventh of the country's landmass, with some 45,000 square miles. By way of comparison, the Casamance is approximately the same size as the state of Pennsylvania in the United States; it is bigger than the kingdom of Belgium; and it is about three times the size of neighboring Gambia.

Due to its situation at the point where The Gambia, Senegal, French Guinea, and Portuguese Guinea meet, the Casamance represents a melting pot where centralized and decentralized populations have cohabited for centuries. They speak different languages, practice different religions, and engage in different socioeconomic activities. Senegalese people have nicknamed the Casamance la "*verte Casamance*" (green Casamance) because its annual precipitation and agro-economic potentialities are unmatched across Senegal. Given its formidable assets, this region is a microcosm of the Greater Senegambia, if we include the two Guineas.[46]

The Berlin Conference (November 1884–February 1885) is the reason why The Gambia forms an enclave that isolates the Casamance from most of the rest of Senegal.[47] This territory comprises three natural regions that present similar ecological features. The Lower Casamance (Basse Casamance) in the west is home to the Diola sedentary wet rice farmers. The Upper Casamance (Haute Casamance) in the east (Fouladou) belongs to the Foula cattle herders. The Middle Casamance (Moyenne Casamance) lays between The Gambia in the north, Guinea-Bissau in the south, the Fouladou in the east, and the Soungrougrou (the Casamance River's biggest tributary in the west.)

The topography of the Middle Casamance is dominated by forest plateaus that rarely exceed thirty meters. These are bordered by wet valleys and mainly covered by beige and red sands, making them perfectly suitable for rice and peanut farming, two crops that hold a central place in the local populations' diet. The region is characterized by a hot and rainy tropical climate, with the permutation between a long dry season from November to June and a short rainy season from July to October. Unlike many Sahelian regions, the Middle Casamance is not too badly exposed to a lack of precipitation. However, heavy rains, the humidity, and the intensive heat easily combine to stimulate the proliferation of the tsetse fly and mosquitoes; these are responsible for sleeping sickness and malaria, the leading cause of death across Africa.[48]

The vegetation is dominated by numerous big species of trees such as silk cotton trees or cheese trees (*ceiba pentrada*), palm groves, palm wine, palm trees, taabo (*cola cordifolia*), tali, and cailcédrats (*kaya Senegalensis)*. Human settlements are preferably constructed near water systems (the Casamance, the Koulountou, and the Soungrougrou Rivers), a reminder of the preponderance of subsistence farming in supporting local economic life. This luxurious vegetation will capture the attention of the most distracted travelers across this region.[49] One of the key ecological features of the region is the Casamance River that begins in the neighborhoods of Kolda in the east and flows westward between Guinea-Bissau and The Gambia before emptying into the Atlantic Ocean. With about two hundred miles in length, the river is navigable during the rainy season until Sédhiou. In addition to being a prosperous source of fish, salt, and other vital products, the river facilitates regional and long-distance trade.

Besides the Kabada, a Foula territory situated in the north of Pakao and the Balantakounda (Balante homeland) on the south bank, the Middle Casamance is a Mandinka country par excellence. Many people use the generic term Pakao when designating the Mandinka country, but Pakao was only one of the seven Bainounk chiefdoms. The others were Boudhié, Yacine, and Sonkoudou on the left bank, and Balmadou, Souna, and Birassou on the right bank. The Mandinka live in overwhelming numbers in and around Sédhiou, which was the capital of the entire Casamance until the dawn of the twentieth century, and which is now the capital of the region of Sédhiou.[50]

## THE EXISTING SCHOLARSHIP

Since the groundbreaking studies by French authors like Jean Girard, Paul Pélissier, and Louis Vincent Thomas between the 1960s and 1980s, the Diola have almost persistently attracted more scholarly interest than all other population groups put together across the Casamance; and they are still front and center in this literature dominated by anthropologists while historians are still lagging behind.[51] Despite some noticeable efforts, there is still a paucity of published sources by historians on the Casamance. Christian Roche's *Histoire de la Casamance* (1985) remains the main reference on the general history of the region, despite being an essentially archive-driven history.[52] This situation is largely imputable to the Diola secessionist movement since its outbreak in the early 1980s. Though human casualties resulting from this armed conflict are still limited to the Lower Casamance where most Diola people live, many researchers have dismissed the entire Casamance as off limits.

Meanwhile, in other areas of Senegambia, scholars have reexamined core but neglected dimensions of Islam, including controversies surrounding Islam, new interpretations of Sufism, and Islamic architecture and epistemology.[53]A number of other studies have reenergized the discussion of Islam, using different approaches, methodologies, and reliable sources. Some have concentrated on relevant issues that have been either misinterpreted or misunderstood in the previous literature.Yet in this essentially Sufi-driven literature, scholars have continued to prioritize the populations of northern Senegambia in the period since the mid-nineteenth century.[54]

This tendency has persisted in more recent investigations of Muslim minority groups, new Sufi rituals, new pathways to God, and the significance of Islamic literacy, among other themes.[55] A few other insightful studies have highlighted previously overlooked features of Islam, the interplay between African Islam and European colonial rule, and new models of religious belonging in southern Senegambia. Other important themes encompass misconceptions about African Muslim societies and pacifist forms of proselytization. Despite their centuries-long existence, the Muslim societies in the Casamance have been neglected in these multidisciplinary studies.[56]

There is no doubt about the importance of the period since the mid-nineteenth century, marked by the beginning of colonial rule, the development of new Sufi orders the fall of the non-Muslim state of Kaabou, and the spread of military jihād. However, there is a strong argument to be made for reimagining some of these dynamics in the light of transformations of beliefs and identities that began much earlier than this period. This book seeks to correct this lacuna by shifting the geographic and historical foci from the northern region to the Casamance in the southern region. Sources include archival documents from the French Ministry of Colonies in Aix-en-Provence (southern France) and the French Ministry of Overseas Territories in Dakar, Senegal; travelers' accounts from the fifteenth to the nineteenth centuries and beyond; published and unpublished scholarship; secondary literature; an old Arabic-written document entitled *Pakao al-qitabo* or *Pakao al-Qurano* (Pakao's holy book); chapters of the Holy Qur'an; participant observation methodology; and oral history and oral traditions mostly collected since the early 2000s.

General reports by Lusophone authors allowed glimpses of Mande groups' role in promoting long-distance trade and Islam, as well as the ethnic interactions and cross-cultural influences in precolonial Senegambia. The Portuguese established the commercial post of Ziguinchor in the Lower Casamance by the mid-seventeenth century. The drastic contrast between the timid growth and the geostrategic value of this post kept annoying French traders living on Gorée Island until the nineteenth century. Lieutenant-governor Jean-Marie Bayol was at this moment the chief administrator of the southern river region. French traders urged their president (Félix Cros) to resolve their collective annoyance by persuading Bayol to acquire Ziguinchor as a French protectorate.[57] The negotiations led to the Franco-Portuguese convention of

May 12, 1886, that forced the French to abandon the Bissago Islands to the Portuguese in return for their exclusive control over Ziguinchor. When the convention became a fait accompli in February 1888 under Captain Bosselard Faidherbe's tenure, the borderline between French Casamance and Portuguese Guinea was delimited. This constrained the Portuguese to move as a slowly growing colonial power to neighboring Guinea-Bissau.[58] Following these fruitful negotiations, French authors like Emmanuel Bertrand-Bocandé and Hyacinthe Hecquard began playing a more prolific role in informing our knowledge of Islam across the Casamance; the former replaced Jean Baudin as French resident on Karabane Island in 1849, while the latter cast himself as the first European to set foot in Karantaba in the 1840s.

The oldest Mandinka clerical lineages have possessed their own family archives since their eponymous ancestors immigrated to southern Senegal. These include their memorabilia (Qur'anic copies, prayer rugs, beads, walking sticks, wooden tablets, tools, cloths, hats, and pens) and documents called *ladiamio* or *ladiami*, local corruptions of *ajami*, the writing of non-Arabic languages with the Arabic script. Sources are unclear about when this calligraphic style first appeared in the region, but scholar genealogies date it back to around Fodé Hérapa's lifetime.[59] As is to be expected, these documents are still jealously kept and passed down from one generation of leaders to the next within the same lineage. Some are intentionally masked with complicated signs so that untrusted outsiders would find it difficult to decipher the esoteric knowledge they contain.[60] Even people gifted with perfect Arabic or Mandingo would need to know "the secret code" indispensable for accessing the meaning of these documents. Others relate to the founders of the early clerical lineages, the first Bainounk communities who hosted them in the Middle Casamance, the relationships they developed with other clerics, and the mosques and Qur'anic schools they built.[61]

Certain documents relate to divinatory performances called *katoumha* and *kamathara* or *tabdith*, the equivalents of what the Wolof call *khatim*. These are done by associating Qur'anic letters, specific meditations and sacrifices, in addition to tree leaves and other secret materials. Some community elders used these performances in the past for self-defense purposes, including protecting themselves against collectors of the French colonial tax as well as cursing disrespectful neighbors. Interestingly, Demba Souané was once the custodian of such precious archives, including some *ajami* documents in the clerical township of Dianaba. Shortly before his death, he surprised his compatriots by unilaterally deciding to dump these into a public well (*kolong thiossan*), arguing that he had no children and trusted nobody across Dianaba.[62] Souané's regrettable gesture was the exception rather than the rule, because elders agreed that such "precious documents" have generally been lost to heavy rains, termite infestations, and wildfires across the Mandinka country.[63]

This tragedy happened to the *tarikh* (book) of Harounaba Dramé, a celebrated cleric who lived in the Bainounk township of Dioudoubou, as we shall see in chapter 3. Similarly, in my base of operations during fieldwork (Karantaba) a portion of the *Pakao al-qurano* written since the tenure of imam Fodé Sitokoto Dramé in the first half of the nineteenth century met the same fate. My host, the late El Hadji Manding Dramé, showed me some segments of the manuscript rescued from a series of devastating wildfires in the 1960s and 1970s. These unpredictable natural calamities, he said, prompted local authorities to authorize the allotment of Karantaba in the 1990s, which irritated their most conservative colleagues.[64]

The *Pakao al-qurano* encompasses Fodé Héraba's family life stories, including his male children and spouses; the listing of the first mosques established in the Mandinka country and the names of their first imams; and the founders of the first Islamic communities in the Middle Casamance. Ndiama, Darsilamé, Diatouma, Mankonoba, and Dianaba are among other townships that have copies of the manuscript, but the one I found in Fodékounda (the Dramé ancestral home in Karantaba) is rumored to be the original document. Dramé clerics are still reluctant to provide anyone with a copy of this "irreplaceable document," and I was no exception. When I asked them to explain the rationale behind this secrecy, they responded by saying that Karantaba welcomes a considerable number of pilgrims during the most attended Mandinka Muslim festival across the Casamance. Because of it, lineage authorities agreed to protect the sacred manuscript, making additional copies of it and keeping them in undisclosed villages.[65] El Hadji Manding himself could hardly remember the last time the manuscript was exhibited in public, but he shared its content with me on several occasions, holding the manuscript in his hands.[66]

Many critics of oral traditions as historical sources in sub-Saharan Africa prioritize the ways traditions are reworked and adapted as living memory linking the past to the present; and sometimes on highly stylized renditions that convey information about the distant past. Some conclude that oral performances teach us more about idealized core values and exemplary human beings than about "real" events or people.[67] While many of these criticisms are valid, they are better taken as precautions about the study of oral traditions than as reasons for undermining oral traditions or highly stylized narratives altogether. In addition, scholars have long been much less preoccupied with

African religions than with Islam and Christianity in Africa. This is largely attributable to the preconceived ideas of explorers, missionaries, and colonial agents, who dismissed Africans as lacking real "history" and "religion" up until their contact with Europeans.[68] Historians singularly have shown less interest in the importance of African "traditional" religions than in the narratives of oral traditions. Still, studies of Senegambia have demonstrated that religion still constitutes a good analytical lens for apprehending different societies, including those lacking real states or aristocracies.[69]

Oral traditions used in this book were exceedingly valuable in adding new perspectives in interpreting most European written sources, which did not begin until the nineteenth century: they help understand how religious beliefs, models of social organization, political systems, and life-cycle ceremonies can define ethnic identity, and close some omissions and gaps existing in written sources. For instance, French archival sources were quintessential in my conceptualization of the Pakao jihãd, but I connected its successive episodes only by combining a myriad of oral renditions on this issue. And some scholars deal with oral traditions as historical sources while prioritizing centralized societies over decentralized societies. This partly derives from the notion that small-scale societies lack a caste system, social stratification, and kingship, contrary to centralized ones. The underlying implication is that the absence of qualified oral experts renders the collection of oral data too hazardous in decentralized societies. Yet, I encountered a number of Mandinka and non-Mandinka informants who displayed the same oratory skills and historical knowledge as the professional *diéli* or *fina*.[70] Because of it, I sought to maximize my chances of success by interviewing people from multiple backgrounds: rich and poor, members of ruling classes and ordinary citizens, Karantaba's inhabitants and outsiders, Muslim and non-Muslims, and Mandinka and non-Mandinka.

## CHAPTER OUTLINE

I have divided the book thematically into four core chapters, each comprising its own introduction and conclusion. The general introduction presents my approach to the topic, my research methodology, an overview of the Middle Casamance, an assessment of the existing scholarship, and a chapter outline. Chapter 1 explores the models of social and religious organizations that existed in the region before the development of Islam, and the ways different local populations reacted to attempts by Muslims and other immigrants to integrate the regional economy. Chapter 2 examines the correlation between a tradition of interfaith marriages and the first phase of the landlord paradigm of Islamization. Special attention is given to the strategies used by Fodé Héraba and his contemporary clerics to lay the foundation of the Dar al-Islam in the Middle Casamance.

Chapter 3 describes the incentives that softened the ground for Karantaba's early communal life and the role of the tradition of Muslim interlineage marriages in the second phase of the landlord paradigm of Islamization. This includes repeated processes of inclusiveness and dispersal that permitted Muslims to widen the Dar-al-Islam, to the detriment of the preexisting Bainounk religion. Chapter 4 conceptualizes the first military jihād that erupted in the Casamance in the 1840s, highlighting the antagonistic relations between the French, the Mandinka, and the Bainounk during those years. I conclude the book with a discussion of the essentialist notion of "ethnic extinction" that has long been applied to the Bainounk in southern Senegambia,and a description of the religious legacy of Karantaba in the broader Casamance today.

## CHAPTER 1

# *The Middle Casamance before the Development of Islam*

## Society, Religion, and the Regional Economy

Although African religions and ethnicities have changed over time and space in response to new historical circumstances, oral traditions that transmit knowledge and narratives about religion, ethnicity, and culture still offer vital tools for reconstructing history. In the Middle Casamance, the history of sacred rites such as shrines, life-cycle events, the funeral songs of key lineage leaders, prestigious hunters, accomplished warriors, or remembered ancestors, and even names, provide windows into the past. By focusing on the Bainounk, Balante, and Mandinka, who represent three different case studies, this chapter describes the major belief systems that existed in this region since the precolonial period.

The Bainounk were the landowners but in the long run they lost their cohesion as a group through processes of conquest, dispersion, or assimilation as they encountered later immigrant groups. The Balante and Mandinka, the main beneficiaries of this reversal, charted different strategies vis-à-vis the Bainounk indigenous communities.[1] The Balante, who came from neighboring Guinea-Bissau and seized territory from the Bainounk, typify a decentralized, nonhierarchical, and self-isolated society that rejected outright political orders imposed from outside their group. The Mandinka, who emigrated from the Niger River basin, developed a hierarchical model of social organization, concepts of highly centralized government (monarchy), and the teaching of Islam. The Mandinka comprised two separate groups at this moment: the aristocracy of warriors (*nyanchol*) who epitomized monarchy, matrilineal descent, and "traditional" religion; and Mandinka Muslims, who prospered as traders, cotton manufacturers, and proselytizers.[2] This chapter concentrates on the nyanchol through the prism of oral traditions associated with the Kaabou empire.

Given its great geographic situation and economic opportunities, the Middle Casamance was a magnet for diverse populations who sought to improve their living conditions in the much wider Casamance region. The chapter analyzes the conflicts of interest and power struggles over the control of wealth generated by these movements, as well as different ways local populations reacted toward others whose goal was to be part of the regional economy. These developments are vital for helping us better contextualize and understand the emergence of Islam in the Middle Casamance, including Karantaba's leading role in this process.

## THE BAINOUNK: "STRANGERS ARE WELCOMED!"

Reconstructing the ethnogenesis of the Bainounk by retracing their trajectory to the Casamance historically is a daunting task. This difficulty comes from the lack of written documents that survived their geographic dispersal in Senegambia in the course of the past several centuries. Despite this shortcoming, travelers' accounts and oral traditions characterize the Bainounk as the landowners across the Casamance, insisting that their presence in this region predates the arrival of other immigrant groups.[3] Several centuries ago the authentic name of the Bainounk was probably *noûn* before it was changed to Bainounko (those who pushed away, Mandingo).[4] This ethnonym may also have come from *abaii* and *nounko* (the one who is chased away). This alludes to the forced removal of some Bainounk populations from the east by Mandinka warriors followed by their resettlement on the south bank of the Casamance.[5] Whatever the case, this ethnonym change seems to have taken effect between the sixteenth century and the beginning of the seventeenth century. Between 1506 and 1510 Valentim Fernandes mentioned the Banhung (corruption of Bainounk), followed by André D'Alméda in 1595.[6] Biaye, Djignaly, Diatta, Coly, Biaye, Mané, Biagui, and Manga were among the authentic patronyms of the Bainounk in their early history.[7] Two authors have analyzed the concepts of multilingualism, hybridity, and language contact using Bainounk lects as case studies. They have called for a reclassification of the Niger-Congo languages, including the Atlantic branch with which the Bainounk language is genetically affiliated; and they conclude that these languages should be categorized as "independent families."[8]

Land scarcity, interethnic tensions, and the search for better living conditions drew many Bainounk groups out of Guinea-Bissau where they originally lived. These immigrants filtered into the more spacious lands of the Casamance, singling out sites located near commercial crossroads and forest ecological zones, like mangrove swamps near riverbanks.[9] The gateway for Bainounk resettlement in the Casamance was Brikama, an old township situated near the mouth of the Soungrougrou. The Bainounk still venerate palm trees because when immigrating their ancestors carried with them seeds like palm kernels, and planted them around their new homelands in the Casamance.[10] Some Bainounk groups left Brikama to establish offshoots in other areas of the Casamance, while keeping intact their ancestral tradition of planting palm trees. Bambadion, Koling, Bakoum, Pathiabor, Oudoukar, Mandouwari, and Dioudoubou in the Middle Casamance and Niamone, Tobor, Enampor, Balingor, Djibélor, and Ziguinchor in the Lower Casamance were among those offshoots, to mention but a few.[11]

Portuguese sources describe the king of Casa (*casa mansa*) as one of the most powerful rulers in Senegambia between the 1450s and the nineteenth century. He bore the Mandingo title of *mansa* (king) and ruled over the Casamance River named after him; his wealth included gold, many wives, and tight control over the economy around the river; and at this moment the river was the site of many commercial transactions among different "races."[12] But despite their importance in informing our knowledge, Portuguese sources are sometimes confusing in their characterizations of Senegambian societies. For example, they sometimes portray the Cassanke and the Bainounk as branches of the same populations, and sometimes as two distinct populations. In truth, the Casa was ethnically and linguistically the homeland of the Cassanke who belonged to the wider Bainounk group. In Mande languages the suffix *nke* or *nka* is often used to create territorial distinctions among different groups.[13] By the time D'Alméda reached the Casamance in the 1570s, the Casa was the most powerful Bainounk chiefdom in Guinea-Bissau–Casamance zone; and Mandingo was becoming increasingly spoken thanks to the dynamism of Dioula merchants in widening trade networks.[14]

Many European explorers hired African polyglots as interpreters and translators to help them better understand African cultures and societies. Mande-speaking experts who collaborated with authors like Damosto may have created confusion by using the term *mansa* when referring to the Bainounk ruler of Casa. A similar confusion exists in French sources but at a different level: Lieutenant Aristide Vallon, the French governor of Senegal in 1882, drew a map on which "Brucama" is the heartland of the Cassanke country. This spelling is a corruption of the same "Brikama" that served as the Bainounk capital until its destruction by Balante warriors in the 1830s, as we shall see below.[15]

In addition, the accumulation of wealth by diversifying their trading operations motivated many voyages made by European explorers in sub-Saharan Africa. Given this ambition, many followed specific road maps and issued reports prioritizing states that harbored lucrative commercial exchanges over small-scale societies considered marginal in the "making of history."[16] One salient example is the Casa between the fifteenth and seventeenth centuries when many populations between the Cacheu and the Casamance were forced to recognize the suzerainty of this "predatory state."[17] Due to their good relations with Casa, Portuguese dealers were more prolific about Casa than the other populations in this region.[18] In light of the above, I agree with Jean Boulégue that the Cassanke were not a separate ethnic group, but rather a "fraction of the broader Bainounk family."[19]

Charles De Lespinay and Stephan Bühnen have documented the roles of place names and their renaming as historical sources in Africa. Bühnen on his part rejected the notion that the state was nonexistent in Senegambia until the arrival of Mande immigrants. For him, the Bainounk, Kassanga, and Beafada were among local populations ruled by "sacred kings," and these kings could conquer weaker populations to extend their wealth and power base at any given moment. Bühnen concludes that these "lineage-based societies" should be typified as "states," although local customs often barred royal figures from participating in other public activities like warfare.[20]

I agree with the notion that African groups like the Bainounk were neither simple tribes nor stateless or decentralized societies. Meanwhile, they never possessed the core features that have traditionally characterized centralized states, or reached the levels of large-scale political entities called states and kingdoms. The Bainounk model of political organization mirrors the case of the chiefdoms (*chefferies*, French) that Robert L. Carmeiro labeled as independent political entities controlled by mighty chiefs. These experienced cycles of decline caused by internal fights for the monopolization of power, or moments of renaissance by building coalitions with other lineages. Seldom did the level of social stratification of these entities go beyond the cohabitation of two distinct social classes: a small ruling elite forming the upper class that was confined to the ruler, his family, and his immediate entourage; and a mass of commoners representing the lower class who were economically subjugated by the former.[21]

In nineteenth-century French sources the Bainounk political model is specifically depicted as a kind of "monarchy" in which older males were theoretically responsible for speaking truth to power, holding the ruler's authority in check.[22] The devolution of power and leadership roles varied from one chiefdom to another. For example, in Boudhié, this was based on a rotation between Bakoum and Pathiabor, the two alternating capitals until the eruption of the Pakao jihãd; on the south bank of the Casamance power circulated among six powerful lineages based in Binako, Adéane, Niamé, Congolon, Brikama, and Bombota; but in Pakao, only Mandouwari assumed this political function.[23]

In his examination of African cosmologies Robert Horton distinguishes two separate realms: the first (macrocosm) operates as the whole universe and is ruled by a powerful Supreme Being; and the second (microcosm) is the communal life where numerous lesser spirits coexist. Given the remoteness and noninvolvement of the Supreme Being, he argues, the microcosm becomes the alternative entity where worshippers and the invisible forces communicate.[24] Many subsequent studies of African religions were inspired by Horton's interpretation. Two good examples in Senegambia regard the Diola and Sérére-Saféne who are among the last populations who embraced Islam and Christianity. In one of his earliest studies, David Sapir depicts the Diola Supreme Being (*emitai*) as a "distant creative force and an unmoved mover that has nothing to do with people in this life and thereafter."[25] Peter Mark also contends that a Higher Power that rewards good deeds and punishes bad ones is absent in Diola cosmology; neither emitai nor Diola individual spirit shrines (*oukin*) are explicitly preoccupied with human morality; and Christian and Muslim missionaries probably saw emitai as God's equivalent in the Diola country and applied these new concepts to Diola cosmology.[26]

Other scholars like Robert Baum and James Searing have challenged some of these previous interpretations. For Baum, nothing escapes the vigilance of emitai, the incarnation of the "Whole Truth" in Diola cosmology; and while being distant and uninvolved, emitai communicates with worshippers through visions and dreams. These allow emitai to issue specific orders regarding new spirit shrines, the code of moral behavior, and punishments or rewards due to good or bad behavior. While Baum acknowledges the usefulness of the macrocosm, the cosmology he discusses is a macrocosmic one in that the instructions given to worshippers come directly from the emitai.[27] Similarly, Searing approaches the Saféne cosmology from a macrocosmic perspective, suggesting that worshippers seek blessings and protection from the Supreme God (*kookh*), even when pouring libations to their supernatural spirits (*pangol*). These rituals aim at ending drought through rainmaking, or at bringing about social peace and economic prosperity, among other goals. However, these are not the exclusive matter of the group in need, but a common cause whose triumph requires the mobilization of all coreligionists.[28]

Likewise, the pre-Islamic Bainounk communities possessed a macrocosmic cosmology dominated by a Higher Power called *dinoh*. As the creator of the whole universe, dinoh manifested Itself in a spiritual mask (*koumpo*) and protected people during key ceremonies like male circumcision (*fanada*). Dinoh could hide in large bodies of water, the wind, or the wilderness.[29] From a Bainounk standpoint, human behaviors of any kind were either good or bad, irrespective of their motivations. This explains the division of their cosmology into two distinct realms, each ruled by a deity that diligently carried out dinoh's orders. The first, "the incarnation of good," protected, assisted, or blessed individuals whose actions were in harmony with God's will. The second ruled over "the domain of transgressions," punishing people who committed grave mistakes like disrespecting God, offending others, or failing to sacrifice to ancestral spirits. In reality, these lesser spirits had no real names in that dinoh was the same force whose demeanor changed as a result of human behaviors.[30]

Before defending themselves from external attacks, launching military operations, or seeking self-happiness of any kind, the Bainounk first sought dinoh's blessings by holding divination ceremonies dedicated to their spirit shrines (*china*). In so doing, they manipulated sacred objects, including wood sticks, and made sacrifices of palm wine, palm oil, millet, rice, and dog and chicken blood.[31] Some groups celebrated their identity by singing, dancing, and praying together while performing these rituals. Niamone and Tobor in the Lower Casamance and Kaour and Sinkére in the Middle Casamance gained notoriety for harboring such popular rituals.[32] In Kaour, Sinkére, and Gonou, commoners showed me some sites that once harbored these rituals: holes, abandoned bushes, termite mounds, dark wells, species of large trees, and empty lands. Mandinka Muslims who immigrated to those areas later disregarded these pre-Islamic landmarks as irremediably haunted and unfit for human settlement.[33]

Bainounk spirit shrines were versatile and unpredictable because they could strike against the very populations they were supposed to protect. Gaffes that unleashed the wrath of the shrines ranged from poor social behavior, family rivalries, and fights over political power, to mutual jealousy and a lack of consensus among elders on serious community affairs.[34] These offenses could result in tragedies such as persistent drought and bad harvests, inexplicable road accidents, epidemics, infertility, or mysterious death. Throughout history, many local groups suffered serious demographic setbacks due to mass deaths meted out by shrines and their indwelling spirits that obeyed dinoh's command.[35] Like many African groups, the Bainounk believed that the world is populated with good and evil spirits that can either harm or protect innocent human beings in several manners.[36] Thus, elders never ruled out sorcery and witchcraft as potential causes of death. These concepts mean here the recourse to invisible powers to inflict damage on innocent victims because of greed, jealousy, envy, or hatred. Despite the spread of Islam and Christianity, practices of witchcraft and sorcery as well as ceremonies to counter these are still popular across sub-Saharan Africa.[37]

The Bainounk saw witches as radically different human beings who transformed themselves into wild animals and destroyed innocent people's lives, eating their souls during the night. They coped with this abomination by holding a preburial ritual ceremony called interrogating the corpse (*homo kossi*). The body of the deceased was covered with a black fabric and placed on a flat piece of wood serving as a poorly decorated coffin. The whole community had to attend this ceremony unless they had valid excuses for absenting themselves; any unjustified absence led to a legitimate suspicion of evildoing.[38] This ceremony lasted hours during which the corpse was circulated from one direction to another through the crowd to determine how the person's life ended, following the movement of the deceased's head. Only if the officers of the ceremony found no guilty person by blaming the death on natural causes did the crowd show a sign of relief.[39]

People suspected of such unforgivable offenses as witchcraft, sorcery, and stealing had to prove their innocence, undergoing and passing an ordeal. This was a red poison (*bouroukou chi* or *sikan*) resulting from the mixing of different ingredients, including water and the bark of a tree called *mancône* (*Erytrophleen guineense*). This ceremony was the equivalent of testifying in public court during which people were theoretically considered innocent until proven guilty.[40] Jules Le Prince dismissed as baseless the narrative that the rationale behind this ritual was to promote social justice, contending that the hidden agenda was to eliminate rich people and profit from their wealth.[41] The Jesuit Balthasar explained how the Cassanga king (Masatamba) took the pretext of witchcraft and other "offenses" to physically eliminate wealthy rivals among the Balante in Guinea-Bissau. For him, the ruler's intention was to sell "guilty" individuals into slavery or to impose on them the deadly red poison and then inherit their wealth; and guilty individuals were those who automatically vomited the red poison.[42] The opposite was true among the Bainounk of the Middle Casamance: people who vomited the poison were considered innocent, whereas those who resisted it were guilty and could use no subterfuge to escape punishment. These unlucky individuals then lost their citizenship by being sold into slavery alongside some family members, or were thrown alive into a massive fire in the dark forest (*soutou*) and were denied rights to adequate funerals.[43]

The importance of Bainounk men's and women's funerals depended on the amount of wealth they left behind. The gender division of labor shaped these services only in principle because in concrete practice the toughest duties were shouldered by women. Gathered on one side of the mourning compound, they collectively remembered the departed soul, endlessly crying and moving from the back to the front of the compound. Some periodically fell to the ground, bursting into tears, throwing dirt on their bodies and shaking violently, as if they were in a spiritual trance and wanted to hurt themselves purposefully.[44] While impatiently awaiting their delicious meals cooked by women, men sat on the other side of the compound, without any female presence. They danced, drank palm wine, chanted, and fired guns into the sky to scare any looming evil forces.[45]

Africans have historically reacted to immigrants who reached their homelands in many different ways, depending on the geographic and historical circumstances. In some regions, Muslims propagated Islam by capitalizing on their dual expertise as agents for economic prosperity and specialists in the resolution of mundane needs.[46] But where Islam was perceived as a menace to local communities' independence Muslims found it more challenging to win hearts and minds. In Senegambia, groups like the Sérére-Saféne in western Bawol and the Balante on the Upper Guinea coast fall in this category. Both elaborated several strategies to avoid assimilation by the Wolof (Wolofization) and the Mandinka (Mandinkization); and relocating to new ecological niches that were difficult to access was central in the strategies they used in this process.[47] Likewise, in the Lower Casamance, the Diola used the Casamance and Soungrougrou Rivers as natural shields to keep at bay their provocative Mandinka neighbors.[48]

When it comes to issues of integration into the regional economy of the Middle Casamance, the Bainounk adopted a different position in their dealings with others. In the precolonial era, they surrounded their homestead with individual and collective fields where they grew a large amount of crops; and they possessed many rice fields (*farol*) such as Minambassé and Bakiang.[49] Mandinka records indicate that the Mandinka who immigrated to the Middle Casamance promoted a "small-scale cotton industry" across the region, but they learned this technique from the Bainounk landowners. Cotton farming required labor-intensive operations supervised by women from the beginning to the end of the process, but the heaviest burdens rested on slaves' shoulders. The commercialization of cotton helped the Bainounk maintain a decent level of economic prosperity.[50] Another labor-intensive task was the harvesting of palm wine and palm oil, a perilous activity that often resulted in fatal accidents. Thus, Bainounk elders delegated this task to slaves, who had to rely on their personal dexterity to bring down the fresh liquid, without dropping or spilling any of it.[51]

The significance of Bainounk economic prosperity is underlined in eighteenth-century French travelers' accounts, including that of Sylvain Golbéry. He sojourned in Senegambia in 1785–87 but spent most of his time visiting the Bambouck, Galam, and Bouré. Nonetheless, the Frenchman mentioned the mutually beneficial partnership between the Portuguese and the Bainounk in Ziguinchor, including among other items slaves, leather, woods, and beeswax.[52] Thanks to these valuable assets the Bainounk were credible power players in the regional economy of the Middle Casamance and surrounding areas. This began with the dynamic role played by local groups in the weekly markets (*louma*) that took place alternatively from one place to another across this region.[53] Through their self-identified status as "the hospitable, welcoming" (*oudiahére*), the Bainounk hosted foreign traders who pledged to respect their customary laws during these gatherings; they made substantial profits in exchange for their hospitality. In some areas, Muslim merchant- scholars were given preferential treatment thanks to their ability to boost Bainounk economic life in meaningful ways.[54] In others, the *lançados* or Luso-Africans gained citizenship through intermarriage with commoners, education, commercial transactions, and rites of passage.[55] Through these commercial exchanges, the Bainounk accumulated a substantial amount of wealth by trading kola nut, chili pepper, and iron with active trading partners like the Mandinka.[56]

Bambadion, Dioudoubou, Pathiabor, Bakoum, Koling, and Badounga were among old Bainounk townships that epitomized *oudiahére* in the Middle Casamance.[57] Verbal arguments, thefts, and physical altercations were commonplace in these markets. Besides welcoming foreign dealers by affording them food, drinks, and housing, local communities guaranteed their safety, using sophisticated mystical performances.[58] Commenting in the 1570s, D'Àlméda highlighted the dynamism of the *lançados*, Portuguese, and Cape Verdeans who traded along coastal West Africa. For him, in the Guinea-Bissau–Casamance zone foreign dealers protected themselves and their merchandise, reckoning with the divinatory practices of local Banyun and Papel groups. In some cases, these rituals were performed by eating dogs and sacrificing blood to their deities.[59] French sources corroborate this culture of hospitality and inclusiveness by profiling the Bainounk as a society whose doors were left open to facilitate the integration of strangers. For example, Laurent Bérenger-Féraud portrayed the Bainounk as a "soft, hospitable and submissive" society whose citizens were fond of palm wine.[60]

I would like to end this section with what I call the powers of prayer and royal curse. In popular imagination across southern Senegambia, the historic downfall of the Bainounk is paradoxically not blamed on the military conquests of Bainounk homelands by later immigrant groups. Instead, these infringements are viewed as the inevitable outcomes of a self-inflicted wound that intervened during the tenure of a Bainounk ruler called Gana Sira Bana Biaye (Masoboti). Because oral traditions obstinately portray his lifetime as the root cause of the Bainounk's downfall, I conducted an in-depth investigation of this complex political character. I wanted to know whether Masoboti's epic grew out of deliberate efforts by other later immigrant groups like the Mandinka to rewrite history to the detriment of the Bainounk. Simply put, why would the Bainounk "blame themselves" rather than those who abused their generosity, pushing them away or assimilating them after conquering their lands?

Given the total silence of written sources on this issue, I conceptualized Masoboti's life experience, combining many versatile and sometimes contradictory oral narratives. Most of those I interviewed defined themselves linguistically and ethnically as Bainounk whose families accepted Islam a few generations ago. For them, Masoboti's lifetime was a new era during which the tragic fate of the Bainounk was sealed at many different levels. He was a brutal, selfish dictator, with boundless authority and no compassion for others, including his constituents, and a "paranoid" and "narcissistic" monarch who used everything at his disposal to solidify his political power base.[61]

Masoboti excelled in the art of manipulating his closest entourage, including the elders' council whose mission was to regulate his powers. One of his deadliest habits was to order human sacrifices every year, choosing his innocent victims among young girls whose numbers changed with his personal mood. After consulting his mystical powers, Masoboti once told his constituents that he foresaw the imminent arrival of powerful "yellow-skinned people" (Europeans) committed to conquering the Bainounk country. Because only human sacrifices would prevent this tragedy from happening, he dictated the killing of dozens of girls, creating generalized anger among his subjects.[62]

If the plot to get rid of Masoboti's terrorizing regime was orchestrated by his own brothers and other male conspirators, at no time were women on the sidelines when men conspired to eliminate him in Brikama where his palace was located. Inspired by their emotional attachment to their victimized daughters, women ignited much of this social uprising, pressuring their husbands to terminate the monarch's exactions.[63] One day when the Bainounk organized a refreshment party after a successful palm wine harvest, the conspirators cleverly dug a deep hole behind the monarch's chair and covered it with a fancy mat. Despite being gifted in divination and magic, Masoboti knew nothing about the ongoing plot until he fell straight into the hole, and died while wearing his royal clothes and red hat and carrying his spear.[64]

Before his painful death by stoning, the betrayed ruler was granted permission to formulate his final prayers and seized this opportunity to curse his own people: as the direct intermediary between humans and spirit shrines executing dinoh's orders, Masoboti prayed for the geographic dispersion of the Bainounk; their loss of power to other ethnic groups; the dismantlement of their civilization; and the failure of his successors to recover any shred of authority forever.[65] For Bainounk elders, the power of the "royal curse" marked the beginning of the "irremediable downfall" of the Bainounk. Successive generations of leaders strived to recover from the curse by showering the *chinas* with gifts and animal sacrifices, but their efforts unluckily bore no fruit. The following vignette by Sanoussy best sums up how the curse is remembered in popular memory across southern Senegambia: "The malediction following the Bainounk people to this day, their dispersal over time and space, and their inability to regroup are the direct outcomes of the curse. Indeed, Masoboti was in total control of the spirit shrines until the very end of his life and relentlessly used them as weapons to retaliate against his own people."[66]

Knowing when and how long Masoboti ruled over the Bainounk is one blind spot in his chronology. Two scholars have established two hypotheses in an attempt to solve this puzzle. Christian Roche situates Masoboti's chronology before the Portuguese reached Senegambia by the mid-fifteenth century. This is a plausible argument since neither early Portuguese nor French sources make explicit reference to Masoboti.[67] Sékené Mody Cissoko affirms that Masoboti extended his jurisdiction over Pakao and other "kingdoms," and could have been the "last Bainounk king in the Casamance." This implies that in the post-Masoboti era, non-Bainounk kings, who were either Mandinka or Mandinkized, ruled over "kingdoms" such as Pakao.[68] One refrain in oral records consists of branding Masoboti not as "the last king," but as the "most powerful ruler" in Bainounk history. But there is no foregone conclusion that these Bainounk societies were totally centralized under one political authority, as indicated above.

Between 1666 and 1684, Francisco de Lemos Coelho counted the Bainounk "kingdoms" of southern Senegambia, but he only listed Sandedougou, Jase (Yacine), Bichangor, and Quinguin.[69] In reality, the number of Bainounk chiefdoms that existed in the precolonial period goes beyond the count of Coelho. Masoboti could have been the most powerful ruler on the south bank of the Casamance where he lived. In fact, a tradition reported by Gérald Gaillard recalls that when the Mandinka expelled the Bainounk from the east, they hid on the south bank under Masoboti's leadership.[70] Cissoko's informants probably confused Masoboti with other rulers because oral narratives signal other powerful rulers in the 1830s and 1840s, including Bodia Danfa of Bakoum and Niadoumassani of Mandouwari, as we shall see in chapter 4.

Oral sources emphasize the importance of the trickle-down effect of Masoboti's curse by indiscriminately affecting all the Bainounk groups living across the Casamance. However, logically speaking, the curse should have been limited to the populations of Brikama who carried out the plot without foreign interference. No informants narrated the epic of Masoboti more prolifically than did *dialloloo and finoloo* (pl. of *diéli eli* and *fina*). In some communities interviews were delayed because local authorities requested the presence of oral historians to help them set straight Masoboti's record. Through their encyclopedic knowledge and personal charisma, these gatekeepers of popular memory may have propagated the Masoboti epic across the Casamance.[71] It is not impossible that while narrating this malediction, some prioritized the self-inflicted wound over the process of territorial conquests. Mandink agriots in particular have often stressed the last warning Masoboti reportedly gave to the conspirators against him, reiterating his final words: "Every now and then, my royal chair will emerge from the bottom to the top of my grave. Unfortunately, it will not be occupied by a Bainounk, but by someone from another ethnic group."[72]

After hearing these perplexing statements many times, I was eager to know whether the epic of Masoboti was an invented popular tradition geared toward whitewashing wrongdoings committed against the Bainounk by other populations . While responding to my inquiries, the populace of Sinkére, Bakoum, and Gonou recalled that Masoboti was not a "mythological figure": that he ruled with an iron fist over an immense territory in the period before the coming of the "white man" (*toubabo*); that he only trusted and nominated his own sons as his lieutenants, right-hand men, and special envoys;[73] and that Masoboti was buried in Brikama, but "his graveyard vanished in the sand" when Balante warriors conquered this territory and denied people access to the whereabouts of his graveyard.[74]

The aftermath of the curse led to a slow dispersal of numerous Bainounk groups in the wider Senegambia, while other immigrant groups were looking for better ecological niches in the region. The Bainounk tried to overcome these challenges by targeting any sites where they could re-create new farming communities and political centers. This resilience galvanized some groups to create a new township called Brikama in the Combo kingdom, on the south bank of the Gambia River.[75] As insightfully stated by Séga Sagna, this self-preservation explains the existence of Bainounk townships that share the same name, like Brikama, Pakao (Bakaw), and Kiang in the Middle Casamance, The Gambia, and Guinea-Bissau.[76] The Masoboti curse had often "come back" to haunt the Bainounk, weakening their agency, or their capacity, to act vis-à-vis other populations. For example, when the Diola invaded the Lower Casamance in the sixteenth and seventeenth centuries, the preexisting Bainounk groups were progressively assimilated into this embryonic Diola society.[77] As will be shown below, the resettlement of Mandinka and Balante immigrants in the Middle Casamance generated a similar outcome.

## THE BALANTE: "THE SAFETY OF OUR HOMELAND COMES FIRST!"

In the past few decades there has been an upsurge of scholarly interest in decentralized societies in the Greater Senegambia, but the Balante of the Casamance are still relegated to the periphery of this scholarship.[78] In the existing English literature, Walter Hawthorne's ethnography still stands out as the most detailed historical analysis of this group, but he concentrates on

Guinea-Bissau where the Balante are the majority group.[79] In the Casamance, the Balante are the fourth largest group, and the second largest in the Middle Casamance behind the Mandinka. Linguistically, the Balante are classified in the West Atlantic group of the Niger-Congo languages, and speak several dialects that present tonal and lexical variations from one physical milieu to another.[80] These include the Balante Naaga, Balante-Mané, and Balante Brassa (sing. *arassa*) or Manodj who live in substantial numbers in Guinea-Bissau; the Gandia who are more numerous in the Casamance; the Binaka or gardeners in Mandingo; and the Bidia Alip or Woyé Bilanté whose name recalls their reluctance to cross the river in pirogues when immigrating to the Casamance.[81]

The Balante were historically depicted in derogatory terms by Western explorers as well as by neighboring groups like the Mandinka. For instance, they were accused of rejecting ideas of modernization by using a strategy of "conservative change" and by prioritizing innovations that benefited their own communities. Given their "warlike" and "backward" attitude, the Balante were pushed to the edge of "civilized societies" by belligerent neighbors like the Mandinka.[82] Some Mandinka sources have profiled them as "stubborn" and "belligerent" individuals due to their rejection of "progress and modernization."[83] Balante self-descriptions contradict these "ill-founded characterizations," rather describing this so-called "negative" attitude as the manifestation of Balante people's determination to be free from domination by others.[84]

Additionally, the Balante rejected foreign authority, while seeking to exploit the weaknesses shown by other populations. Some oral data depict the original Balante as slaves from Fouta Tooro, a Foula kingdom located in the Senegal River valley. When they were mobilized to collect palm wine and pick fruits in Guinea-Bissau, they felt in love with this new environment and refused to return home.[85] Others paint the Balante as former soldiers of Koli Tenguella who in the fifteenth century founded the Dénianké dynasty that ruled Fouta Tooro until the Toorodo Revolution in 1776.[86] Following his father's example, Tenguella Bâ, he put together a professional army of dedicated soldiers and invaded the Ferlo, the Falémé, and the Gambia and Senegal River regions. Tenguella wanted to develop his influence in the wider Senegambia, but his countless military expeditions exhausted some of his soldiers, who fled to start a new life in Guinea-Bissau.[87] Likewise, oral material collected by Cornelia Giesing among the Bidia in Guinea-Bissau brands the Balante as "escaped slaves" or "resistant warriors" who were eager to recover their freedom; and on coastal Guinea-Bissau they avoided political subjugation, immigrating to an inland location.[88] For Balla Moussa Sadio, the first Balante name is Bidia or Beeja (in reference to the people of Dia). Dia is probably the pathway for Balante immigration to Guinea-Bissau from an unknown region; and the Balante were not originally acephalous societies, but were led by abusive kings who were eventually replaced by other chiefs (*alama*).[89] One common denominator among these accounts is Balante's propensity to reject political leadership and royal authority.

Oral accounts I collected in the Middle Casamance corroborate some of these sources, portraying the Balante as "outsiders," "former slaves" or warriors," and "immigrants" to Guinea-Bissau. They also explain the previous "Foula identity" ascribed to the Balante, observing that these "warriors or slaves" were gradually assimilated into the Balante in Guinea; and that mounting tensions with the Foula and Mandinka contributed to the relocation of the Balante from the Cacheu and Geba regions to the Casamance.[90] Balante ancestral homelands included Samodji, Boundi, Magar, Youroum, Dia, Gounio, and Binaga; and Mangaroungou, Sayan, and Kouniara were among their first settlements in the Middle Casamance.[91]

I found no tangible evidence of Balante royalty in the Middle Casamance. Sadio's informants probably confused such "royal authorities" with powerful leaders in the early phase of Balante history.[92] Some oral data rather link the Balante ethnonym to "we the men" in the military sense of the term (*ba bilanté*), or to the men (*bilanté*). Others persist that this ethnonym came "from without," implying the Balante's refusal of Mandinkization. In effect, in Mandingo *abalanta* signifies "those who have refused," which implies that the Mandinka ultimately dismissed the Balante as "stubborn people" due to their rejection of Mandinkization. A few other narratives associate the origin of the Balante ethnonym with the refusal of "Balante slaves" to follow Tenguella back to his native Fouta.[93]

Laurent Bérenger-Féraud dated Balante presence in the Casamance in the fifteenth century, but in the Middle Casamance their numbers did not increase until the first part of the nineteenth century. It is not a random act that Bainounk and Balante groups living side by side in this region still share many popular patronyms.[94] In fact, Balante warriors invaded the Bainounk homeland at a time when endless internal feuds crippled the stability of communal life.[95] They annihilated local resistance, expelled those who challenged their legitimacy, adopted some preexisting patronyms, and rebaptized this territory home of the Balante (Balantakounda, Mandingo).[96] Némou

Samanangou is remembered as one of the legendary warriors who created the Balante regiments and coordinated these military assaults.[97]

By the 1830s, Balante warriors tightened the noose around the remnant Bainounk groups by launching additional military expeditions, culminating in the destruction of the Bainounk palace in Brikama. Balante farmers told me that some portions of this land became farms where various crops are still grown; and that while preparing their fields for the new farming season, they occasionally find some vestiges of the once powerful Bainounk civilization: water jars, pipes, bones, and pottery shards near wells and baobab trees (*adansonia digitata*), and one day a golden scepter that belonged to early Bainounk rulers.[98] After conquering Brikama, like the Bainounk before them, the Balante gradually created offshoots in other areas across the Casamance.[99] Today the Balantakounda is a small strip of territory that spans some thirty-two miles, between the Boudhié in the north, Guinea-Bissau in the south, Adéane in the east, and Simbandi Birassou in the west.

The Balante model of organization was characterized by a horizontal social structure in which personal merits and seniority took precedence over family ties in attributing leadership roles. Though the Balante formed scores of autonomous villages, they quickly built a united front whenever their collective safety as a group was jeopardized.[100] Three major organs dominated decision-making processes in a typical Balante township. The first, the elders' council, was exclusively comprised of a carefully selected groups of older men. The second, the women's council, regrouped those who had reached menopause, and was led a woman called "men's friend" (*nteer bilanté*); she was selected among elders who stood out from their peers for their impressive gifts. At times, some younger women with incredible talents were exceptionally permitted to become a part of this highly selective group. The third comprised young soldiers under the leadership of a warrior (*atenga bilanté*) whose patriotism and fighting skills were indisputable. This tripartite division did little to alter the gerontocratic, male-dominated nature of Balante society in that the powers invested in women and youth were more nominative than deliberative. In other words, male elders secretly met at the cabaret to resolve the most complex community matters before making their decisions public.[101]

The Balante held in the highest esteem the ancestral spirits (*bouhoulé*) that dominated their cosmology because they considered these the intermediaries between worshippers and the Balante Supreme Being (*khaala*).[102] Whenever the Balante wanted to obtain military success, bless their life-cycle events, or surmount ecological disasters, they organized specific rites at their sacred groves (*boisé*). A carefully selected group of professionals whose knowledge and public loyalty were irreproachable was responsible for supervising these groves. The sacrifices performed included cattle, white and red hens, palm wine, and a portion of their harvest.[103] The deaths of prominent lineage members like patriarchs and matriarchs resulted in public mobilization. A man carrying a special drum (*degnna ndangué*) alerted the public and commoners deciphered the nature of his message by carefully listening to the sound of his instrument.[104] Following the death of a man, his widow(s) had to automatically shave their heads before the interment, but this rule did not apply to widowers who completed this ritual before the big male circumcision ceremony.[105]

From a Balante viewpoint, the loss of a male or female elder who had enjoyed a long life and left behind children and grandchildren was a normal life occurrence, whereas the death of a child or a young adult who never commenced household life and had never borne children was suspicious. Thus, elders diagnosed the real cause of death before the burial, using supernatural techniques to determine whether evildoers like witches (*awera*) had caused any premature loss of life.[106] The deceased's corpse was interrogated on these occasions by placing it on a piece of wood and covering it with a black fabric. This was a type of autopsy during which the key witness to be cross-examined was the corpse itself.[107] Like Jules Le Prince in the case of the Bainounk, Doctor Alexandre Lasnet characterized this ritual as an ethnic cleansing (*épuration de la nation*), or a witch hunt solely designed to harm innocent citizens.[108]

Another old Balante ritual was the *tali* ordeal whose function was to detect public wrongdoings with a deadly red poison. This resulted from the mixture of water and other ingredients, including the bitter bark of a tree botanically classified as *Erythrophleine guineense*. Devastating wars, epidemics, droughts, and bad harvests were among calamities that might give rise to this ordeal. Some communities became famous thanks to their association with the tali, but they learned it from Ngoré or *ingoré*, an old township situated in northern Guinea-Bissau.[109] One native of Ngoré volunteered that the location of the Balantakounda at a working distance from Ngoré facilitated the spread of the tali in the Middle Casamance. He vehemently denounced the large number of people who unjustifiably lost their lives to this practice, calling Ngoré a "village-cemetery."[110]

Many full-fledged experts in magic and divination consulted during these stressful moments blamed evil forces hiding inside or outside the Balante homeland. People suspected of any intolerable misconduct had to demonstrate their innocence, drinking the "poison of truth" from a calabash or a water jar.[111] The suspects were stripped of their clothes and carefully watched throughout this process so that they would not escape to use counterpoisons leading to their false exoneration.[112] Those who vomited the poison proudly sang and danced while happily returning home. Guilty individuals could not vomit the poison and suffered unbearable abdominal cramps until they died by cardiac arrest within a few hours. As in the case of the Bainounk mentioned above, they were denied any rights to proper funerals and were buried in the forest (*ndjiné*) or eaten by wild animals.[113]

The tali is seemingly one of the old rituals that survived Balante resettlement in the Casamance, but oral sources are unclear about when it was first performed in the Casamance. Between the latter part of the nineteenth century and the opening decades of the twentieth century the tali claimed countless innocent lives between Guinea-Bissau and the Casamance. In the Balantakounda, where it killed some 3,500 people; 57 percent of those who underwent the ordeal succumbed to the poison.[114] These grave casualties irritated French officials so profoundly that they ordered a detailed report on the tali from a team of experts; but despite their efforts, the practice persisted for many more decades.[115] A similar technique of death by poisoning existed among the Diola of Boulouf, Fogny, and Kombo in the Lower Casamance, until its official interdiction by the French administration.[116] Other African groups like the Dinka of Soudan, the Pangwe and Bafia of Cameroun, the Nguni of South Africa, and the Lefana of central Togo were familiar with analogous punishments.[117]

The original Balante buried their dead with plenty of food and drinks, believing in the immortality of human souls. For them, the deceased needed these ingredients while transitioning from the world of the living to the world of the dead. During the burial the body was placed in a seated position, holding in his or her right hand a calabash of palm wine, and in the left hand a cow tail to keep the flies away. Another large calabash (*guignadou*) filled with foods and wine was also attached to a solid rope and hung on the wall.[118] There were times when men were buried with their preferred protective charms, musical instrument, sharp knife, red hat, and guns nicely decorated with cowry shells; and women with some of their prettiest wedding dresses, jewelry, and dishes. The dead bodies were washed with lemon leaves, covered with fine fabrics, placed horizontally inside the tomb, and surrounded with solid tree leaves and branches. This slowed down the decomposition of the bodies by limiting their contact with the soil around them.[119]

The Balante immortalized their patriarchs by burying them at the entrance to their original family house, the best way for everybody to remember them while entering or exiting the house. Unlike their male counterparts, matriarchs were buried in the same public cemeteries as their other family members. Balante funeral services involved a typical dance (*mboumbourou*) designed to accompany the deceased's soul to the realm of ancestral spirits. Much of the wealth belonging to the deceased (pigs, goats, chickens, and crops) was consumed the day of their funeral. Collective singing, dancing, and drinking animated these funerals, which lasted weeks if the mourning family was among the wealthiest ones.[120]

In French sources raiding or stealing is described as a hallmark in the Balante code of moral values, but Balante self-descriptions categorize this practice most essentially as the specialty of Manodj people.[121] Some subgroups like the Gargay have also acquired notoriety thanks to their great raiding skills. Gargay men prided themselves on their expertise in plundering harvests and cattle belonging to their neighbors during the heaviest rains or in the darkness. Neighboring groups dismissed them because of their ability to steal without being caught, but the Gargay perceived this skill as an irrefutable sign of manhood.[122] For them, raiding was a male activity par excellence and one of the most admirable "moral virtues" Balante men could brag about. In some cases, if accidental death and raiding occurred simultaneously, during the eulogy the victim was not criticized but glorified with dances, songs, and eating and drinking. In others, no funerals were celebrated unless the raiding skills of the deceased were indisputably proven. The exhibition of one's raiding talents was one of the straightest paths toward male social acceptance. For example, single women perceived this prowess as the proof for a prosperous household life, believing that men who demonstrated such prowess would take good care of their families. One proof of manhood was to steal a dog without its master's knowledge. Aided by their trustworthy friends, grooms also would take their wives to a secret location for about a month, without the knowledge of their in-laws. Balante parents compensated expert thieves who instructed their children "in the art of stealing."[123]

In the 1830s, while evaluating the social atmosphere in the neighborhood of the fort of Sédhiou (discussed in chapter 4), French officials portrayed "stealing" as a vicious Balante habit. Neither oral traditions nor written sources are clear about when raiding became "a high-ranking virtue" in the Balantakounda. A few accounts collected in Sédhiou indicate that raiding was originally considered an "act of bravery," not a "shameful behavior."[124]

During times of war in Guinea-Bissau, Balante men were recruited en masse as fighters thanks to their unflinching bravery, discretion, and sophisticated raiding skills;[125] and "when a male child is born, a cord is often placed in the doorway of the house, signifying that the child will have the courage to steal many cows."[126] We can draw from these statements that raiding was probably a benchmark in the formation of male identity before the Balante immigrated to the Casamance.

The role played by the Balante in the regional economy of the Middle Casamance contrasted drastically with that of the Bainounk. This was much more similar to the strategy of "exclusiveness" adopted by other decentralized societies in Senegambia. For example, in the course of the nineteenth century the Diola improvised a new defensive system to complicate the layout of the townships they took away from the Bainounk in the Lower Casamance. This architecture was a shelter against the infringements of aggressive groups like the Mandinka. At this moment, some Diola districts like Fogny, Mark indicates, possessed small houses that were difficult to see by attacking cavalry because they were "half-buried in the earth."[127]

Likewise, the Balante suspected that the Mandinka and Europeans were hatching plots to convert them to Islam or to enslave them, respectively. They consequently denied suspicious strangers access to the Balantakounda by making three strategic choices that deserve emphasis.[128] First, the Balante augmented the dimensions of their new homeland in the Middle Casamance, intentionally targeting large, luxurious forests with big vegetal species like silk cotton trees, baobabs, palm wine, and palm oil trees. This gigantic landscape helped them limit the risks of external attacks that were commonplace in the Casamance in the precolonial period.[129] Second, inside this dense vegetation Balante elders set up sophisticated camps where young soldiers underwent intense military training. Soldiers learned the fighting skills that helped them defend their homeland at a time when *la guerre des races* or interethnic wars were numerous in this region.

Balante rituals encompassed a traditional ceremony called the dance of warriors (*ndiokta*) that was exclusively reserved for male warriors. Led by the *nteer bilanté*, women were tasked with making the protective charms that rendered male warriors invulnerable on the battlefield.[130] The purpose of the *ndiokta* was to uplift warriors' spirits by sowing in their souls, minds, and spirits the seeds of a renewed patriotism whenever it was performed to the rhythm of the balafon, the most sacred Balante musical instrument. During their performance warriors bragged about their past or future military prowess, dancing, singing, and pointing their swords to the sky as a sign of victory. In Brikama, praise-songs dedicated to legendary warriors are still fresh in popular memory.[131] Thanks to their unshakable courage, these elite warriors were the first to appear on the battlefield and the last to return home, intimidating their enemies through their invisible powers. During these military sessions elders intentionally lauded warriors like Matabélé in order to trigger the patriotism and perseverance of the youngest soldiers.[132]

Third, the Balante retaliated against any strangers who dared to enter the Balantakounda without their authorization. They were brilliant, passionate hunters who singled out deer and elephants for local consumption and the acquisition of highly prized products like ivory;[133] they grew large amounts of rice, beans, millet, and yams and harvested palm oil and palm wine; they fished in the deep waters of the Soungrougrou River; and they raised many animals such cows, goats, pigs, and hens. Thanks to this combined wealth, the Balante sustained their local economic life and participated in the commercial exchanges in the broader Casamance, but only if these occurred outside the Balantakounda.[134]

Michel Jajolet de La Courbe succeeded Louis Moreau de Chambonneau as the commandant of Senegal from 1688 to 1690 and from 1709 to 1710. He gathered some of his knowledge from his trips to the southern rivers region and his reports inspired later French written accounts on Senegambia. This included that of the Dominican father Jean Baptiste Labat (1664–1738) who never set foot in Africa. Prosper Cultru demonstrated how Labat wrote a multivolume description of Africa, plagiarizing La Courbe on some accounts. Labat also wrongly attributed a significant amount of La Courbe's early work to André Brue, the director of the "Compagnie du Sénégal" from 1697 to 1702 and from 1714 to 1720. La Courbe warned explorers about the toughness of the Balante closed-border policy.[135] For him, strangers were denied access to the Balantakounda probably because it contained substantial gold mines; and whites and blacks captured within this territory were killed or sold into slavery. The Balante avoided similar painful treatments through self-inflicted harm, such as starving themselves to death.[136]

Another Frenchman, Jean Baptiste Duran, made the same negative portrait of the Balante in the 1780s. For him, the Balante sold rice, millet, vegetables, cows, chickens, and gold, among other commodities, to Europeans and Africans, but only outside the Balantakounda; and this region was packed with gold mines more valuable than the mineral resources of Galam, a major gold and slave entrepôt situated on the upper reaches of the Senegal

River.[137] The abundance of these riches, Duran added, galvanized the Balante to give strangers persona non grata status across the Balantakounda. Some of these allegations do not seem grounded in reality; no empirical evidence lends credence to the existence of such an amount of wealth in gold in this region.[138] Before the arrival of the French, the Portuguese too had planned incursions into this same territory to find these same valuable resources. They were defeated by Balante warriors who benefitted from the bad weather conditions, as well as their great fighting skills and better familiarity with local topography. Bearing in mind the Balante's "extraordinary fury," Duran advised explorers willing to reach the Balantakounda to act with negotiation and diplomacy, not violence and intimidation.[139]

At the local level, the Balante suspected that the Mandinka represented a bigger danger for them than any other African group, beginning with their risk of being victims of Mandinkization. Filidjié Mané alluded to this sentiment: "Our elders clearly and totally knew that Mandinka Muslims wanted to marry Balante women for the sole purpose of converting them to Islam, as they did with generations of Bainounk women across in the Middle Casamance. Thus, while drinking palm wine together our elders legitimately debated the best strategies to safeguard our ancestral heritage."[140] In group interviews many participants corroborated Filidjié's statement, repeating that this lack of confidence was the reason why the Balantakounda remained an unfriendly territory to "suspicious strangers" for centuries; and that Mandinka Muslims were first among those suspects.[141] Doua clarified this longstanding suspicion, saying:"it would be wrong to suggest that intermarriage between the two groups [Mandinka and Balante] was totally impossible; but this was much harder than with the Bainounk because our Balante ancestors hated the subterfuges used by Mandinka Muslims to mislead others."[142] In the Woyi region of Guinea-Bissau as well Balante community elders painted the same negative picture; they accused the Mandinka of eagerly wanting to marry local Balante women, while refusing the "rule of reciprocity" in the name of Islam.[143]

## THE MANDINKA: CONQUERING THE WEST

The Mandinka are one of the largest ethno-linguistic groups in West Africa and their language (Mandingo) belongs to the Mande branch of the widely spoken Niger-Congo family. They have been active agents in propagating long-distance trade and Islam in West Africa for several centuries.[144] The Mandinka are the third largest ethnic group in the Casamance after the Diola and the Foula, and the majority in the Middle Casamance, despite their immigrant status.[145]An accurate analysis of the Mandinka's redeployment from the Niger River basin to other African regions should go back at least to the debut of the Mali Empire. This immigration toward the West particularly comprised two watershed moments: the first coincided with the advent of the Mali Empire in the fourteenth century, while the second occurred in the aftermath of its decline, followed by the expansion of the trans-Saharan trade in the sixteenth and seventeenth centuries.[146] This chapter focuses on the first stage of this historical sequence, when Soundiata's military ambitions generated trends of immigration westward led by his war general, Tiramakha Traoré.[147]

Two major accounts on Mandinka immigration from east (*tilibo*) to west (*tilidji*) merit consideration. The first, mostly known in Mali, signals a correlation between horses and Soundiata's imperial projects. At this moment, horses were becoming influential in the commercial transactions that existed in the West African savanna. The Venetian Alvise Cadamosto reported that Portuguese dealers could exchange as many as fifteen slaves for one horse in Senegambia.[148] In addition, Western Soudanic states like Mali, Songhay, and Djolof obtained a variable level of military power and political prestige through their acquisition of strong cavalries; and horses were instrumental in the payments imposed by the Djolof confederacy on tributary states until its decline in the middle of the seventeenth century.[149]

Robin Law spoke about a lack of evidence regarding the reliance on horses in West Africa until reports by Arab chroniclers like Al-Omari and Ibn Battuta in the fourteenth century.[150] However, Mande oral records classify Soundiata among rulers for whom obtaining horses was a precondition for becoming power players in Western Soudan. This ambition explains his idea to extend his influence beyond Mali's borders after the Kirina battle in 1255 when he defeated the Sosso king, Soumangourou Kanté. The emperor subsequently sent his half-brother Solimani to purchase warhorses in the Ferlo region of Senegal.[151] Testing Soundiata's level of tenacity, the ruler of Djolof confiscated the horses, forcing Solimani to go back home empty-handed.[152] Soundiata ipso facto planned a military retaliation against the Wolof king who committed this unprecedented offense. Tiramakha volunteered to lead this patriotic mission and threatened to take his own life if the ruler denied his request; he luckily achieved his wish thanks to the royal griot Balla Fasséké who persuaded Soundiata through his charisma. After fulfilling his mission, Tiramakha was welcomed home as a war hero. Soundiata was so proud of his warrior that on this occasion he "composed twelve songs" in his honor, before ordering him to return to the west and administer some lands in the name of Mali.[153]

The second version, generally known in southern Senegambia, emphasizes Soundiata's change of religious identity. After the Kirina battle, he showed gratitude to Islam by granting some privileges to five clerical families who prayed for him, converted to Islam, and designated it as the state religion of Mali. Tiramakha and some of his constituents, including his children, refused to follow the emperor's lead, and chose the path of self-imposed exile in protest and to spare their own lives. While leaving Mali Tiramakha reportedly said, "I'm not tired," (*kanan toro*), implying he did not mind returning to the west one more time.[154]

Despite their differences, these two versions agree that Tiramakha's campaigns led to the creation of Mandinka states in *tilidji*. One of these, Kaabou, served as the western wing of Mali until the sixteenth century, when it became independent.[155] Kaabou's name was probably coined by Duarte Pereira D'Almeida, the first known Lusophone author who revealed its existence in the course of the sixteenth century.[156] Arab chroniclers, like Battuta who had visited Mali by 1354 during the rule of Mansa Souleymane, issued insightful reports about Western Soudan; but they were remarkably mute about Kaabou's history perhaps because of its non-Muslim status at this time. A multidisciplinary group of researchers has thrown light on some obscure aspects of Kaabou's history and legacy. Despite their considerable resolve, there are still lingering questions, including the circumstances of its emergence, its concrete status as a slave-raiding state, its geographic limits, and its chronology.[157] Some scholars have blamed the European colonial partition that arbitrarily divided Kaabou into three distinct territorial units: British Gambia in the north, Portuguese Guinea in the south, and French Casamance in the middle.[158] This puzzle may also be explained by Kaabou's excessive physical dimension: a federation of more than a dozen provinces stretching from the Gambia River in the north to the borders of Fouta Diallon in the south. This encompassed parts of the Casamance, but the heartland of the empire was between the Upper Casamance and Guinea-Bissau.[159] The populations who now live in these areas have different languages, religious belief systems, and models of economic and political organization. One of the outcomes of this kaleidoscope is to exacerbate the already vexed oral narratives on Kaabou because local populations instinctively remember Kaabou's legacy through their own prisms.[160]

Interestingly, in the previous several centuries the evolution of African societies was affected by a succession of drought and desiccation that forced many population groups to immigrate from their homelands to less affected regions. Among these were Mande professional groups like traders, smiths, and leatherworkers. They were followed by horse warriors who profited from their military skills to build new states, levy taxes, and impose their mores on local populations in Senegambia.[161] Following the existing water systems, these warriors subdued many communities from the Gambia River to the Bisago Islands. Writing in the 1620s, Richard Jobson described how these warriors forced some Diola and Sérére groups in the Gambia River region to move further north and south in Senegambia.[162] In the Guinea-Bissau–Casamance zone, Mande warriors also pushed back several Bainounk, Balante, Pepel, and Diola populations. By the end of the sixteenth century, they had already extended their hegemony to most areas of the Casamance, but many were incorporated into Kaabou in the seventeenth century.

Furthermore, many human societies have historically explained their experiences on earth by replacing the natural with the supernatural, the ordinary with the extraordinary, or the real with the unreal: religious beliefs, patterns of immigration and resettlement, birth and death, and the rise and fall of empires, for example. This applies to sub-Saharan Africa where orality easily emerges as the alternative medium for elucidating the past in the absence of written sources.[163] Oral sources associated with the Mandinka of Kaabou (Kaabounké) specifically are replete with myths and legends designed to legitimize their domination over the local populations of southern Senegambia. Two myths singularly address the ways matrilineal descent came to dictate the system of devolution of power in Kaabou: the myths of Balaba and Dialansa.[164]

The first concerns a small team of leatherworkers. When one day they went hunting during the rule of a Sané ruler in Kaabou, they saw a porcupine rushing to hide inside a hole. The animal changed from a porcupine into a beautiful young woman when it finally emerged from the hole. Despite being collectively shocked, the hunters jumped on the woman without panicking and took her to the king, who automatically ordered special sacrifices to know more about the woman named Balaba. She still refused to talk and was kept in a room with a tiny hole through which she was fed. After months of detention, Balaba shocked the Kaabounké once again, miraculously giving birth to four baby girls, which forced the king to marry her and adopt the girls. When they grew up, the girls were married respectively to the Mandinka princes of Djiméra, Patiana, and Sama (Kaabounké provinces in The Gambia), and to the "king of Kahone" in the Sérére Kingdom of Saloum.[165]

The second myth relates to a young orphan called Mamba Koto Sané who became the hostage of a dragon (*ninki nanka*). The boy had to shelter and feed the animal with many meals, but one day the dragon suddenly required human sacrifices. The only person available was Mamba's own sister, but he was unwilling to sacrifice her. Nonetheless, his sister agreed to die for a noble cause if Mamba made the following pledge in front of the dragon: if some day Mamba should become king, his heirs would not be his own children, but his nephews or his sister's sons. Mamba hesitated before accepting these terms and taking his sister to the room. When he came back, the dragon had already eaten his sister before vanishing through the roof.[166]

Other versions complement or contradict these initial stories, depending on how and when they are narrated. For instance, some indicate that while Balaba was detained a member of the Sané royal lineage kept sleeping with her until she became pregnant.[167] Others suggest that the woman's name was not Balaba, but Tenemba, a princess who fled from Mali to Kaabou under King Maforang.[168] The second story seems incomplete due to its nebulosity on how the idea of kingship surfaced. Perhaps the dragon wanted to reward Mamba for being a caring host by making him a king, if he consented to sacrifice his sister. But even in this scenario, Mamba's sister might have already been aware that kingship was at stake when she accepted to die for her children's future.

Kaabou's ruling dynasty (*mansaya*) used many such myths and legends to perpetuate their self-aggrandizement and reflexes of subordination to them by non-*nyancho* people. The empire's pyramidal model was composed of three distinct classes. At the top were the *horon*, who were chosen from the founding families and their direct associates, the nobles, aristocrats, and free people. In the middle were the *nyamakalaw* who were hereditary occupational groups, including leatherworkers (*karanké* or *farba*), blacksmiths (*nounol*), and griots. At the bottom were the slaves (*dion*) who could be prisoners of war or born into slavery.[169] Male slaves could hold public office, serve in the army, marry free women with their consent, and work on their own farms. In the early Kaabounké society the rule of endogamous marriage was strictly enforced.[170] Only the children of Balaba's four daughters formed the ruling dynasty, and only men born to nyancho women were eligible to rule in Kaabou. In the Sérére kingdom of Sine founded by Mbégane Ndour between

1494 and 1514 the last ruling dynasty (*guélewar*) emigrated from Kaabou.[171] This Kaabounké scenario resembles the myths explicating the ascension to power in the Djolof Empire (1220–1550 CE). We have in both cases a chronology of events: the appearance of a stranger with noble and supernatural origins, the disintegration of an established social order and its replacement by a new one, and finally the rise to political prominence.[172] As the direct descendants of Balaba who was half-human and half-spirit, the nyanchol occupied the highest echelon within the *horon* hierarchy, thus setting themselves apart from the rest of the Kaabounké society.[173]

First among the nyanchol was the Great Mansa, supreme judge and king of Kaabou (*mansaba*) whose investiture occurred in the middle of the forests, the ideal holy site for holding key ritual ceremonies.[174] The invisible spirits (*dialan*) that dominated Kaabou's cosmology lived in the forests and took many different forms, including animals, bodies of water, or large trees. Like the Diola grandfathers of forests (*afan gureng*), only experts with proven public loyalty supervised these sacred forests.[175] As in the case of the Diola *oukin*, the Kaabounké suspected that misfortunes, such as sterility, drought, road accidents, and miscarriage, were caused by the wrath of their *dialan*.[176] If the inauguration of the *mansaba* was handled without due diligence, the *dialan* that supervised the whole process would not let him receive the hat symbolizing his royal power (*mansa naffo*). Once the new mansa was officially installed in his functions, the Kaabounké could no longer speak to him without first saying the Great (*mama*). Every new mansa gave a bright speech that emphasized the core episodes that would shape his tenure. After he blessed the crowd and prayed for the country, his personal bard ended the ceremony with a beautiful song in his honor.[177] Like the *tiéddo* (ruling class) in the Wolof kingdoms, nothing interested the nyanchol more than hunting, waging war, drinking, and eating good food; and they had to show no signs of fear for anything and anyone, including death.[178]

Kaabou's immense physical size barred its central administration from mobilizing all the human resources necessary to hold the entire empire under one single authority from the capital, Kansala. The mansaya sought to remedy this structural weakness by inventing a new mechanism of political control called a "system of client-kings. " This consisted of delegating some powers to a group of administrators (*kanta-mansa*) selected among Mané and Sané ruling lineages who descended from Tiramakha and Balaba. Besides representing the *mansaba* in approximatively twelve provinces, these administrators helped the state militarily and economically.[179]

Some Kabounké provinces resulted from political arrangements between the mansaya and powerful local lineages in the broader Casamance like Firdou, a Foula territory in the Upper Casamance; Birassou on the eastern border of the Balantakounda; and Pakao in the Middle Casamance. Golbéry mentioned the case of a "mansa" who lived in the Upper Casamance without giving his name.[180] As in some Gambian kingdoms where political power alternated within Diamé, Mané, and Sonko lineages, the Mandiang of Sonkoudou, Madina, and Kouniara defended the interests of Kaabou in Pakao.[181] Two groups of administrators were the close collaborators of nyanchol in this area: the first (*mansaring*) or offspring of nyancho fathers and non-*nyancho* mothers; and the second (*koringo*) who descended from the Sonko, Sagna, and Mandiang lineages. None of these were eligible for Kaabou's throne, despite having a long tradition of intermarriage with the mansaya.

I saw several *koringo* lineages who continue to enjoy some degree of social prestige in the Middle Casamance thanks to the role played by their ancestors in Kaabou's early administration. For Cissoko, these could well be the direct descendants of the Bainounk; and the powers invested in them may have resulted from pacts that authorized some lineages with proven loyalty to Kaabou's ruling class to administer their own territories.[182] In some accounts the representatives of the mansa of Kaabou (in the Middle Casamance) are described not as real Mandinka, but "nature-Soninquei people" like the Bainounk. I saw other local lineages like Mandiang, Danfa, Bodian, and Diassy who are still considered ethnically and linguistically Mandinka. But their representatives told me that their families underwent a change in ethnic identity (through cultural assimilation) following the Mandinka's resettlement in the region.[183]

Between the seventeenth century and the 1750s Kaabou greatly benefitted from the slave trade between the Casamance and Guinea-Bissau, and reached the peak of its economic prosperity when it boomed in this region.[184] Local sources insist that both the rise and fall of Kaabou were the direct results of the slave trade, and that during this time the Casamance was one of Kaabou's economic outlets in Senegambia.[185] The mansaya took advantage of this situation to abuse the poor peasant communities living in and around Kaabou, regardless of their religious and ethnic identities. For example, in the early 1600s, Kaabou's provincial governors *(farim)* dominated the Balante and the Bainounk and forced the Cassanke king who ruled over the upper waters of the Casamance to make tribute payments to them.[186] At the same time, rainfall shortage, drought, and bad harvests often pushed Foula pastoralists to look for water and pasture for their livestock in wetter and greener ecological spaces; Kaabou was one of the main destinations of these dedicated nomads who migrated seasonally from French Guinea. When they decided to create their own communities in Kaabou (*foulakounda*) instead of traveling back and forth, some governors openly targeted them for enslavement.[187] Others confiscated a portion of wealth produced by Foula agro-pastoralists living under their jurisdiction. The wealth, power, and prestige of these officials depended on the quantity of "gifts" in cattle or harvest products they received from the Foula.[188] These products, euphemistically called "gifts" in some oral records, were indeed "substantial tributes" or "forced gifts" paid by the Foula to the Kabounké, to borrow from one griot in Sonkoudou.

Another humiliation was to confiscate the millet plants grown by Foula farmers so that the Kaabounké could use these not as food but as firewood for cooking delicious meals. These long-standing power abuses inspired a popular Mandinka song that begins with the phrase "mandinka tiéddo, do not finish my millet" (*tiéddo kanama nion bang*).[189] Young children in the Casamance still perform an old game called the "Foula game," sleeping with only half of their bodies in the bed. This painful position was one of the punishments the Kaabounké inflicted upon their Foula subjects to humiliate them at their leisure. The mansaya exchanged many enslaved people and the food items they obtained from their subjects for valuable foreign items such as rifles, gunpowder, and horse saddles. These power abuses accentuated the economic hardships of the already poor peasant communities in the broader Casamance region.[190]

The period from the 1750s onwards was a totally different situation for Kaabou, a change that can be explained by a combination of factors. For example, this was the time when Senegambia was gradually undergoing a transition from the era of the slave trade to an era of legitimate trade. Subsequently, Kaabou ought to invent adequate strategies and adjustments to cope with the new situation created by the fall of the slave trade, but Kansala was unable to meet these serious challenges.[191] After becoming a theocratic state in 1725, Fouta Diallon planned to surmount those same challenges by becoming a more effective power player in the southern rivers region.[192] At this critical juncture, the French, Portuguese, and British were already engaged in a competition for total hegemony over this region. This led the French and the British to sign new treaties with Fouta Diallon, in 1843 and 1844, respectively. This means that the Europeans recognized the importance of Fouta Diallon in these transitory years, contrary to Kaabou whose power was hanging by a thread.[193]

In addition, while controlling the trade networks in the Guinea-Bissau–Casamance zone, Muslim merchant-scholars established their own self-segregated neighborhoods in Kaabou.[194] Islam was tolerated as a minority religion in Kaabou, but the mansaya treated Muslims with contempt by claiming a monarchical power that placed them in opposition to Islam. Muslims could only practice commerce since administrative and military affairs were strongholds of Kaabou's ruling elite, and commoners who accepted Islam lost their privileges in the army or in the central administration.[195] Muslims dealt with these discriminatory practices by choosing to ground their agency in patience and silence. Thanks to this strategy Muslim proselytizers won the confidence of a growing number of Kaabounké at the expense of their pre-existing cult of Dialansa. Many of these were members of the poorest farming communities who were exposed to the same economic exploitation as the Foula by provincial governors.[196] These breakthroughs were among the incentives for some Muslim revolts against the mansaya in the 1840s. Provinces that took this opportunity to unilaterally declare their independence from Kansala included Souna, Birassou, and Pakao where Islam had already been the dominant faith thanks to the collective efforts of the original Muslim settlements mentioned above.[197]

During the nineteenth century, Kaabou's continuous hegemonic ambitions on the Casamance were irreparably crippled by its inability to exert "a total, long-lasting" control over the entire region, given its "remoteness, vastness and inadequate resources."[198] Given these weaknesses, many Europeans and Muslim merchant-scholars carved out commercial and religious niches in the Middle Casamance, by negotiating land concessions not from the Kaabounké but from leaders of the Bainounk chiefdoms."[199] Echoing this argument, one griot said the regional power of Kaabou "had significantly diminished before the fall of the slave trade, followed by its storming by Fouta Diallon in 1867. This gave the Islamization and colonization processes free rein in the Casamance–Guinea-Bissau zone."[200]

This host of detrimental factors led to the inevitable collapse of Kaabou under its most famous ruler, Mansa Dianké Waly Sané. He is eloquently described in Mandinka epic songs as the exemplification of the fearlessness characterizing every true nyancho. Fouta Diallon's expansionism led to a direct military conflict between this theocratic state and Kaabou. The Mandinka call this memorable event "the war that ended the clan" (*tourouban kélo*). During his inaugural speech, like his predecessors, Dianké Waly used his bully pulpit to predict that Kaabou's existence would probably end with him. In 1867, Foula warriors provoked general panic when they suddenly entered Kansala, after spending a lot of time along the way. The noble status of the mansa forbade him from running, especially after some women and girls jumped into public wells, choosing suicide over submission.[201]

When he realized that his palace was irresistibly encircled from all sides, Dianké Waly moved from words to deeds: he demanded that Kansala be burnt to the ground, only sparing his own griot's life because he wanted future generations to appreciate his level of honor and patriotism.[202] At the height of this memorable war, both camps were determined to achieve military success by overcoming the other with sophisticated occult forces. Besides being a military disaster for them, many Kaabounké considered the *tourouban kélo* the litmus test of the superiority of Islam and the Qur'an over their preexisting *dialan* and "traditional religion." This widespread belief facilitated the incorporation of increasing numbers of Kaabounké into the Dar al-Islam.[203]

## CONCLUSION

Oral traditions used in this chapter are vital tools for helping us grasp how ethnicity, religion, and culture shed light on key historical transitions in the Middle Casamance. These sources are reworked to elucidate outcomes such as the "decline" of Bainounk power, the "fall" of the Kaabou monarchy, and Balante "xenophobia." This approach is not intended to erase history and then replace it with a timeless tradition, but rather to create a kind of "periodization" of the past by explicating crucial turning points in the general history of this region.

Although since the precolonial era Islam was developing little by little in this region, local populations had generally remained attached to the preservation of their ancestral heritages. Decentralized societies like the Diola, the Sérére–Saféne, and the Balante may have historically lacked gigantic armed forces, as opposed to highly centralized ones. However, they have always created powerful strategies to deal with those who sought to introduce foreign institutions into their homelands or integrate their regional economy, or both.[204] The Balante repeated many times their long-standing motto, "The security of our homeland comes first," to reiterate the decisiveness of these strategies in preserving their independence from others.

These developments do not mean that groups like the Diola and the Balante were congenitally hostile to any form of foreign presence in their homelands. Showing generous hospitality toward strangers has historically been an integral part of most Senegambian societies.[205] In fact, as Lasnet notes, trustworthy strangers were welcomed, protected, and treated with dignity, hospitality, and respect in the Balatakounda.[206] Oral testimonies also include stories of countless Muslims and other talented immigrants who were warmly welcomed and authorized to settle in the Balante and Diola homelands.[207]

That said, the available oral and written evidence makes clear that in the period under consideration, no ethnic group across the Casamance exhibited more hospitality, inclusiveness, and open-mindedness toward immigrants than the Bainounk. Their old tradition of respecting and welcoming foreigners to their homeland (*oudiahére* )was largely rooted in their strong desire to recruit highly skilled professionals who could help them ameliorate their living conditions in significant ways. Chapters 2 and 3 will show how Fodé Héraba and his fellow clerics took advantage of *oudiahére* to lay the groundwork for the Dar al-Islam in the Middle Casamance. The Karantaba landlord paradigm was a stepping-stone for this process.

# CHAPTER 2

# The Landlord Paradigm of Islamization

## Interfaith Marriage and the Founding of Karantaba (Seventeenth Century)

As highlighted in the previous chapter, one standard practice across sub-Saharan Africa has historically been the accommodation of strangers from multiple backgrounds by affording them food, water, wives, shelter, protection, and other basic human needs. These preferential treatments apply particularly to immigrants who bring with them valuable socio-professional skills, like traders, warriors, smiths, hunters, musicians, Christian theologians, healers, diviners, and Muslim clerics.[1] Through their old tradition of *oudiahére* the Bainounk chiefdoms offer a compelling case study for comprehending this long-standing culture of hospitality in Senegambia.[2]

This chapter describes the first phase of the landlord paradigm of Islamization by concentrating on the personal interactions between early Muslim immigrants who played the role of strangers (*lountang*) and their Bainounk host communities (*diatti yoo*) in the Middle Casamance. The Bainounk found it extremely beneficial to entice talented Muslim newcomers by facilitating their interfaith marriages with local women; Muslims profited from the sacredness of marriage alliances in Bainounk society and culture to acquire land concessions that became the foundation of the Dar al-Islam in this region; and Muslims drew local inhabitants into the orbit of Islam in a piecemeal fashion. These dynamics occurred between the first half of the seventeenth century, when the original Muslim townships began to mushroom in this region, and the 1840s and 1850s when the balance of religious power was increasingly tipping away from the previously dominant Bainounk religion.

In the 1970s, the conflicting paradigms championed by Robin Horton and

Humphrey Fisher provided the blueprints for many subsequent studies of religious outlooks in many regions. In his pioneering model (intellectualist theory), Horton paints the African cosmology as a realm dominated by a Higher Power and lesser spirits, corresponding to the *social macrocosm and microcosm*. For him, the transformation of the basic African cosmology is sparked by external and internal crises, culminating in the breakdown of the social microcosm. By asserting that this cosmology slowly undergoes a change from within, Horton proposes a new version of "syncretism," which means here the symbiosis between Islam and African religion.[3]

In comparison, Fisher, the leader of the "devout opposition" to Horton's paradigm, approaches conversion in Africa as a three-step process. The first, "quarantine," occurs when Muslims immigrate to non-Muslim lands and distance themselves from local "unbelievers" to avoid the corruption of their faith. The second, "mixing," takes shape when host communities solicit Muslims' expertise in such sophisticated divinatory practices as dream interpretation, fortune telling, and the making of protective charms by manipulating the Qur'an; and the third, "reform," starts when Muslims profit from mixing to convert non-Muslims into Islam through violent means. Fisher uses the metaphor of the juggernaut to elucidate how the new worldview, Islam, gradually smashed and swept aside the old worldview, African religion.[4] These two scholars have refined their argument many times to formulate sharper perspectives on this vexed issue. Within the past two decades, some scholars have used core components of this decades-old debate as theoretical frameworks while proposing other models of conversion.[5]

I use Fisher's model as a comparative framework simply because it better suits the ethnic comportments emphasized in this book. Unlike him, I contend that interfaith marriages between Bainounk women and Muslim clerics (mostly Mande-speaking people), rather than "quarantine," fostered the expansion of Islam in the Middle Casamance. Drawing on hagiographic accounts and scholar genealogies, this chapter first retraces the historical circumstances of the founding of Karantaba and the key episodes of Fodé Hérabas peregrination from Mali to southern Senegal. Second, it analyzes the negotiations between the cleric and the Bainounk ruler who hosted him in the Souna-Balmadou region, to explain how together they typify the first part of the landlord paradigm. Third, the chapter explicates the persistence of this paradigm in the Middle Casamance, narrating the untold stories of other prominent Muslim clerics whose course of action mirrored that of Fodé Hérabas on several accounts.

## A DIVINE MISSION: THE FOUNDING OF KARANTABA

Scholars have investigated the importance of many currents of immigration from the Niger River basin to other African regions. Mande-speaking people were the main architects of these currents that accelerated in the aftermath of the fall of Mali in the course of the sixteenth century.[6] Wangara, Dioula, and Maraka are the principal generic names attributed to these trade diasporas that have crisscrossed sub-Saharan Africa since the precolonial period. According to authors like Philip Curtin and Robert Launay, these migratory currents were motivated by long-distance trade and its economic and political repercussions in other African regions.[7] Others have used more nuanced approaches by prioritizing Islamic proselytism in characterizing these transformations. For example, Ivor Wilks comments that besides propagating trade networks Dioula merchants promoted Islamic learning in the forest ecological zone.[8] For Thomas C. Hunter and Lamin Sanneh, proselytism rather than trade was the driving engine behind the dispersal of Diakhanké clerics in West Africa.[9] Nehemia Levtzion contends that Muslim merchants were "the carriers of Islam" rather than "the agents of Islamization," even though their dispersal helped link isolated African populations with broader commercial networks.[10]

These same commercial transactions existed in precolonial southern Senegambia thanks to the dynamism of successive waves of *dioula* merchants and scholars (*mori*). Because these experts generally shared the same ethnic and religious backgrounds, they have often been lumped together as members of the same socio-professional category in local scholar genealogies and oral traditions.[11] In these same sources Fodé Héraba is classified among the "devout Mande merchant-scholars" who popularized Islam in the midst of non-Muslim populations via incentives that differed from military jihãd.[12] Early Arab travelers like Al-Bekri mentioned Muslim functionaries who worked at the royal court in pre-Almoravid Ghana. The ruler (*tounka*) returned the favor by authorizing Muslims to live and worship freely in their own quarter.[13] Before the arrival of Portuguese mariners, some African rulers in other areas gave Muslim clerics land grants where they created and ran their own communities.[14] Following mentions by André Àlvares de Almada in the 1580s, Balthasar Barreira in the early seventeenth century signaled the existence of independent Muslim settlements with mosques and Qur'anic schools in Africa. These were led by preachers called *bixirin*, the same experts Richard Jobson termed "*mary-bucks*," a corruption of marabouts.[15]

Fodé Héraba was one of the African clerics who perpetrated these patron-client relationships in southern Senegambia in the first half of the seventeenth century, like the "professional guild of clerics" documented by Sanneh. For him, Diakhanké clerics were active agents in this process since the time of their "clerical prototype," El Hadji Salim Souwaré.[16] Fodé Héraba's hagiographers depict him not as a "Diakhanké" but as a "Mandinka and sometimes a Sarakholé." It would be too risky for us to compare the *Pakao al-kitaabo* to such substantial manuscripts as the chronicles of Timbuktu in Mali, Gonja in Ghana, and Kano in Nigeria for the reasons aforementioned. But given the absence of contemporaneous written documentation on Fodé Héraba, I reconstructed the most decisive aspects of his lifetime, drawing on the *Pakao al-kitaabo*, scholar genealogies, and oral traditions.[17] In Letvzion's opinion, studies of the march of Islam that are based on local traditions and Muslim chronicles, tend to emphasize the role of Muslim clerics and downplay that of Muslim merchants; but the opposite is true in European written sources because for Western traders who communicated with African merchants nothing mattered more than the accumulation of wealth.[18]

This description may explain why Fodé Héraba's hagiographers persist that while he was born to a family of merchant-scholars, he was dedicated to the propagation of Islam, profiting from long-distance trade, like many of his fellow clerics.[19] His father, Abdoul Rahmane (or Mamadou Lamine), was a merchant-scholar in Fass, a Senegalese corruption of the town of Fés, Morocco. During his lifetime, Timbuktu was a vibrant Islamic and commercial metropolis that attracted a myriad of teachers, students, and traders.[20] By the sixteenth century Timbuktu may have counted about 180 Qur'anic centers and 9,000 students, impressive numbers by the standards of that time.[21] When Abdoul Rahmane moved to Timbuktu, he rapidly submitted to an old Islamic custom by marrying a local woman to commence his own family life.[22] Regrettably, oral traditions give us scarce information on Fodé Héraba's paternal and maternal ancestry, only relating that his mother (Aicha Tounkara) belonged to a respected Muslim lineage in Timbuktu. According to Iman Fodé Almamy Dramé of Karantaba, when his ancestor reached the Casamance, he was impeccably fluent in several languages, including Mandingo and Sarakholé.[23] As in the case of Cheikh Ahmadou Bamba, Fodé Héraba's father instructed him in the Qur'an and introduced him to the Khadiriyya before he departed from Mali with his *wird* (special litanies).[24] Before his death, Fodé Héraba's father asked him to follow another old Mande custom by marrying Yassa Tounkara, the daughter of his maternal uncle.

Since Prophet Muhammad's groundbreaking meditations on the Mountain of Light (*jabaal al-noor*) located outside Mecca, the road maps of many Muslim clerics have included dreams and visions, resulting in the fulfillment of their divine missions.[25] Fodé Hérabaʼs mission began when night after night he experienced a mystical illumination summoning him to relocate from east to west. This was to lay the groundwork for a new Muslim township that would become a cornerstone for the diffusion of Islam between the Casamance and the Gambia, the two rivers flowing through the heart of the Mandinka country in Senegambia.[26] After a long moment of soul searching, Fodé Héraba consulted his extended family as well as his closest friends and left Daramane, a town founded by Dramé clerics from Timbuktu.[27] André Brue (1654–1738), the director of the Compagnie du Sénégal, sojourned in Kayes by the late seventeenth century. He portrayed Daramane as "a very populous clerical township where local Dramé and Yatabaré lineages were among the best-educated" elements across this region.[28]

Fodé Héraba was in the middle of his life (*fondiké*) when he started his spiritual journey on foot, accompanied by his wife and by a slave. They first sojourned in Kaabou (Mandinka term for Guinea-Bissau) where a tiny minority of Muslim merchant-scholars lived, as mentioned above. The region between the Casamance and Guinea-Bissau was at this moment populated by many different Bainounk groups. The trio stopped in some Bainounk townships to recuperate from a physically fatiguing trip and pay tribute to some "brothers in Islam" who preceded the cleric in this region.[29] Throughout his journey, Fodé Héraba often lost sight of the "divine light" (*nooro*) that guided his nightly meditations whenever dawn arrived. This painstaking experience prevented him from pinning down an ideal site for the settlement of a Muslim village, but did not crush the spirit of Fodé Héraba, as he knew the precarious mission ahead of him from the outset.[30] In Mandinka historical consciousness, the ordeals surrounding this "forced relocation" are considered expected occurrences; sometimes these are compared to the Prophetic predicaments during his *hijira* and sometimes to hagiographic accounts explicating the ethnogenesis of Muslim settlements in West Africa.[31]

In the Middle Casamance, Fodé Héraba was hosted in Bambadion (*wild crocodiles*, Bainounko), an old township laying on the south bank of the Casamance River. In the mid-seventeenth century local populations were devoted to their ancestral traditions, including harvesting, drinking palm wine (*dolo*), and sacrificing to their *china*.[32] Though Bahoumba Daffé, the ruler of Bambadion at this time, had never seen or known Fodé Héraba before, he welcomed him as a distinguished guest, thanks to his honorable clerical status. Daffé was pleased to listen to his guest read from his Qur'anic manuscripts, or to watch him write "sophisticated calligraphy" on his wooden tablets (*wallal*) on a daily basis. This behavior is consistent with John Hunwick's and Jack Goody's ideas that the populations of Western Soudan were fascinated by Islam due to Muslims' ability to read, write, count, and speak in various languages; and that Muslim experts in divination exercised a powerful influence on illiterate African cultures and societies thanks to their magico-religious practices. Likewise, the Bainounk were impressed by Muslim divinatory performances and perceived Qur'anic schools as "fast avenues for overcoming illiteracy.[33]

While the holy man's reputation resonated across the region, Daffé's demeanor episodically shifted to "legitimate fear and suspicion."[34] This psychology is shared by many African authorities implicated in the settlement of Muslim communities within their jurisdiction. For instance, this is a clear theme in Wolof hagiographic records on the gentlemen's agreement between Serigne Khaly Amar Fall and Damel Makhourédia Khouli Fall, two men who were both born into the same royal dynasty of Kayor. Nonetheless, the Damel did not initially take the cleric's declaration at face value, when in the early seventeenth century he requested a space in Saniakhor (now Pire) where he could teach the Qur'an. Rather, before granting his request, the Damel demanded that he obtain the marabout's honorable word (*kadou*, Wolof) that he would never seek to overthrow his regime, and that he would protect him against any foreign aggression.[35] This same psychology seems to have animated the dialogue between King Yimba of Tamba, in eastern Senegal, and the highly regarded Foula marabout El Hadji Oumar Tall, when he mobilized his disciples to establish a village school in Dingiraye.[36]

Notwithstanding his vacillating feelings, Chief Daffé applied *oudiahére* by ordering his assistants to ascertain that his guest "lacked no food, water, shelter, or other material he needed to appropriately practice his faith in Bambadion." This recommendation was particularly apparent when Daffé was persuaded of the cleric's apoliticism. Fodé Héraba reciprocated by initiating the populace to the basic Qur'anic tenets, befriending top dignitaries, and praying for Daffé's good health and for social harmony and economic prosperity in Bambadion.[37] After months of peaceful coexistence, Daffé consulted his closest advisers and granted his distinguished guest a concession to settle on empty land. This was a large forest laying less than four miles to the northeast of Bambadion, between the rice fields of Minanbassé and

Bakiang.[38] The *nooro* that had accompanied Fodé Héraba since the beginning of his peregrination led him straight to a taabo tree. This became the site of Karantaba whose name derives from knowledge (*karan*) and taabo, signifying in Mandingo the taabo under whose shade knowledge (Islamic knowledge) is transmitted. The Mandinka strongly believe that what is now the Mandinka country was already a holy land since the early history of Islam, when seven "saints" came from Arabia to the Middle Casamance as a blessing for Muslims. These saints are remembered in popular imagination as the "seven Abdoul" who have no descendants in the region. Sometimes they are portrayed as invisible spirits (*ginol*) and sometimes as holy men, based on the narrator and the location; and each of these saints is believed to have been buried in a specific village: Abdoul Khadir (Karantaba), Abdoul Rakhman (Saliguénié), Abdoul Wakhab (Badounga), Abdoul Aziz (Katabina), Abdoul Yékini (Ndiama), Abdoul Khoudoss (Diana-Sonkoudou), and Abdoul Karim (Bassaf). Abdoul Kadir is reportedly the one who softened the ground for Fodé Héraba and his companions in Karantaba.[39]

These long-held narratives may have arisen from invented traditions, considering the fact that most oral accounts, including those associated with Fodékounda in Karantaba, have totally denied the veracity of the "seven Abdoul." Fodé Almamy Dramé, Karantaba's caliph general (1956–90) in particular dismissed tales of the physical presence of the "seven Abdoul" as a total aberration. For him, this story began as a "persistent rumor" that ultimately became a "truth" in popular memory. Similarly, recollections by respected oral experts like Fina Kéba Dakhaba and Fina Malang Faty made no explicit reference to this story. In other words, the guardians of Islamic traditions and the gatekeepers of human memory have both rejected the truthfulness of this story. Nonetheless, these tales by dint of repetition have over time enhanced the spiritual image of these seven townships, classifying them as "holy lands" for thousands of individuals.

The question of the "seven Abdoul" emerged again in another interview I had with El Hadji Manding on the spiritual value ascribed to the taabo. My host said whenever he asked his father his opinion on this issue, he always answered with the same strong sense of confidence: "If this story was true, don't you think that somebody like me would know about it. This is not grounded in reality; do not believe it, do not believe it."[40]

While building Karantaba Fodé Héraba and his associates sought divine blessings, interminably reciting the Holy Qur'an under the taabo. Karantabans have since then considered the taabo the heart of their sacred geography,

**Table 1. These villages are considered the burial grounds of the "Seven Abdoul"**

| | |
|---|---|
| Karantaba | Abdoul Khadir |
| Saliguénié | Abdoul Rakhman |
| Badounga | Abdoul Wahab |
| Katabina | Abdoul Aziz |
| Ndiama | Abdoul Yékini |
| Diana-Sonkoudou | Abdoul Khoudos |
| Bassaf | Abdoul Karim |

given its status as the gateway of Qur'anic education. The taabo is sometimes characterized as the "chaperone" or the "watchdog" for the township founded by the cleric in God's name. For Diéli Sirifo Kouyaté, the taabo instilled in Fodé Héraba the courage he needed to excel in the Dar al-koufr.[41] We will discuss later how the taabo was incorporated into the emerging Dar al-Islam, like the Muslim holy shrine in Mecca (*kaaba*). But whether the taabo was initially an abode of Bainounk spirits is unclear in oral sources.[42]

Dealing with the periodization and the chronology of historical events is one of the burdensome tasks for those who are doing fieldwork research in sub-Saharan Africa. Indeed, these exercises are replete with distortions, variabilities, misconceptions, omissions, and anachronisms, and must consequently be executed diligently to maximize the chances of success. Even the most outspoken informants struggled while attempting to determine the exact date of Karantaba's founding. Some linked this discomfort to its antiquity over the other Islamic townships.[43] Others confirmed this antiquity by suggesting that before Karantaba the Bainounk knew almost nothing about Islam. Certain oral records correlating the founding of Karantaba with key historical transitions insist on the erection of the Fort of Sédhiou some 200 years after Karantaba, meaning in around 1637.[44]

Other accounts recall the aftermath of Timbuktu's invasion by the Moroccan army that terminated the era of the Western Soudanic empires by the 1590s.[45] This generated chaos and caused the displacement of some members of Timbuktu's Muslim intelligentsia. This harassment was prolonged from one generation to the next until the time of Fodé Héraba, who immigrated to Senegambia following divine revelation.[46] It is worth recalling that Timbuktu's storming intervened against a backdrop of internal feuds within the Askia ruling dynasty; they spent too much time fighting each other over

Figure 2. The fallen lenko tree planted across the street from the taabo. (Photo by the author, October 2003.)

the mechanisms of devolution of power rather than attacking their common foe. This diversion helped King al-Mansour of Morocco fulfill his dream of occupying the wealthy salt mines of Teghazza. The *Tarikh al-sudan* furnishes vivid details on these military assaults that resulted in the deportation of local scholars like Ahmad Baba (1556–1627 CE) to Marrakech. The Moroccan armed forces terrorized Timbuktu's inhabitants, pillaged their houses, stole their wealth, and annihilated any attempt at public uprising.[47]

Some scholars have attempted to determine approximately when Karantaba was founded. For example, in the 1960s, when Christian Roche posed this question to Chief Fodé Almamy, he replied that "the village was founded three hundred and forty five years ago by Fodé Héraba," meaning in around 1625.[48] In 1988, in his resourceful master's thesis, Fossar Souané depicted his ancestral homeland as a 356-year-old village, retracing its existence back to 1632.[49] Similarly, in oral data collected by Djibril T. Niane, "the first Mande Muslim townships in the Casamance, including Karantaba, date back to the 1620s."[50]

Despite the proximity of these dates, I deepened my knowledge of this complex issue by examining the family tree of the Dramé founding lineage. I concentrated on the period between Fodé Héraba, the eponymous ancestor, and Fodé Almamy, the longest-serving imam until his death in 1990. I further looked at the available raw data gleaned from scholar genealogies and oral records collected by other local lineages. As a result of my inquiries, I discovered a total of six different generations of leaders between these two men, the average being forty years from one generation to the next.[51] In light of these sources, Karantaba was likely established between the 1620s and the 1640s, but this date is more suggestive than conclusive.

## INTERFAITH MARRIAGE: FODÉ HÉRABA AND CHIEF BAHOUMBA DAFFÉ

Many studies of religious conversion in sub-Saharan Africa now tend to focus chronologically on the contemporary period. The meaning, motivations, moment, trajectories, and outcomes of conversion as well as the interactions between different religious outlooks are among the critical themes emphasized in this literature.[52] Scholars of Senegambia have used multidisciplinary approaches to shed new light on new methods of affiliation that mostly occurred in the northern region between the nineteenth and twentieth centuries. Gender, sexuality, intermarriage, conversion, global and local appropriations of Islam, transnational practices, and the battles of orthodoxy between Islamic "tradition" and "modernity" are dominant themes in this scholarship.[53] In some cases, conversion involves generational conflicts in which elders act like guardians of tradition while youth serve as agents of change. In others, conversion is a switch of membership from one Islamic denomination to another.[54] By building on my previous work, I provide here a long-term view of conversion to highlight a tradition of interfaith marriage bonds that began in the Middle Casamance in the precolonial period. These were short-lived experiences in the sense that Bainounk women involved in these marriage ties accepted Islam right after joining their Muslim husbands.[55]

With his general theory of exchange (the alliance theory), Claude Lévi-Strauss deeply influenced many studies on kinship relations in non-Western societies. For him, the prohibition of incest as an immoral behavior by local customs and traditions, encourages members of such societies to seek to marry outside their own kins or lineages.[56] However, in the Middle Casamance, besides the prerogatives that emanated from Muslims' expertise in long-distance trade and divinatory practices, interfaith marriages were stimulated by other considerations. The first and most obvious is shariah which authorizes Muslim men to marry outside of their religion, if their offspring would follow their father's religion.[57] In fact, broadening the Islamic community (*ummah*) by bringing in new converts is considered one of Muslims' finest undertakings that would be rewarded by God on Judgment Day.[58] Next, Muslims who resettled in non-Muslim lands like the Bainounk country considerably decreased their chances of finding Muslim wives in their new homelands. So, local host communities became the primary "wife-giving groups" for Muslim newcomers.[59] Finally, and most importantly, as one of the most sacrosanct social institutions in Bainounk society, marriage ties led to land concessions designed to entice skillful strangers, instead of letting them move to different areas. This combination of factors helped Muslim clerics like Fodé Héraba propagate Islam in the Middle Casamance and surrounding areas.[60]

Historically, Muslim and non-Muslim rulers both contributed to the Islamization of sub-Saharan Africa in various ways. This sometimes grew out of Muslims' spirit of compromise by deliberately targeting rulers for conversion, or at least for friendly alliances that could best serve their interests. As Levtzion notes, the spread of Muslims was the first step in conversion to Islam in Africa; the second was the moment when clerics began to communicate with host kings; and in some instances, rulers were directly the "early recipients of Islam."[61] One classical example in Senegambia is the king of Malal (Musulmani) who embraced Islam and subsequently dismantled local shrines after the meditations of a visiting cleric ended a terrible drought in this country. War Diabi, who was probably the first known Muslim ruler of Tékrour in northern Senegal, asked his subjects to accept Islam before his death in around 1040 CE.. Around the same time, the ruler of neighboring Silla personally attacked his non-Muslim neighbors.[62]

Other rulers acted like what I term *king-facilitators* by helping create new Muslim settlements inside or near their own homelands without abandoning their non-Muslim identity. Indeed, this practice is as old as the inception of Islam, considering the case of the Negus of Abyssinia (Ethiopia); he offered sanctuary to some of Prophet Muhammad's followers when they fled Mecca; these refugees later returned home instead of staying in Abyssinia for good.[63] Again, Arab travelers like Ibn Hawkal and Al-Idrissi mentioned the case of Muslim interpreters, accountants, and translators in pre-Almoravid Ghana.[64] During the seventeenth and eighteenth centuries, Nomré, Kokki, and Louga were prestigious Islamic townships (*dekkou serigne*, Wolof) created in Senegambia by the Muslim intelligentsia (*serigne lamb* and *serigne faakh taal*).[65]

These resulted from land grants (*lew*, Wolof) by Lat Soukabé Fall (1697–1719) and like-minded rulers who wanted to find ways to regulate the impact of Islam.[66] The same politically motivated arrangements existed in Tékrour before the outbreak of the Islamic revolution of 1776.[67]

Chief Daffé was among "the early recipients of Islam." Because Fodé Héraba and his first wife had no children by the time they arrived in the Middle Casamance, he chose most of his spouses among Bainounk women, including Némouna Diakoumba, Daffé's own daughter.[68] Traditions recall that Fodé Héraba performed sophisticated prayers for his host on multiple occasions. His repeated successes inspired Daffé and his daughter to accept Islam before the founding of Karantaba, setting the tone for many commoners in Bambadion. In addition to giving Fodé Héraba his daughter in marriage, Daffé granted him the wild forest that became the site of the first Muslim village and first mosque across the Casamance.[69]

Moreover, the march of Islam led to the reconfiguration of the political and religious landscapes in many African regions. This culminated in the coexistence of two separate quarters: the old one (*dar al-kufr*), where the non-Muslim majority lived, served as the temporal center; and the new one (*dar al-Islam*), where the minority of Muslims resided, was the Islamic periphery. This separation between center and periphery was partly motivated by a mutually advantageous wish to avoid both religious interference and "political meddling," and to create a sense of "neutrality" and "autonomy," without ruling out the possibility of collaboration through mutual protection.[70] Mauro Nobili has recently revisited the relationship between "religious" and "secular" authorities, or "dependence" or "independence" between these two protagonists in sub-Saharan Africa. For him, it is much more appropriate to frame this dichotomy championed by scholars like John Hunwick in terms of "the separation of spheres and autonomy and embodiment."[71]

Still, the relationship between Muslim clerics and Bainounk rulers described here fits better the paradigm formulated by Hunwick, for several reasons. My inquiries about the power dynamics and the physical distance between these two radically different entities led to three important revelations regarding the formation of immigrant communities in the Middle Casamance. First, while Bainounk rulers wanted to accommodate Muslim clerics, they were unenthusiastic about letting them settle for good in the heart of their own communities.[72] At times, I found it difficult to grasp concretely notions of "remoteness" or "nearness" emphasized in oral sources on the settlements of new communities. Perhaps this intentional frontier came from a modus vivendi designed to minimize the short-term risks of conflicts of legitimacy. This enabled secular leaders to reduce their risks of vulnerability, at least for the short term, while simultaneously giving Muslims freedom to administer their new territory based on an Islamic ethos.[73]

Second, Bainounk rulers found it too risky to let Muslims settle too far away from the temporal center, which could throw gifted clerics into the hands of rival groups who could better profit from their valuable services. Gambian rulers who hosted some "Taal, Fatty and Darboe" clerics between the late sixteenth century and the 1750s seem to have shared this mindset.[74] Third, Bainounk rulers disdained the idea of permitting Muslims to occupy their most fertile lands. The land tenure system in Senegambia includes two types of landowners: humans beings who populate the natural space where life is much safer; and invisible spirits that occupy the supernatural space where life is full of unpredictable dangers.[75] As noted above, these old beliefs explain why the Bainounk never dug a hole, cut a tree, slaughtered animals, uprooted a tree, planted a crop, started warfare, or crossed a river without first seeking to make the proper sacrifices. Oral records encompass captivating stories about Muslim clerics and other skilled professionals who created their own townships in the Bainounk country. But these sites were initially classified as parts of the "wildness," the "supernatural world," or the "no man's land" by local rulers who authorized these settlements.[76]

Given these restrictions and predicaments, Muslims had to know how to "purge" or "decontaminate" these dangerous areas, combining their personal courage and "God-given gifts." Those who surmounted such a daunting challenge as transforming a haunted forest into a safe human settlement gained additional prestige by having more disciples and sympathizers.[77] Meanwhile, at no time did Bainounk rulers expect Muslims to equate this authorization to settle with a blank check for lawlessness. Aided by his companions, Fodé Héraba expulsed the bad spirits that inhabited the land around Karantaba by reciting the Holy Qur'an, pouring holy waters on the ground, burying amulets, and performing prayers overnight. As a result, Karantaba became a magnet for increasing Bainounk groups who viewed these gestures as a clear demonstration of courage, power, and knowledge.[78]

Even though Chief Daffé's acceptance of Islam did not immediately translate into a conversion en masse among his constituents, his unprecedented gesture motivated many individuals in Bambadion to move in this direction over time.[79] "Besides their proven expertise, according to Boubacar Dabo, the marabouts profited from the sacredness of *foutouwo* to introduce our ancestors to Islam. Fodé Héraba himself remained in our village [Bambadion] until he tied the marriage knot with the chief's daughter, like other clerics across the Middle Casamance."[80] While the majority of Daffé's constituents had remained loyal to their pre-Islamic heritage for a long time, the citizens of Karantaba and Bambadion never quarantined themselves from one another. Instead, the new affine relationship between the Dramé and Daffé lineages inaugurated a tradition of intermarriage between the two communities. Many interviewers designated one village or the other as their maternal or paternal homeland when explaining how these old marriage bonds transformed them into "members of the same extended family."[81]

Throughout his public speeches and Friday sermons (*khutbah*), Fodé Héraba frequently recalled his solid friendship with Daffé. He reminded his audience that thanks to their great affine ties moving from Souna to another chiefdom never crossed his mind.[82] Henceforth, he instructed Karantabans to treat their Muslim and non-Muslim neighbors with the utmost respect, insisting that special treatment be given to Bambadion's sons and daughters who took care of him impeccably since his first day in the Casamance. Bambadion and Karantaba still commemorate this centuries-old tradition, grounded in mutual consideration, friendship, hospitality, and altruism.[83] Even today gift exchanges between them are reminiscent of this old relationship. For instance, a significant portion of the wealth, including food donations, brought by pilgrims to Karantaba's annual festival goes to Bambadion's households.[84]

## INTERFAITH MARRIAGE: OTHER NEGOTIATED CASE STUDIES

Plenty of empirical evidence demonstrates that the role of marriage ties in the settlement of strangers in foreign lands was not circumscribed to either Muslims or to the Middle Casamance in the period under consideration. For example, if we focus on the wider Senegambia, as George Brooks notes, following their intermarriage with *lançados* some Bainounk women acquired additional wealth by inheriting the fortunes of their deceased husbands.[85] When the slave trade attracted European businessmen to Saint Louis and Gorée Islands, they facilitated their integration by intermarrying with attractive women called *signares* (corruption of female traders, Portuguese). These unions were celebrated according to local customs (*mariage à la mode du pays*, French), and the *signares* inherited their husbands' wealth when they died or returned to Europe.[86] When writing in the 1730s, Francis Moore mentioned intermarriages between Portuguese dealers and African women in the Gambia River region.[87] As stated by Emily Osborn, the peaceful principles of *nabaya* (welcome here) and *fudunyolu* (people with whom to marry) cherished by Muslim clerics like Alpha Kabiné Kaba helped Muslim bachelors to find spouses and start a household life in eastern Guinea.[88]

The intermarriage bonds I describe have never been fully considered in historical studies of Islam in Senegambia. These were like rites of passage in the process of immigration, resettlement, and integration of Muslims in this region. Numerous informants spoke about their double identity to reiterate the importance of these old patterns of intermarriage bonds.[89] They mentioned generations of Bainounk women who intermarried with clerics who charted the same course of action as Fodé Héraba. However, for two major reasons these women's names are confusing or unclear in Mandinka and Bainounk oral records. The first is the same "masculinist tone" that existed in the Kétu communities of southern Benin, as highlighted by Lorelle Denise Semley.[90] Matt Schaffer also contends that in Darsilamé, one of Karantaba's offshoots, three wives of Syllaba who led the Pakao jihãd (discussed in chapter 4) are absent from historical recollections.[91] The reality is that Mandinka men are mainly responsible for reworking oral traditions regarding the founding of new communities; and the general rule among them consists of narrating history, using a binary approach based on male centrality and female marginality. More precisely, the narrators concentrate on the great deeds of male legendary figures by repeating their full names throughout their renditions. By contrast, they simply refer to women as the "wife," "daughter," "sister," or "grandmother" of such or such a warrior, healer, diviner, hunter, or cleric. Regardless of the narrators' personal motivations and level of knowledge, this approach overshadows women who may have played praiseworthy roles in history.[92]

The second reason is the mindset that still profiles the Bainounk in negative terms in southern Senegambia. In the Casamance alone, it is hard to find today many Mandinka, Diola, Balante, or Foula people who are not full or partial descendants of the Bainounk landowners. But because of the continuous tendency to equate "Bainounkness" with backwardness, many Casamançais (people of the Casamance) will refuse to discuss their Bainounk ancestry in public. One of my fieldwork assistants were among those who typified this lack of pride, dissimulating his Bainounk ancestral heritage until the day his own brother in-law uncovered the truth.[93] These lingering stereotypes are the more appealing elements in explaining the ubiquitous censorship faced by women in Mandinka and Bainounk historical recollections.

Despite these inconveniences, oral traditions emphasize the names of other "men of God" who spearheaded the institutionalization of Islam in other areas of the Middle Casamance. Because of space constraints, I will concentrate on the cases of four men, beginning with Harounaba Dramé, due to his seniority. This Qur'anic schoolteacher and expert in healing and divination migrated from Mali before Fodé Héraba Dramé's arrival in the Middle Casamance. He brought with him several Qur'anic copies and a personal document remembered as Harounaba's *tarikh*.[94] He and Fodé Héraba called each other "brother" due to their common patronym and national origins, but they were not biological siblings. Harounaba is considered a household name in Dioudoubou (*honey jar*, Bainounk) where he was hosted by a powerful ruler, Badokoré.[95] Through his charisma, formidable erudition, and great expertise in dream interpretation, Harounaba rapidly impressed local communities. He secluded himself for periods of forty consecutive days to conduct sophisticated nocturnal prayers and mediations (*istikhara*) for his growing number of clients in the Souna-Balmadou region.[96]

After introducing Chief Badokoré to Islam and teaching the populace the basic Islamic pillars for years, Harounaba thought about becoming an itinerant marabout. The chief forced him to postpone his decision when he gave him a wife followed by a land grant where he started his household life (*sinkiro*). Sinkiro, which in Mandingo means a triangular cooking fire made of iron, is metaphorically used here to say a new marriage or a household life.[97] At this moment, Dioudoubou possessed several public squares where the marabout and his oldest sons (Dala and Doumbé) instructed the public in the rudiments of the Qur'an; the students rewarded them with precious gifts by the end of the rainy season.[98] Harounaba also performed "rainmaking prayers" to help farmers surmount fears of drought and bad harvests, which consolidated his prestige in a region where rainfed farming was the foundation of life.[99]

Once his sons were sufficiently well trained professionally to carry on his educational legacy, Harounaba relocated from Dioudoubou to other townships where Qur'anic experts of his caliber were lacking. He sojourned alternatively in several villages before his venerated age constrained him to settle definitively in Koling (Koly's house, Bainounk), a township founded in Boudhié by a famous, wealthy hunter called Koly Mané. One day, the marabout selected his burial ground in the dark forest (*soutou*) and ordered his trusted assistants to keep this spot secret; he did not wish the public, including his constituents to turn his graveyard into a place of worship.[100] One matriarch said Koling's inhabitants do not know the exact date of the marabout's death, but their ancestors said he was nothing short of a holy man (*wali*). She added that "Harounaba personified respect and humility towards all human beings, not just Muslims; he generously shared his massive Qur'anic knowledge with others; and the forest where he is buried still produces *nooro*, a clear reminder of his holiness."[101]

The second cleric, Fodé Bourama Kadiali Dia Seydi, emigrated from Aéro Lao, a Foula town situated in northern Senegal. This itinerant scholar first began his public consultations as a specialist of divinatory practices among the Bainounk of Fanty, Yacine. He spent a great deal of time performing *istikhara* for local dignitaries in Yacine and surrounding areas.[102] Asides showering Seydi with good donations due to his proven expertise, they arranged his marriages with three local women remembered as "the mothers of Muslims" in Yacine: Kaaba Baba Dabo, Ardié Daffé, and Kourou Dabo.[103] Thus, local dignitaries granted Seydi permission to settle on empty land between two large trees (*salylinko* and *kabanla banta*) situated in the north of the forest of Bari.[104] This neighborhood was previously inhabited by supernatural spirits hostile to any form of human presence. Like Fodé Héraba before him, Seydi expelled the bad spirits from this forest zone through sacrifices and prayers, in addition to his personal bravery. This mystically purged zone became the site of a new village baptized Ndiama, or Muslims' paradise (short for *dianatoul mouslimin*, Arabic).[105] Some years later Seydi was joined by two clerics, Fodé Moulaye Dabo and Fodé Kharia Daffé who helped him expand Qur'anic education in Yacine. This explains why in oral narratives Ndiama is portrayed as the "the gateway of Islam into Yacine."[106]

The third cleric, Boubacar Sadikh Souané (or Moussa Bakari), immigrated from Timbuktu to the Casamance. He spent part of his early career in Kaabou and Tamba, a multiethnic town in southeastern Senegal. A Bainounk leader called Kérési hosted the cleric when he first arrived in Pakao. He greatly admired Souané's ability to read and write the Qur'an as well as his gifts in healing the sick, mixing Qur'anic verses and herbal medicine he brought with him. After befriending each other for "two rainy seasons," Kérési converted to Islam before helping Souané freely acquire an abandoned forest in eastern Pakao.[107] Aided by two Qura'nic schoolteachers who predated him in Pakao, Souané built on this site a new Muslim village baptized Dianaba (short for *dianatoul mounawara*, bright paradise, Arabic).[108] A decade later, another cleric, Almamy Sadiyya Souané, immigrated to Dianaba from Bassey, in southeastern Gambia. Together, they peacefully promoted Islam and Qur'anic education thanks to their collective sense of hard work and brotherhood. In Dianaba's early history, females slightly outnumbered their male counterparts.[109] Clerics gradually solved this gender gap by intermarrying (through the system of polygyny) with the generation of Basso Bajinka in eastern Pakao, and with women in neighboring countries. Their top destination was The Gambia where they went annually to recruit Qur'anic students and exchange esoteric knowledge with their peers.[110] Oral records are unclear about when Karantaba, Ndiama, and Dianaba were exactly established, but lengthy interviews with Mandinka and Bainounk elders reveal two clear points of consensus among them: Ndiama was settled after Karantaba, followed by Dianaba a few generations later; and unlike Mandinka communities whose populations were originally Bainounk and non-Muslim before undergoing conversion, these three townships were "all born Muslim," to paraphrase one elder.[111]

This tradition of interfaith marriage followed by the settlement of Muslims in the Middle Casamance persisted in the following centuries thanks to the dedication of later generations of Muslims including Ndoura Kamara. He was looking for a place where he could teach the Qur'an in the first half of the nineteenth century when he moved from Pakao to Boudhié. Ndoura was hosted in Bakoum whose inhabitants annually crossed the river to meet their neighbors of Sandiniéri. They proudly celebrated their common Bainounk heritage, eating, dancing, playing games, and drinking palm wine under a large baobab tree.[112] On one such occasion, Ndoura was an honorable guest and noticed in the large sitting crowd an attractive woman, Yéri Danfa. After conducting the customary negotiations with her relatives, Ndoura married the young woman who immediately became Muslim. Elders in Bakoum and Pathiabor were so delighted by Ndoura's noble gesture that they authorized him to settle freely between the two townships. This led to his relocation from Bakoum to a Muslim quarter (Morikounda) in Sédhiou, which etymologically derives from *si dié*, or "sit right there," in Mandingo.[113] Like Harounaba, Ndoura never created his own village, but he rapidly became a dynamic community organizer for his coreligionists in Morikounda; the other quarter (Mansakounda) belonged to secular power where most non-Muslims lived.[114] In 1849, a decade after the completion of the fort of Sédhiou, French officials appointed Ndoura as the chief of Boudhié. The motivations and implications of this political decision will be amply discussed in chapter 4.

Female informants were more excited than men when it comes to the household lives that resulted from these old marriage ties. For them, the mere fact that Muslim clerics targeted Bainounk women for intermarriage does not mean that they totally excluded non-Bainounk women. They backed up their arguments by narrating the untold stories of other women who had affine ties with prestigious Muslim families across the Middle Casamance. Some of the generations included the Balante Sireng Sadio, the Mandiago Moti Dolinko, and the Foula Mouso Sabaly.[115]

Furthermore, Muslim experts, particularly known for their gifts in the Islamic art of divination, easily accumulated substantial wealth through the payments and donations made by numerous clients in exchange for their services; another source of wealth accumulation for them was the agricultural farms they successfully ran, aided by their relatives, disciples, and sympathizers. This combined wealth included foods, animals, cloths, fabrics, jewelry, land plots, and any other products considered valuable by the standards of the Middle Casamance at this moment. Many clerics used a portion of this wealth to pay the bride-wealth as part of their marriage arrangements, but the amount of this wealth generally depended on the personal status of the bride's family.[116]

Songs, dance, hand clapping, laughter, and banter were paramount in animating these highly attended weddings throughout the day until the bride was accompanied to her husband's house by members of her generation. But most of the marriage alliances described by women concerned their grandparents and great-grandparents, who lived between the nineteenth and the twentieth centuries, not the "original generation of Muslim clerics," as one woman said.[117]

Normally, it should take no more than two sentences in the form of a testimony of faith, formulated with conviction, to be considered Muslim. This act (*shahada*) consists of saying "there is no God but God and Muhammad is God's messenger."[118] In the Bainounk country, new converts who could not accurately memorize the *shahada* only needed to repeat the words of the officers who performed the ritual.[119] Afterwards, they were taught the knowledge either mandatory or necessary for practicing the basic Islamic recommendations: purifying their bodies, fasting, praying, and reciting simple Qur'anic verses.[120] Additionally, these converts did not immediately undergo a name change from their "previous names" to "new Islamic ones" at the very moment of conversion; this change generally happened with the birth of their first Muslim children.[121]

I was preoccupied with knowing how the Bainounk reacted to the risks of losing their preexisting heritage as Islamization was gaining ground in the Middle Casamance. Mandinka and Bainounk respondents agreed that this Islamization process was a mutually advantageous relationship in many respects. Without a doubt, *oudiahére* permitted Muslims get the Bainounk wives who became "the mothers of Muslims," followed by land concessions where they built their new homelands, with mosques and Qur'anic schools.[122] Conversely, Muslim merchant-scholars helped their Bainounk ameliorate their living conditions in significant ways through their expertise in the art of divination, fortune telling and making talismans, as well as long-distance trade in the broader Middle Casamance. Many Bainounk converts who graduated from the Qur'anic schools run by Mandinka Muslims became respected imams and Qur'anic teachers; and others with an excellent level of Islamic education married women from prestigious Mandinka clerical lineages.[123]

Moreover, this Islamization process was not always a linear movement or a quick societal change, because some Bainounk groups feared that embracing Islam might profoundly offend their forebears; provoke the retaliation of their ancestral spirits; anger their non-Muslim kin members; or legitimize their ostracism and elimination for being "bad blood."[124] Because these "well-founded fears," the spread of Islam did not result in a systematic abandonment of the spaces that had previously been integral parts of local sacred geography in some Bainounk townships. This change happened with the arrival of Mandinka Muslims in these areas.[125] One consensus suggests that most Bainounk communities responded to this Islamization process by adopting a syncretic religious worldview, as happened in many African regions: blending their old beliefs and practices with the new Islamic ones, as investigated by Marc David Baer in his categorization of conversion.[126]

## CONCLUSION

Muslim clerics who promoted the development of Islam in the Middle Casamance adopted strikingly similar roadmaps and strategies from their homelands to their host lands: immigration, demonstration of knowledge, negotiations of marriage alliances, inheritance of land grants, creation of Islamic infrastructures, teaching of the Qur'an, and finally a change of the local spiritual geography from African religion to Islam. The soft approach that enabled this successful Muslim agency was couched in patience, pacific coexistence, and interfaith dialogue with local host communities. This "jihad without the sword" was a leitmotiv in scholar genealogies and oral renditions by prominent griots.In comparison, aristocratic groups like the *nyanchol* in Kaabou, the *tiéddo* in the Wolof states, and the *dénianké* in Fouta Tooro had long accused Muslim clerics living within their jurisdiction of using "begging and collecting alms" as ways of making a living; and they treated Muslims with contempt and denied them access to political office and intermarriage with members of the ruling elites.[127] This characterization does not fit the modus operandi of the Bainounk for whom intermarriage with talented immigrants who respected their customary laws was beneficial in the long term.

According to Roche, Mande immigrants and French businessmen were expected to pay taxes to the Bainounk chiefs of the Casamance. As we shall see in chapter 4, some archival documents lend credence to the plausibility of this statement.[128] Yet, there is no tangible evidence of "payments of taxes" from Muslim clerics to their Bainounk political overlords in the Middle Casamance, despite the gift exchanges explicitly mentioned in historical recollections. Perhaps the "payments of taxes" began after the original Islamic settlements were established, or these gifts were real payments of taxes, as happened in other regions of Senegambia.[129] Whatever the case, the Muslim agency could have generated an entirely different outcome, without the hospitality and willingness of Bainounk authorities to behave as king-facilitators in this process. I strongly believe that the affine ties between Fodé Héraba and his contemporary clerics and the "Bainounk mothers of Muslims" is another valid paradigm of Islamization in Senegambia that deserves serious consideration. The correlation between Muslim interlineage marriages and the second phase of the landlord paradigm will be the focus of the next chapter.

# CHAPTER 3

# *The Landlord Paradigm of Islamization*

## Muslim Intermarriage, Sanoyya, and Dispersal

This chapter delineates the second phase of the landlord paradigm by drawing on scholar genealogies, family trees of local founding lineages, oral testimonies from persons willing to narrate their own life stories, and participant observation methodology. Intermarriage has historically been among the oldest, most widespread social institutions in sub-Saharan Africa. For instance, in some regions, this practice is motivated by the desire to safeguard the interests of the ruling elites who want to bar low-ranking classes from attaining prestigious status.[1] In others, "ethnic insiders" (indigenous communities) practice intermarriage among themselves to avoid losing their lands to "ethnic outsiders" (immigrants) looking for better living conditions.[2] In the Mande world, caste groups have often relied on intermarriage to deny untrustworthy individuals access to their secret knowledge, passing it down only within their own lineages or kinships.[3]

During the second phase of the landlord paradigm Muslim immigrants changed position as time passed by becoming the landlords for other immigrants to the nascent Dar al-Islam in the Middle Casamance. At the same time Muslims put their faith in a type of joking relationship (*sanawwo* or *sanoyya*) based on the practice of interlineage marriages to sustain their new homelands as much as posible.[4] The chapter begins with the principal beliefs and practices that framed the worldview of Fodé Héréba, including his preferred method of conversion to Islam. Next, it discusses the major factors that facilitated early communal life in Karantaba, including the distribution of land and administrative responsibilities, the Mandinka Qur'anic school system, and the importance of sanoyya through interlineage marriage bonds in this process. Lastly, the chapter examines the strategy of geographic dispersal by later generations of Muslims from their homelands to other regions to expand the borders of the Dar al-Islam.

## THE WORLDVIEW OF FODÉ HÉRABA

Fodé Héraba's paradigm of Islamic development unequivocally rules out recourse to any form of physical brutality as a tool of proselytism. From his perspective, no new converts can reach the level of genuine Muslim citizenship without first internalizing *shahada*, the most sacred pillar in Islam.[5] In both Muslim and non-Muslim societies, people who are dedicated to spreading Islam can achieve long-lasting change through peaceful coexistence among neighbors from distinct religious outlooks.[6] Fodé Héraba's favorite "jihãd" is not a short episode in which people strive to preserve the authenticity of their faith or impose their will on others. Instead, this is an experience of a lifetime throughout which educated Muslims help spread knowledge (*karan*) among those who live in ignorance (*jahiliyya*).[7] Armed with these firm beliefs, the cleric relentlessly urged his constituents, lineage members, and Qur'anic students to behave as role models, including by treating their fellow humans as equals.[8]

In his public conversations and *jumuah* sermons, during Friday congregational prayers when most worshippers were present, Fodé Héraba backed his antimilitary-jihâd ideology by frequently citing one of his favorite Qur'anic verses: "Force is not required when it comes to changing people's minds, hearts and souls."[9] One of his descendants elucidated this pacifist orientation by making the following remark: "We have never forced people to Islam. Negotiations, persuasion, and prayers were central in the stratagems used by our forebears with non-Muslims." He then added, "I have personally been criticized by some conservative clerics for eating, drinking beverages, and chatting with people who had initially rejected Islam. However, after developing sincere affinities with me, these individuals switched allegiance to Islam by the grace of God. We have learned this strategic patience and interfaith dialogue from our founders for whom military jihãd must be used only for self-defense purposes."[10]

These statements raise the question of whether such systematic opposition to physical violence was bolstered by the fact that Muslims represented a tiny minority in the Middle Casamance during the seventeenth century. In this disadvantageous demographic context, pursuing military jihãd would have been a risky, unaffordable proposition, as in the case of Dioula migrants in northern Ivory Coast.[11] Still, Fodé Héraba's hagiographers maintained that for him religious tolerance and the peaceful teaching of Islamic values sufficed to generate durable change, and that the practice of the daily prayers, the exegesis of the Qur'an (*tafsir*), the forging of brotherhood and solidarity among Muslims, and the observance of the prophetic tradition (*sunna*) were the cornerstones of his pedagogic system.[12]

As documented by Igor Kopytoff, African histories include the movements of "disgruntled" individuals, like "refugees, the ambitious, the adventurous and the victimized" who seek to overcome wrongdoings committed against them by immigrating elsewhere.[13] Koly Diémé, who was barred from replacing his father on the throne in the Mandinka kingdom of Badibu in The Gambia, embodied this sentiment. When he came to grips with this unbearable discrimination and took the path of a self-imposed exile in protest, Fodé Héraba welcomed him with open arms to Karantaba. From the time of Diémé's arrival, the cleric used the same religious tolerance he enjoyed while living among non-Muslims in Bambadion; he allowed Diémé to follow his ancestral heritage, including harvesting palm wine in the village's outskirts.[14] Despite their doctrinal differences, the two men never quarantined themselves from one another, but developed great affinities grounded in mutual respect until Diémé felt comfortable enough to become Muslim. Following his conversion, Fodé Héraba prayed for him and encouraged him to establish his own village named Bougnadou (*house of honor*), right across the river from Karantaba.[15]

I found one striking philosophical commonality between Fodé Héraba and El Hadji Salim Souwaré whose biographical dates are somewhat obscure, but who probably lived between the fourteenth and the fifteenth centuries.[16] From Souwaré's viewpoint, the existence of two separate worlds, one for Muslims (Dar al-Islam) and one for non-Muslims (Dar-al-kufr) is the manifestation of "the will of God." Thus, as the Master of the whole universe, God alone could change the status of non-Muslims, enabling their entry into the Dar al-Islam. Furthermore, Muslims might legitimately live under any non-Muslim authority, if this cohabitation would not impede their ability to follow the sunna and serve as role models for "unbelievers" (*al-qafiruun*). Disdain for violent jihād and noninvolvement in politics are the twin doctrinal pillars of the Souwarian model that inspired his disciples in the centuries following Souwaré's death.[17]

Both Souwaré and Fodé Héraba belonged to the Khadiriyya, dismissed physical violence as a method of proselytism, and forcefully advocated for tolerance and respect for non-Muslims; In spite of these commonalities, I found no proof of a direct pedagogical connection between the two men.[18] While Fodé Héraba's father exercised the most direct impact on his initial Islamic career, his hagiographers associate him with no specific spiritual master or no exclusive school of jurisprudence.[19] Besides depicting the cleric's knowledge as the by-product of divine blessing (*baraka*), they categorize him as a holy man (*wali* ) whose direction is the Kaaba, whose preferred book is the Holy Qur'an, whose role model is Prophet Muhammad, and whose ascetic life rests upon two sacred things besides farming: "self-denial of worldly things, and teaching Islamic values to others."[20]

Interestingly, Fodé Héraba incentivized the demographic growth of Karantaba by opting for the same strategies of inclusiveness and hospitality that Chief Daffé had previously used with him. This positivity turned Karantaba into a magnet for groups of immigrants from diverse backgrounds: political dissidents wishing to commence a new life elsewhere, emancipated slaves looking for safer social niches, landless farmers interested in new economic opportunities, Qur'anic teachers willing to open new schools, and merchants seeking additional wealth, to mention but a few.[21] It is critically important to stress that Fodé Héraba benefited from the tremendous help and support by a quartet of "big men": Matiakou Wandifa Diba, Fodé Moussa Soly, Fodé Barro, and Fodé Sakho. These men's contributions in this Islamization process is a refrain in Mandinka and Bainounk sources. We shall see below some of the methods of enticement used by Fodé Héraba with them to help him carry out his dreams and visions.[22]

## EARLY COMMUNAL LIFE IN KARANTABA

There is a substantial body of literature on the vitality of land tenure systems in modifying the trajectory of history in sub-Saharan Africa. Land ownership, questions of precedence, the value of land, trends of settlements and resettlements, and the modalities of land inheritance are among the important questions examined in this literature. Many studies focusing on Africa were influenced by the land paradigm previously elaborated by anthropologist Jack Goody.[23] Another influential paradigm was Kopytoff's reevaluation of the concept of the frontier in the reproduction of "traditional" societies. For him, the notion of "first comers" is generally not an absolute fact of chronology, but in African societies "the principle of precedence does not determine authority, but authority must accommodate to it in some way."[24]

Following Kopytoff, others have produced more nuanced analyses demonstrating that the value and the meaning of land surpass its material dimensions.[25] When it comes to Senegambia, for example, one scholar has challenged some dominant conceptual frameworks concerning the place of land in African history. Using the Gambia River region as a case study, he shows that land could be viewed as a mechanism of control and as a bargaining tool for the acquisition of power, the building of social networks, and the renewal of political and social alliances.[26]

The populations of the Casamance have possessed a code of chronological presence since the precolonial period, one of the main exceptions being areas where landowners were subdued by powerful intruders. More holistically speaking, terms like first comers, next comers, last comers, or strangers and hosts are not randomly parts of the lexicons of Senegambian societies.[27] Instead, these are key components of nonwritten codes that have traditionally been used to determine land ownership and political legitimacy at the local level. These codes help identify and classify people coexisting in the same territory, considering their respective times of arrival. So, if interlineage antagonisms over complex issues such as wealth or political legitimacy break out, for example, the codes theoretically play an arbitration role, turning to the historical record.[28]

In the early Mandinka society land was plentiful but not free if free means that one could settle anywhere, at any time, and under any conditions, while disregarding those who predated them in this specific milieu. Land ownership and political legitimacy were based on an old rule: those who cleared any land and founded a village were de facto the landowners (*banko tiyyol*) and village owners (*saté tiyyol*).[29] Depending on the place of rendition of the story or the narrator' s social identity, some oral versions on these issues downplay or overemphasize certain events, whereas others are vague or more exhaustive on some episodes.[30] While keeping in mind these variations, I investigated the ethnogenesis of Karantaba, looking at two different versions that are rich in detail in popular memory. My investigations revealed that "questions of land ownership and land administration" were the first challenges facing the stability of early communal life in Karantaba. But Fodé Héraba and his early companions fortunately found the peace, harmony, and compromise they needed to overcome these challenges.

One version that emanates from the Diba extended lineage in Karantaba prioritizes the role of hunters in creating human communities. Matt Schaffer mistakably suggests that Matiakou Wandifa Diba, who hailed from Farfegniey in Badibu and founded this lineage, was "the son of Fodé Héraba's sister."[31] He was always accompanied by a "mysterious" dog during his hunting adventures. This version goes on to brand Diba as a cleric who constructed a mosque in his homeland before coming to the Middle Casamance. One day, Diba left his residential village of Babadion to escape the summer heat, sitting under the taabo tree. A man (Fodé Héraba) passed by Diba three times and greeted him. After exchanging cordial words, the two men discovered that they were pursuing "the same goal" and agreed to build a new village together.[32] The pivotal moment here is when Diba's "mysterious" dog somehow showed them the appropriate site for the settlement of the village, but the version does not specify how this revelation occurred. Diba's intention was to go back home after Karantaba's founding, but Fodé Héraba dissuaded him when he characterized the village as their "shared property" and married his daughter to him. The implication is that Diba predated Fodé Héraba on Karantaba's site and must be viewed as the village's cofounder and co-owner.[33]

The other version, which originates from the Dramé ruling lineage, asserts that the whole story began with Fodé Héraba's divine revelation in his native Daramane. He consequently extensively read from his Qur'an and prayed overnight for the success of his mission. The cleric's nocturnal prayers advised him to begin his settlement wherever he would find a "dog sleeping" near a taabo. This version clearly acknowledges Diba's great hunting skills, his hardworking spirit and respect for his fellow humans, as well as the role he and his dog played in the birth of Karantaba; but it excludes Diba's status as a mosque builder and designates Bambadion, not the taabo, as the site where the two men first met.[34]

This means that knowledge about which man first discovered the site of Karantaba is subject to conflicting interpretations. Meanwhile, the correlation between "the principle of precedence" and landownership and chronological presence clearly appears in both versions. Additional interviews with other individuals with no direct family ties with either side corroborated the contributions of Diba to the founding of Karantaba; they qualify Fodé Héraba as the village founder (*saté kourala*) and his descendants as landowners (*saté tiyyol*),[35] and they insist on the firm collaboration between the Dramé and Diba lineages for the expansion of Islam in the Souna-Balmadou region.[36]

Fodé Moussa Soly (a corruption of the Foula patronym Sow) founded Solykunda, one of the most educated clerical lineages across the Casamance. This bachelor and bright Qur'anic teacher migrated from Macina, a town laying halfway between Ségou and Timbuktu, Mali. Throughout his journey, Soly stopped in several villages where he greatly impressed commoners thanks to his esoteric knowledge and admirable piety. Through his solidly grounded erudition, Soly astounded those who had met him since he first set foot in Karantaba. This quality incentivized Fodé Hérаba's decision to host Soly and to give him his daughter in marriage.[37] While visiting his son in Karantaba, Soly's father (Moussa Sow) was content with the news of his marriage. He congratulated Soly on fulfilling his obligation as a Muslim man, exhorted him to work closely with his father in-law, prayed for peace in Karantaba, and returned home.[38]

Fodé Barro was a merchant-scholar who is commonly remembered as Barroba (Barro the Great). When he traveled to the Casamance, he only wanted to pay a visit of courtesy to his maternal uncle (Fodé Moussa Soly) and return home. In public discourse, the Barro lineage is praiseworthily referred to as "Barro did not come to stay" (*barro mansiola*), because only when Fodé Héraba married his daughter to him did Barroba settle in Karantaba for good.[39] Contrary to Diba, Soly, and Barro, Fodé Sakho and Fodé Héraba shared the same mother, a consanguinity that forbade their lineages from having affine ties, even if shariah tolerates some of these close relationships.[40] In some African regions like the Upper Guinea coast Mandinka and Foula businessmen were sometimes hosted by their fellow Muslims in exchange for a commission from their profits.[41] I found no proof of similar payments between Fodé Héraba and these "big men" in Karantaba.

Another commonality between Fodé Héraba and Souwaré regards the model of political and social organization in their respective homelands. Diakha Bamboukhou, the Diakhanké's ancestral home, was divided into clerical lineages called *kabilas*: Souwaré Kounda, Darame Kounda, Fofona-Guirassi Kounda, and Fadiga Kounda.[42] For Lamin Sanneh, "within each Qabilah section a certain amount of fluidity existed so that newcomers could be incorporated and given precise functions; and an important feature of Jahanke settlements was the principle of an open and undefended center to which outsiders might, if they wished, come for an adoption as clients or members of the community, although full adoption into the clerical vocation was strictly confined to a small section of Islamized Serakhulle."[43] Similarly, Karantaba initially had five original extended lineage units called kabilas: Fodékounda, Kantiakou, Solykounda, Sakhokounda, and Barrokounda. These were composed of men and women who lived in the same territorial units and shared the same paternal ancestor, as happened in the Diakhanké country and other regions.[44] These units regrouped "those who shared the same kola nut, attended mosque prayers together and cultivated good relationships with one another."[45]

Each of these kabilas was tasked with specific responsibilities in Karantaba's early administration. At the top of this hierarchy was Fodékounda whose members monopolized the offices of imam and village chief. These male-dominated offices were the most prestigious social institutions in the Mandinka country at this time; but their powers were local in character, irrespective of the village's dimension and population.[46] The village chief (*alkaly*) was the top officer who collected taxes, led military activities, solved interlineage disputes, supervised farming performance, and welcomed newcomers. Mungo Park depicted the *alkaid* (alkaly) as an administrator found in Mandinka towns where this "chief magistrate levies taxes on travelers, preserve order and leads conferences."[47] Given the importance of land ownership, the *alkaly* was selected from the founding lineage whose members inherited the office via the rule of male primogeniture.

This rule did not apply to the religious guide (*almamy*) who led jumuah and performed other public rituals like newborn naming ceremonies and funeral services, in addition to helping the populace with diverse personal matters. Unlike the *alkaly,* the *almamy* might be recruited from another township, but he would not receive the stick symbolizing his official power (*almamy doko*), unless his expertise and piety were proven beyond reasonable doubt.[48] According to one of his descendants, Fodé Héraba himself invented the political model in which the two most senior members of his kabila, Fodékounda, assumed the functions of village chief and imam. Theoretically, neither one could concentrate both powers in his own hands; in the event of a power vacancy caused by death or a terminal illness, the next man in line was invested; and the other kabilas abided by the same male gerontocratic rule.[49]

Interestingly, in some Mandinka Muslim communities, the local political system has traditionally obeyed a system of rotation among the oldest lineages by contrast to Karantaba. When I asked Fodékounda to explain the rationale behind the monopolization of power by Dramé clerics, one leader said: "Here [in Karantaba] no mechanisms or institutions are set up to regulate the powers of these two officers who are appointed for life. The elders' council (*kéba kaafo*), our most venerated social institution, stands as the mouthpiece of public opinion and provides wise advice to our leaders. Still, council members can do nothing against these officers whose powers emanated from Fodé Héraba. In the meantime, any of these two men who selfishly rules counter to his teachings would face negative consequences; and after his death this punishment might even continue to affect his descendants."[50]

The masters of social ceremonies (baptisms, funerals, weddings, and the distribution of charity and almsgiving), land officers, and managers of the imam's official investiture were selected from Kantiakou. One legitimate question consists of knowing whether as Karantaba's "cofounders" Kantiakou received a fair share of power, without inheriting any of these prestigious offices.[51] Sékouba Diba, their spokesperson, replied to this question with a tirade: "Do not think that the Diba got the short end of the stick. Fodé Héraba initially asked him to choose between the positions of imam or village chief since Karantaba belonged to both of them. Matiakou refused to violate conventional wisdom, knowing that a son-in-law could not take precedence over his father in-law. Fodé Héraba returned the favor by choosing the Tiakou kabila as the land managers, which explains why our seal of approval is still indispensable for these officers' nomination. Given Matiakou's allegiance to Fodé Héraba, we [the Diba] will eternally be the servants of the Dramé, who are our leaders until today. However, given our long-standing affine relationship, any Dramé who refuses to share their wealth with us will pay a heavy price for disregarding our ancestral will."[52]

Diba's tirade was not intended to question Fodé Héraba's legitimacy, but rather to recall the debt of mutual gratitude that linked their two lineages since Karantaba's founding. Two important things are highlighted in a few other recollections. First, as stated by Diba, from the outset Fodé Héraba recommended a decentralization of power, seeking to appoint others outside the Dramé lineage—but "those he had in mind" preferred to live under his leadership and declined his offer.[53] Second, Fodé Moussa Soly is the only man who "has ever exercised the *almamiyya*" outside the Dramé lineage. This appointment stemmed from the mutual trust and respect between Soly and Fodé Héraba. As the lead instructor of Karantaba's first Qur'anic school, Soly quickly became a full-fledged pedagogical master thanks to his exuberance and impressive teaching skills.[54]

Soly's proven expertise also begs the question of knowing why his lineage did not continue to inherit the almamiyya. Some sources suggest that the Dramé later recovered this function from the Soly because they were already performing remarkable duties in the administrative apparatus. The two lineages later found common ground to avoid harming the community's equilibrium: Dramé clerics would provide the *almamy*, but his nomination would be official only with Soly's nod of approval.[55] Other sources indicate that unlike Diba, when Fodé Héraba first appointed Soly as head of religious affairs, he accepted out of respect for his father in-law, and that later on mystical revelations predicted that Soly could someday become the most powerful spiritual leader in the region. Thus, Fodé Héraba profited from one of Soly's absences to strip him of his initial powers, but how long Soly assumed this function is not clear in these sources.[56]

Ultimately, the two lineages agreed to "build a bridge of understanding," allowing Solykounda to manage the imam's official investiture, in addition to being the village's spokespersons. Fodé Barro's kabila served among the Qur'anic teachers and callers to prayers (*wandanela*). Fodé Sakho's kabila provided the direct advisers and right hand of the imam; they escorted him during *jumuah* and the celebrations of the Day of Sacrifice (*baana saalo*) and the end of Ramadan (*sounkar saalo*). Additionally, each of these kabilas received a large portion of land where they built their ancestral hamlet and a Qur'anic school, while using the remotest part of it as their personal lineage farm.[57]

Today a popular Mandinka saying, "Do not brag about yourself as if you were the Dramé or Djité," insinuates that these two lineages may be the first clerical groups in the Middle Casamance.[58] In Schaffer's view, Karantaba's "religious antiquity" explains the monopolization of powers by Dramé clerics and their status as the "owners of Pakao," meaning the Mandinka homeland.[59] However, some clerical lineages, such as the Souané in Dianaba and the Seydi in Ndiama have the same "religious antiquity" in their respective townships, but not the privileges claimed by Dramé clerics.

Perhaps this rotation of power became a popular model in the region long after the founding of Karantaba. In some old Bainounk settlements whose inhabitants later accepted Islam, the devolution of power is still based on a rotation from one lineage to another. Exceptions include Dioudoubou where Harounaba's descendants now control both the temporal and spiritual powers, despite their originally foreign status.[60] It is also possible that this system of power sharing in Karantaba was effective as early as the time of Fodé Héraba, who appointed Soly as imam; that after their deaths the Dramé used their sense of entitlement to recover the almamiyya from Soly clerics; and that the two kabilas worked out a compromise, including giving the other kabilas specific administrative tasks. This hypothesis echoes Chief Fodé Almamy's observation that: "If you clear the land, build your village and appear to be as knowledgeable [religiously] as others, you do not want to choose the chief and the imam outside your own family."[61]

The demographic growth of Karantaba was stimulated by three critical factors. The first was the patrilocal character of Mandinka society in which new married couples and their offspring lived with the husband's extended family, if land was available for them to start a *sinkiro*. Second, Mandinka men could marry up to four wives (polygyny) to satisfy their personal desire, overcome a shortage in field labor by augmenting their progenitors, or follow local mores, marrying their siblings' widows.[62] Third, outsiders profited from the kabilas' porosity and integrate them in specific ways. For instance, after a successful war each soldier returned home with a slave, but after her or his emancipation this slave could negotiate their integration into their former master's kabila, adopting the corresponding patronym.[63] Landless farmers who borrowed a plot of land could also become members of their lending kabila, following a similar procedure.[64] However, while newcomers could acquire citizenship by adopting the patronyms Dramé, Soly, Diba, Sakho, and Barro, only the biological members of these lineages were eligible for the prestigious offices mentioned above. These arrangements occurred at the hamlets where the eponymous ancestors resided. Regardless of their kabila affiliation, all Karantabans who were physically and mentally fit had to contribute to farming and Qur'anic education, two vital activities in their communal life.[65]

Through interkabila dialogue and cooperation, local leaders initiated additional courses of action that helped Karantabans grow and expand as a respected Muslim minority in the Middle Casamance. For example, when Karantaba was first created, local Muslims used a small prayer compound (*misero*) as their common place of worship. But as their number grew bigger and bigger local authorities built one of the oldest mosques in Senegambia in the northeastern part of the village (*domassou*).[66] Fodé Héraba was among African clerics who never performed the pilgrimage to Mecca, like Cheikh Ahmadou Bamba or Seku Usman Dan Fodio. One of his close associates who accomplished this ritual brought with him a sample of Mecca's soil to Karantaba. The mud used to construct the mosque was mixed with some sample of this soil and a protective verse from the Qur'an, *ayatal koursiyou*. This product was then carefully inscribed in all the material used for the building of the mosque.[67]

The mosque, which still exists, is designed in a rectangular fashion and has no decorations on the walls, or the towers of embellishment known as minarets. It includes a niche on the wall (*mihrab*) pointing in the direction of the Kaaba (*qibla*) and a pulpit (*minbar*) from which the imam gives his *khutbah*. The mosque has nine doors that communicate with one another, and each is associated with one of the nine kabilas now existing in Karantaba; but the village only had five kabilas when the mosque was first built. Originally, when filled to capacity, the mosque could accommodate up to fifty people, an impressive number by the standards of the Casamance at this time. During prayer sessions, worshippers formed three distinct lines separated by walls and doors so that only those standing in the same lines (*sapé*) could see each other.[68]

In his illuminating study of the Mouriddiya, Eric Ross mentions the growing competition between trees and mosques as the center of the public square in West African Islam. He notes that the leading role between these two landmarks shifted from the palaver tree to the mosque as Islam expanded in this region.[69] Ross' description perfectly fits the case of Muslims in the Souna-Balmadou region; they had first held the taabo in the highest esteem due to its status as Fodé Hérаba's guiding light and the place where Qur'anic education in Karantaba began. However, once the mosque was created, Muslims followed the recommendation of the Qur'an, automatically placing the mosque above the taabo in terms of religious importance.[70]

When reflecting on this spiritual priority, one dignitary lauded the mosque as "the center of the public square," without minimizing the spiritual value of the taabo.[71] Another depicted the mosque as "the doorway to Islam and the living symbol of Islam in the Middle Casamance."[72] Other dignitaries used the generic term of untouchable (*kamathra*) when referring to the mosque. This implies that, given the mosques' sacredness, the fence around it can be occasionally remodeled to resolve physical damage caused by soil erosion, heavy rains, wildfire, and termite infestations; but that changing the mosque's original layout would irremediably cause "social chaos and destruction" for local communities.[73] Like many other mosques, Karantaba's was originally used for the five daily prayers, annual festivals, *jumuah*, and the recitation of the Qur'an during the holy month of Ramadan.[74]

By dint of working hard for the dissemination of Qur'anic education Karantaba's founding lineages became progressively known as kabila schools in the Middle Casamance. Local Bainounk communities and Muslim families provided their largest student bodies, but others came from distant areas in the Casamance and neighboring countries like The Gambia and Guinea-Bissau. Although both adults and children were involved in this educational process, I would like to focus essentially on the latter. The general rule was to enroll children in Qur'anic school when they turned seven or when they

Figure 3. The new mosque in Karantaba constructed around the original one in the early 2000s. (Photo by the author, September 2003.)

Figure 4. Some seniors are talking to the imam inside the old mosque after the Friday congregational prayer. (Photo by the author, October 2003.)

could count from one (*killing*) to ten (*tang*). The teaching curriculum began with a ritual called *boulsafé*. This was the day when the knowledge-seeker (*karanding*) and the knowledge-giver (*karamo*) were introduced to one another; legal custody of children was transferred from the students' parents to their new teachers on this same day.[75]

One bright schoolteacher characterized boulsafé as more or less the equivalent of baptism among Catholics, although a naming ceremony happened on the seventh day following the birth of a Muslim baby.[76] Boulsafé was also a moment of spiritual rebirth during which children's heads were shaved, as if they were newborn babies, but this rite does not apply to girls.[77] Using ink (*doua*) the teachers wrote three letters of the Arabic alphabet (*ba, sin, mimara*) on the right palm of each student, and ordered them to lick it with their tongues three consecutive times before it dried. The bitterness of this ink was intended to alert students to the challenging voyage of discovery awaiting them.[78]

From a Mandinka perspective, boulsafé inaugurated the debut of a collective journey during which students had to show total respect to their *karamol* (plural of karamo), a precondition to earn their blessing (*baraka*). *Karamol* reciprocated by instilling in students the amount of knowledge and beliefs that would help them become genuine Muslims.[79] This ceremony ended with the recital of the Qur'an, hand shaking, tears of joy, and the sharing of foods and beverages among attendees. On the day of boulsafé God would erase the totality of sins committed by all the individuals who were involved in this educational process. And on Judgment Day, negligent schoolteachers would be held accountable for their students' underperformance. Given the spiritual bond linking students and teachers during life and thereafter, in many communities the funeral services of deceased students were officiated by their original teachers.[80]

The teaching curriculum used in these kabila-schools comprised three daily sessions: one in the morning, one in the afternoon, and one in the evening. These were separated by short breaks so that both students and teachers could observe the daily prayers and enjoy a little recess.[81] In terms of curriculum, after boulsafé came the rote memorization of the twenty-eight letters of the Arabic alphabet. This prepared students to begin learning to read and write the Qur'an correctly, but many teachers also used this phase to teach them how to make ablution (*wudu*), pray (*salat*), and fast (*sawn*).

The third phase was the rote memorization followed by the recitation of the 114 chapters of the Qur'an, beginning with the opening chapter (*al-fatiyya*). Students dedicated to a long-term career continued on during this third phase, whereas others ended their education once they acquired some rudiments of Qur'anic knowledge. Memorization moved from one group of verses (*ayyat*) to another, until the whole chapter is memorized. The idea was to start with the least complicated chapters before moving on to the most complicated ones. This phase was extremely challenging for most students, as it encompassed the correct spelling and writing of Qur'anic verses and a good understanding of proper punctuation (*siro*).[82]

Students were off from Thursday morning to Friday afternoon when lessons resumed as soon as *jumuah* ended. Elders were unsure about when this choice began in the Mandinka country, but many believed it may be the remnant of a Muslim practice as old as the tenure of Umar Ibn al-khatab, Islam's second caliph. (634–44 C.E.) In the aftermath of his conquest of Jerusalem, some oral accounts indicate, young Qur'anic students were authorized to take the day off and be part of his homecoming ceremony.[83] In the Mandinka country the social arrangements between schoolteachers and their students' families were that students had to perform field work for their teachers, in exchange for their services. Because subsistence farming is the foundation of economic life throughout the Casamance, these performances helped schoolteachers take care of their families and students. Parents who wanted their own children to perform such work for them had to get permission from their Qur'anic teachers, out of respect.[84]

Apart from excelling in the Qur'anic school, hardworking students were those who exhibited physical courage in the fields. This included always returning home from the farms with bundles of firewood (*karanta*), the equivalent of *takhan matt* among the Wolof traditional schools (*daara thiossan*) in northern Senegambia. In this rural environment, in the absence of moonlight, firewood guarantees the continuation of Qur'anic education during the night (*karanta-dimba*). The old belief that the burning of *karanta* is a divine weapon against deadly thunderstorms and lightning during the rainy season reinforced the value of firewood.[85]

During their brief passage in Qur'anic school, girls performed the same domestic chores they would normally do at home, such as cleaning the schoolyard, washing dishes, and refilling water jars. Unlike boys, girls were never expected to go beyond the sum of knowledge allowing them to practice the basic recommendations of Islam. This is the rule rather than the exception in the Dar al-Islam where the acquisition of higher education is still a male preserve, despite its inconsistency with the teachings of shariah.[86] Besides fixing broken fences, herding cattle, building huts, or running errands for elders, boys supplied two of the three didactic tools required for their education. One was the harvesting, and the making of the ink (*doua*) needed to write daily lessons by boiling the bark of a mango tree many times to make the liquid as dark as possible. The predominant technique was to collect the soot from cooking pots by wiping them with a wet cloth.

Another way to obtain ink was to ask mothers to cook various meals so that students would not return to school empty-handed on the day of collection. This solidarity generally happened after a successful rainy season when local household granaries are full.[87] The boys cleaned their hands well before going to work on the ink, to prevent oil from contaminating the liquid. They targeted old cooking pots of extremely dark color in their search for quality and collected the soot, wringing their wet piece of cloth into a bottle. Teachers preferred a *doua* as sticky as possible, otherwise the words inscribed on the wooden tablets could be easily removed; some mixed the liquid with sugar or gum Arabic if the product looked too watery and of weak quality.[88]

Boys also made the wooden pen (*kalla*, local corruption of *khlam* or pen, Arabic) needed to write on their wooden tablets. This material originally came from the same wood used to make house fences in the poorest areas in Senegambia. The clarity of the calligraphy inscribed on the wooden tablets depended on boys' ability to select the best pieces of wood and cut them with a sharp knife.[89] But neither teachers nor students could produce the wooden tablet (*walla*, Arabic deformation of *allouwwa* or tablet), the third vital tool used in the Qur'anic school. This wood was cut from one of the most beautiful species of tree called *kéno*, or from the whitest segments of an orange tree. Like the wood stick (*almamy doko*) carried by the imam, the *walla* had to be carved by a master carpenter to avoid the bumps that would damage the quality of the calligraphy. Woodcarvers accommodated students of diverse age groups by fashioning the *wallal* (pl. of *walla*) in rectangular or oval shapes and in different sizes. On top of the *wallal* they placed a hole where a thin cord is attached, to limit the risks of mistakenly erasing the sacred words they contain.[90]

After assimilating their lessons on both sides, students washed their tablets with clean water and sand before letting them dry in the sun. They returned to their teachers that same day or the next for the inscription of new lessons. While washing their tablets, students drunk a small amount of the *doua* coming off their tablets, ignoring the ink's disagreeable taste, a source of physical and spiritual blessings. As noted by Al Fouseyni Cissé in one of our private conversations, many wooden tablets did not originally retire with their original user, who was generally a gifted scholar or the lineage's founder. Instead, the tablets were passed down to another lineage member as a source of blessing; and the carpenters who crafted them were carefully selected because any lack of piety on his part may result in the young pupil's counterperformance.[91]

The average length of study for Qur'anic students committed to a longtern career was about seven years. Those who finished the Qur'an with proof of fluency in reading, writing, and recitation were eligible for graduation. This was a moment of pride for the kabila school, as well as for the graduating students and their loved ones who escorted them during this solemn ceremony. Wearing their finest outfits, the graduating students received the title of *arfang*, the equivalent of someone who knows how to read and write the entire Qur'an *(hafizul Qur'an*, Arabic). Before their departure bright students were sometimes asked to write out the entire Qur'an without copying from the original book, the equivalent of the *bindeu kaamil* among the Wolof. This intellectual feat was a demonstration of accomplished learning and a clever way to help remedy the shortage of teaching tools in areas where Qur'anic manuscripts were scarce.[92] In some cases, schoolteachers, proud of their graduating students, offered them some "highly classified esoteric secrets" extracted from the Qur'an for them to use in their future divinatory practices.[93] In others, these relationships were consolidated through marriage alliances: a teacher gave his daughter to one of his favorite students, or a graduating student arranged a marriage between his teacher and one of his relatives. One French colonial administrator, who visited the Casamance in 1883–84, mentioned the religious importance of Karantaba. For him, this was a holy place and the biggest Mandinka village (in the Casamance) with many Qur'anic schools, but he wrongly suggested that Karantaba had no mosque probably because he underestimated its size.[94]

Nobody could be inducted in the *fodé* hall of fame, without overcoming exceedingly tough hurdles first. *Fodéyya,* or the act of becoming *fodé*, was the most prestigious title in Mandinka Islam. This coronation was reserved for men who established proof of their piety, scholarship, and wisdom.[95] Metaphorically, *fodéyya* was a swan song in that this honorable title was bestowed late in the life of those who had mastered the Qur'an and the most complicated branches of Islamic sciences. This burden of proof included the exegesis of the Qur'an (*kawando*), Islamic jurisprudence (*fiqh*), and adequate punctuation (*siro*).[96] During this public ceremony held at the main mosque, the seminal moment was when a selected jury covered the head and chin of the recipient with a long white turban (*kan minindang*) and placed a red hat on top of his head. This ended with the recital of the Qur'an (*soukouwo*), hugging, hand shaking, tears of joy, and a lavish celebration among those who attended to witness history.[97]

This form of canonization may be the remnant of an old Muslim practice going back to Prophet Muhammad; he is believed to have once turbaned one of his war generals to protect him from evil; and Gabriel was among the thousands of angels turbaned as Muslim allies at the battle of Badr in around 624 CE.[98] Fodéyya may have also resulted from ritual practices associated with the Khadiriyya. Well before Cheikh Bou Kounta (1844–1914) established the holy city of Ndiassane, most Mandinka, Diakhanké, and Bidan scholars living between the Casamance and Guinea-Bissau were affiliated with this order.[99]

Because *fodéyya* emblematized social prestige, scholars who reached this level of Islamic expertise were automatically placed on a pedestal.[100] As a result, they spent the reminder of their lives performing prayers, advising their neighbors, converting people to Islam, mediating disputes, and acting as role models to youngsters. The male descendants of these "men of God" inherited their congregations after their deaths.[101] Scholar genealogies make clear that across the Mandinka country *fodéyya* was originally created as a male-dominated, meritocratic, gerontocratic, elitist social institution.[102]

Karantabans confessed that they were times when tough challenges dangerously affected the equilibrium of their communal life at the kabila and at the village level; and that rivalries and power struggles over complex issues such as the modalities of political or religious power transmission, matrimonial disputes and the resolution of economic hardships were among the driving forces behind these challenges. However, the council of elders (*kéba kaffo*) always found adequate ways to overcome these challenges; and the "power of sanoyya" rested at the heart of the strategies used by elders to bring back peace and harmony in the community. Because these repeated oral narratives I wanted to better apprehend the significance of this concept of sanoyya. This is the Mandinka version of the ritualized forms of banter whose names change from one African population to the next.[103] These standardized joking relationships (*parenteés á plaisanteries*, French) caught the imagination of European authors who conducted ethnographic fieldwork in Africa.[104] Depending on local cultural contexts, these have been called "blood pacts," "social contracts," "tools for conflict resolutions," or "kin-based alliances";

and their multiple purposes include accusation, ownership, mediation, praising and integration.. In spite of these variations, joking relationships have traditionally been used to create more integrated communities, by sowing the seeds of peace, respect, altruism, harmony, and friendliness among relatives, neighbors, and other individuals.[105]

Even today, anybody who goes to a public place in the Mandinka country will hear somebody use sanoyya to make an argument: women seeking a better price at the fish market; farmers trying to reenergize their teammates in the fields; grandparents willing to teach their grandchildren good moral virtues; elders settling a land dispute under the palaver tree; and imams summoning their congregants to attend *jumuah* on time, to mention but a few examples. Youth are endowed by custom to mock their seniors if they are legitimate joking partners (*sanos*). Strangers may enter a house inhabited by their *sanos* and claim possession of their host family, saying words such as "your king has come" (*allaa mansa ké nata*). Sanoyya transcends age, marital status, wealth, religion, gender, ethnicity, education, and caste; and it is almost impossible to find Mandinka people who do not have many *sanos* inside and outside of their homeland.[106]

While it is difficult to determine the origins of sanoyya, Mandinka oral records make mention of two important ones that deserve special attention, given their ubiquity in the Casamance.[107] First, sanoyya could derive from a fortunate or unfortunate circumstance that radically changed the relations among coexisting lineages. One classical example was when the ancestors of the Bayo and Kouyaté lineages gave birth to two babies the same night. The delivery coincided with a thunderstorm that plunged the community into disarray, forcing the nurses to put the newborns away from any potential danger. When it came time for the mothers to take care of their babies, they could not identify them in the dark and agreed to breastfeed them without distinction. The Mandinka vertical social structure categorizes the Bayo in the noble group of *horon* whereas the Kouyaté belong to the *nyamakalaw*. Nevertheless, the extraordinary sense of sisterhood shown by these two mothers generated sanoyya relations between the two lineages; since this momentous event their members have been required by custom to live exclusively in mutual peace and tolerance, including the sharing of wealth and jokes.[108]

Second, sanoyya could emanate from old trends of intermarriage and joking relationships among neighboring lineages. Karantabans have exemplified this reality since the time of their forebears in the seventeenth century. For them, thanks to sanoyya successive generations of Karantabans have lived happily in a region where they were surrounded by non-Muslims.[109] Some dated the roots of sanoyya back to at least the affine relationship between the Dramé and Daffé lineages. This explains why the citizens of Karantaba and Bambadion still call themselves "one and indivisible" (*gnin saaté foulo bé ba killing néti*).

Others correlated the importance of sanoyya with the system of interlineage marriages, describing it as "the key" that permitted Karantabans to safeguard the internal cohesion and unity in Karantaba. Many emphasized the *kéba kaffo's* ability to surmount these challenges by eloquently reminding conflicting parties that "you are all members of the same family" (*ali téli bé baa kaa bili killing*). Regardless of the complexity of these challenges, these negotiations ended with shaking hands, joking, laughing, and the sharing of foods and beverages, to elders' greatest delight.[110] One senior who belongs to the Dramé and Barro kabilas through intermarriage characterized this sentence as a "rallying cry" before adding, "Our founders consistently reminded that any Karantaban who hurts the feelings of another has committed a self-inflicted wound."[111]

This culture of interlineage marriage was perpetuated and solidified by successive generations until most individuals involved in these relationships viewed themselves as members of the same kabila.[112] As time passed, these interlineage alliances generated increasing patterns of cross-cousin marriages (*systéme du cousinage*, French): women married the sons of their mothers' brothers (*sanoma ké*) or men took the daughters of their fathers' sisters (*sanoma mousso*). I heard many times such closely related individuals banter with one another, sarcastically calling each other "lazy" (*barkantang*) or "greedy" (*domorolaaba*), for the sake of having fun.[113]

While explaining the advantages of cross-cousin marriages, two men included the cultivation of strategic alliances by specific lineages. They evoked how the marriage of their own children cemented their friendship, characterizing it as a continuous tradition initiated by their forebears. For them, saying Karantabans belong to different kabilas would be correct only in theory, one of them concluded , because in practice "our bloods have interminably been mixed since the founding of Karantaba. This has a lot to do with the power of sanoyya."[114]

Given this centuries-old tradition of cross-cousin marriages, I never heard any Karantabans mention their male or female ancestries without the Barro, Soly, Sakho, Diba, and Dramé patronyms. My analysis of sanoyya concentrates on Karantaba in the Souna-Balmadou region, but these same afinal and nonaffinal intermarriages and cross-cousin marriages have also existed for generations in other areas in the Middle Casamance.[115] The late Fodé Fossar Souané summed up perfectly well "the power of sanoyya," saying: "We [Muslim immigrants] incorporated the Bainounk country into the Dar al-Islam through generally peaceful means; and we strengthened our newly created communities with a tradition of interlineage marriages among us."[116] In group interviews with women in Dioudoubou and Sinkére-Bainounk, they recalled the same culture of intermarriage between the Bainounk and the Mandinka (*djibé silla*, Bainounk), calling it "a powerful milestone in our common history," to paraphrase one of them.[117]

Like many Muslim groups, the Mandinka have traditionally perceived sainthood as a powerful source of physical and spiritual blessing, which explains the sanctification of their distinguished clerics, by turning their burial grounds into sites of memory and pilgrimage. Many Sufi centers of northern Senegambia have huge mausoleums (*khabrou*) belonging to their cheikhs' families and closest associates. Many are generally beautiful buildings, decorated with rugs, Qur'anic scriptures, gold, fabrics, and other expensive items that force the admiration of their visitors.[118] By contrast, one will find two kinds of burial grounds in Karantaba: one public cemetery where commoners are buried, and private holy shrines whose owners conducted special prayers (*khalwa*) to determine where they would like to be laid to rest. The holy shrines I visited belong to male clerics who operated some of the most famous Qur'anic schools and who had more disciples than many educators during their lives.[119] These are nothing short of hut-tombs possessing a water jar at their entrance where visitors make their ablutions (*wudu*) before entering the huts and washing their hands before going home. Visitors will be shocked by the sharp contrast between the sobriety and the cleanliness of these hut-tombs, which are always covered with massive amount of sand. In front of each shrine sits a man who welcomes visitors and collects donations for himself and for the maintenance of the shrine, while the rest goes to the deceased cleric's family.[120]

My instinct as a researcher was to know if the sobriety of this architecture was the direct result of a lack of monetary means, considering the decent amount of wealth accumulated by these famous clerics during their lives; and if the secrecy surrounding the burial grounds of Karantaba's founders were just rumors and speculations. When I learned about the esoteric nature of these "holy graves" in the 1990s, I thought of three possible hypotheses: given Karantaba's age, the sites of the graves probably disappeared from popular memory over time; like Harounaba Dramé in Koling, perhaps the grave owners asked their heirs to keep them secret in order to prevent worship at their tombs; and probably the local marabouts intentionally hid these sites so that they could use them as bargaining tools with their impressive number of clients. Many individuals said they know the general whereabouts of these "holy graves" but not their exact locations.[121]

I investigated these issues by tapping into scholar genealogies and oral testimonies by Karantabans from different kabila affiliations. I found two outstanding answers as a result of my inquiries: the secrecy of these graves emanated from elders' refusal to elevate any humans to a level unacceptable to God, a strict recommendation of their forebears; and the original intention of elders was to make it extremely difficult to use these sites as "weapons against one another," fearing that God may accept prayers made in these locations. This explains why up until a few generations ago Karantabans who knew these sites did not exceed the "nine wisest men" in a kabila; and as they got older, they transmitted this secret to their younger relatives, if they deserved their trust.[122]

Karantabans who know the exact site of Fodé Hérabа's burial ground were not shy about their legitimate bragging rights. El Hadji Manding of Fodékounda surmounted this mystery only when his father took him to this site; and El Hadji Khadiry Barro of Barrokounda was handpicked by his grandfather following "a tough competition with his contemporaries."[123] Both men agreed that guessing the whereabouts of the graves is a good way to start, but the most important thing would be to pinpoint the gravesites accurately. This could only be done by measuring correctly the grave's length from the head to the feet of the deceased, a sine qua non for performing fruitful prayers on these sites. Following the founders' deaths, there were times when pious visits to their graves were scheduled on Thursday night; pilgrims wrapped two sheets of traditional woven cloth around their bodies, like Muslims wearing their robe (*ihram*) during the hajj in Mecca.[124]

## MUSLIMS' STRATEGY OF DISPERSAL

The trajectory of religious change I describe moved from the Bainounk religion to Islam, not the other way around. Men and women who were engaged in this double tradition of interfaith marriage and Muslim intermarriage, "the Bainounk mothers of Muslims" who accepted Islam as a result of these unions and their offspring, and individuals who obtained new spaces of affiliation by integrating the original Muslim settlements together constituted the building blocks for the nascent Dar al-Islam in the Middle Casamance. I retraced the roots of the Mandinka Muslim diaspora, looking at the pedigree of contemporary clerics, including imams, judges, village chiefs, Qur'anic teachers, as well as ordinary citizens.

For them, across time and space a host of factors triggered the dispersal of Muslims from their new homelands to other regions. Power struggles resulting from the mode of political succession, regional and long-distance trade, land scarcity caused by overpopulation or natural calamities, and the instinct to avoid competition by other Muslims were central in stimulating these movements.[125] Meanwhile, despite the big leap forward accomplished by Islam, Muslim founders understood that much more needed to be done to radically change the spiritual geography of the Middle Casamance in favor of Islam. As a consequence, before their deaths they advised the next generations of Muslims to take the additional steps necessary to accomplish this goal.[126] Their mission was specifically to "return to success," to paraphrase Fodé Almamy Fossar Souané by doing other things favorable for the development of Islam: seeking to increase their knowledge of God and the Qur'an, a precondition for getting respect from their fellow non-Muslims and Muslims; being foot soldiers of Islam by relocating to the remotest areas where they could attract new adherents to Islam at the grassroots level; behaving as genuine role models in other communities through the "gifts" of peace, love, and respect toward others, as well as interfaith marriage; promoting brotherhood, solidarity, unity, and intermarriage among Muslims, regardless of people's personal status; and augmenting the number of mosques and Qur'anic schools run by qualified scholars.[127] Founders premised these recommendations on their firm conviction that the proliferation of Islamic institutions and the teaching of the Qur'an would ultimately spur social change. These were pivotal in the articles of faith of the legacy Fodé Héraba transmitted to his son and successor, Fodé Saloum. Clerics who belonged to the chain of transmission (*silsila*) in the Soly, Sakho, Barro, and Diba kabilas pledged allegiance to keeping alive this same tradition.[128]

The centuries following the founders' deaths were marked by considerable efforts by the next generations of Muslims to widen the Dar al-Islam. This explains the existence of three groups of Muslim settlements in the Mandinka country today. I have so far mentioned the first two groups: the old Bainounk settlements like Dioudoubou, Bakoum, Pathiabor, Mandouwari, Koling, and

Bambadion whose populations embraced Islam as a result of their encounter with peaceful proselytizers like Fodé Héraba; and the original Muslim townships like Ndiama, Karantaba, and Dianaba. The third group comprises the offshoots of both of these previous settlements, but the exact dates of their creations are nebulous in local sources. This spatial mobility captured the attention of Bocandé who called "the creation and re-creation of new Mandinka villages a benchmark" in the Casamance history.[129]

Like Ndiama and Dianaba, Karantaba left its fingerprints on these additional Islamic breakthroughs in multiple ways. For example, besides Bougnadou founded by Koly Diemé, many other Muslim settlements had direct or indirect connections with Karantaba. Among these were Darsilamé in central Pakao, Sitaba and Diareng in eastern Pakao, Karantaba-Sonkoundou in Sonkoudou, Karantaba-Boudhié in Boudhié, and Kounayan whose older generations of clerics were schooled in Saliguénié, one of Karantaba's oldest offshoots.[130]

After finishing his Qur'anic education in Karantaba, Siaka Karimou Dramé moved to central Pakao where Bainounk authorities helped him freely acquire a land concession. This became the village of Darsilamé (local corruption of Dar al-Islam) located near Mandouwari, the Bainounk capital destroyed during the jihād, as we shall see in chapter 4.[131] Sanoba Dramé, a Bainounk convert, undertook his Qur'anic studies in Karantaba and became a dynamic schoolteacher. He spent some years in Diareng, another village that descended from Karantaba, before resettling in Boudhié, where he was hosted by the Mansali and Biaye ruling lineages. After several rounds of negotiations, Sanoba freely obtained from his hosts an abandoned plot of land in western Boudhié. This site became a new Muslim village baptized Diatouma ("new house," Bainounk).[132] El Hadji Ibrahima Djitté, one of the first men across the Casamance to make the pilgrimage to Mecca twice by foot, was the first scholar who joined Sanoba in Diatouma, followed by four others years later.[133]

Diatouma's elders led by Chief Mansani Dramé said many Bainounk lineages in this area accepted Islam around the time the French were building the fort of Sédhiou in the late 1830s; they wanted to show that their village is very young compared to many other Bainounk villages created in this area before Diatouma.[134] Another elder paid tribute to the "Bainounk grandmothers and mothers of Muslims." He said intermarriage is the reason why "the blood of these remarkable women is still running in the veins of all Mandinka; and no man sitting under this tree now would deny this historical fact."[135]

Moreover, Karantaba is the alma mater of many Qur'anic students from neighboring countries like Guinea-Bissau and The Gambia. This generation included Fodé El Hadji Salim and Fodé Sané Saadi, two contemporaries of Fodé Sitokoto and Fodé Sétama who graduated before the jihãd broke out in 1843. At this moment, graduating students never left Karantaba without a sample of the soil so that they could use it as a blessing when establishing new villages or schools. Salim and Saadi abided by this popular ritual when they each established a new village baptized Karantaba, between Soma and Senoba in The Gambia and near the Guinea-Bissau-Casamance border, respectively.[136] Scholar genealogies do no tell us when exactly these settlements were created, but according to J. M. Gray, Jarra-Karantaba was probably founded by 1785.[137] Salim and Saadi never cut "the umbilical cord" with Karantaba, and before their deaths they both were elevated to the honorable rank of *fodé*. How they transformed Karantaba-Jarra and Karantaba-Guinea into famous Qur'anic centers in their respective countries is omnipresent in popular memory in Pakao and Souna.[138] Likewise, Bagadadji (Mandinka corruption of Baghdad in Iraq), one of Ndiama's most famous offshoots, was founded by Fodé Kémo Kadiali. He studied the Qur'an under Karamokho Qoutoubo in Fouta Touba and Cheikh Sidiyya in Boutilimit, Mauritania, and was one of the most respected marabouts of his generation.[139]

Generally speaking, these new Muslim offshoots ran their local institutions with minimal external pressure, as happened in Darsilamé after the jihãd when Dramé clerics kept the *alkaliyya* for themselves but reserved the almamiyya for Sylla clerics.[140] Despite this flexibility, the center (Karantaba) and the periphery (offshoots) maintained good relationships at various levels: the search for spiritual advice, the exchange of Qur'anic students, interlineage marriages, and mutual assistance during turbulent times, for instance. In case of a power vacancy, those who belonged to any ruling lineage in Karantaba while living abroad could return home and exercise their legitimate rights.

The *Pakao al-Qurano* provides the chronological order of the first twenty-seven mosques erected in the Middle Casamance since the precolonial era, beginning with the mosque of Karantaba and ending with that of Diakha. Nothing indicates that this classification respects the order in which the villages mentioned on the list became chronologically part of the Dar al-Islam. Nor does this list imply that the transmission of Islamic knowledge in the region was the preserve of Dramé, Cissé, Kamara, and Souané lineages, given their strong presence on the list. Many respected clerical lineages are not included on the list, because they had chosen the *alkaliyya* over the almami-

**Table 2. The first twenty-seven mosques and their original imams in the Mandinka country, according to the Pakao al-Qurano**

| Villages | Imams |
|---|---|
| Karantaba | Fodé Diané Koye Dramé |
| Kounkaly | Fodé Diané Bourama |
| Badoungha | Fodé Lamine Kagny |
| Diana Sonkoudou | Fodé Diané Dramé |
| Maradaw | Fodé Mamai Kéréra |
| Saliguenié | Sissao Dialima Cissé |
| Dianaba | Fodé Lamine Souané |
| Diombaty | Fodé Bouran Fané |
| Ndiama | Fodé Lamine Daffé |
| Missira Sonkoudou | Fodé Dialma Daffé |
| Bayamba | Fodé Hirama Dramé |
| Bary | Lang Tida Ba |
| Bassaf | Fodé Saloum Dramé |
| Babady | Fodé Balancoundji Cissé |
| Darsilamé | Fodé Bourang Daffé |
| Sitaba | Fodé Makounda Dramé |
| Bougnadou | Fodé Bourang Camara |
| Soumboundou | Fodé Dialima Dramé |
| Manconoba | Fodé Bamba Fofona |
| Oudoukar | Fodé Amoro Camara |
| Kirakounda | Fodé Bandey Touré |
| Diareng | Fodé Bourahima Siré Dramé |
| Bambadion | Fodé Toumani Dramé |
| Sandiniéri | Fodé Ibrahima Dramé |
| Koumbony | Fodé Ibrahima Cissé |
| Kafour | Fodé Ibrahima Cissé |
| Diakha | Fodé Ousmane Kaba |

yya in their own villages. Thus, if the classification had been solely based on the *alkaliyya*, the list would have included other important clerical lineages.

In one group discussions of this list, some participants reiterated the religious importance of Karantaba, recalling that when Bougnadou's first mosque of was built, the Diémé ruling lineage was mindful of the solid landlord-stranger relationship between Fodé Héraba and the Gambian Koly Diémé; they then reserved the almamiyya for Dramé clerics who resettled among them, out of gratitude. In Mankononba the maternal ancestor of the Dramé lineage belonged to the Sagna founding lineage, whereas their paternal ancestor, most erudite scholar, Fodé Aladji Dramé, migrated from Karantaba generations ago. After his death, his sons returned to Mankonoba to create the first local mosque and led religious affairs.[141] The overwhelming number of imams whose name starts with *fodé* on the list, participants concurred, is indicative of their commitment to following the recommendation of their founders, acquiring the highest level of Islamic expertise possible.

Many scholars on the list undertook their initial Qur'anic studies based on the teaching models that had long been used in the old kabila-schools mentioned above. At some point in their professional careers, some resettled to other areas where Muslim experts were needed. Others sought to improve their credentials, performing the pilgrimage to Mecca, exchanging esoteric knowledge with colleagues living in remote areas, or traveling abroad to acquire higher education. Between the eighteenth and nineteenth centuries essentially such study abroad programs sparked the prestige of Mandinka clerics. Notable among them were Ibrahima Sylla of Darsilamé and Diébatéba of Dianaba who traveled to Fouta Diallon and Fouta Touba before the 1840s.[142]

Another, Fodé Kadiali of Ndiama, whom Paul Marty described as "the most important Mandinka marabout in the Casamance" in French sources, studied under Koutobo, the grandson of Karamba Diaby who founded Fouta Touba in French Guinea.[143] Between 1890 and 1905, another generation of Mandinka men from The Gambia and the Casamance were among Koutobo's students in Fouta Touba.[144] Reflecting on the social impacts of these trips, one member of the Barro kabila said their founders wanted both their direct heir-apparent and disciples to expand the cognitive repertoire, to the best of their ability. He characterized this "ancestral recommendation" as consistent with the teachings of Islam, associating these long-distance endeavors with one hadith: "Those who travel in search of Qur'anic knowledge are walking in the path of Allah until the day they return home."[145]

In light of the above, whether Muslim immigrants resettled near or away from their Bainounk host communities in the Middle Casamance, there is no irrefutable evidence that they quarantined themselves to safeguard the originality of their faith. Muslims rather wanted to find the best strategies to manage their new communities in accord with Islamic tenets. In some African regions, the interactions between first comers and latecomers resulted in the assimilation of the latter, as in the case of the Dangara frontiersmen in the Black Volta region.[146] But in the Middle Casamance, the porosity of ethnic boundaries helped Muslims keep extensive contacts with the Bainounk communities, despite episodic tensions. This comportment resembles the course of action of the Dioula minority who achieved a commanding role in the West Volta region. As Robert Griffeth notes, in this region, "the immigrant managed to preserve his particular linguistic, cultural, and religious identity, while maintaining extensive contacts with the indigenous pagan people among whom they settled, and who were initially his recognized political overlords. This pattern persisted even when considerable marriage occurred."[147]

Indubitably, "mixing" and "reform" were decisive steps in the institutionalization of Islam in Africa, including the Middle Casamance. But in this particular region non-Muslim and Muslims were accustomed to maintaining contacts in numerous ways: commercial exchanges, intermarriage, the solicitation of the Islamic art of divination, the benefits resulting from Qur'anic education, and the participation in public rituals like the circumcision ceremony (*kouyamba*). These collaborations are incompatible with any notion of ethnic and religious quarantine.

While investigating the impacts of political Islam, Anne Frances Leary drew a different picture of ethnic and religious encounters in the Lower Casamance. For her, intermarriage between Dioula traders and local women occurred in the Diola region of Fogny; but these new wives neither embraced Islam after their marriages, nor did their Muslim offspring who pursued their Islamic education abroad return home. This means that Muslim migrants were not necessarily propagators of Islam and were not obligated to convert others in the Diola country.[148]

This scenario can be partly explained by the Diola's long-standing dedication to maintaining their independence from foreign institutions. It is not a simple coincidence that the Diola were among the last Senegambian populations who succumbed to French colonial rule.[149] Two other factors may be taken into consideration in explaining this situation: whereas some Muslim immigrants to the Diola country profited from their commercial activities to engage in Islamic proselytism, others only focused on the accumulation of wealth; and Diola youth and elders envisioned conversion through diametrically opposed prisms. As stated by Peter Mark, like the Sérére-Saféne in western Bawol, Diola youth viewed conversion as a great chance to reject unwanted customary practices, while male and female elders feared that the implementation of shariah would lead to a redistribution of social roles, inexorably nullifying their preexisting privileges.[150]

The situation of the Bainounk differed entirely. Based on French sources and oral records, ethnic interactions and the influence of Islam in the Middle Casamance persisted well into the nineteenth and twentieth centuries. Bocandé, who witnessed these interactions through his dynamism and mobility, underlined the persistence of intermarriage between Mandinka men and Bainounk women. For him, local non-Muslim women were fascinated by the ways Muslim men dressed their new wives according to Islamic mores, and imitated the same dress code, like some Diola women who embraced Islam in other areas like Thionck Essyl, in the Lower Casamance.[151] These developments show some level of popularity of Islam among women in the Casamance. In the same vein, Hecquard reported that between the 1840s and 1850s Karantabans warmly welcomed him when he was hosted by the venerated cleric Fodé Sétama; and that during his short visit both Muslims and non-Muslims, as well as insiders and outsiders, rewarded the "holy man" with valuable gifts in exchange for his teachings and prayers.[152]

## CONCLUSION

The double tradition of interfaith marriages and Muslim intermarriages emphasized in this chapter facilitated the landlord paradigm of Islamization that occurred in the Middle Casamance since the precolonial era. This was a time of "jihād without the sword" in the sense that Muslim immigrants negotiated and acquired a new homeland in this region through peaceful means. The significance of quarantine exceeds the creation of separate territories between the populations involved in this process. To be fully effective, quarantine must include, if not a complete absence of contact, at least minimal interactions between these populations. This paramount dimension was lacking in the Middle Casamance where no real buffer zone in the military sense of the term existed because Muslims and non-Muslims needed each other and exchanged multiple favors.[153]

The language of social change took an exceedingly violent overtone with the eruption of the Pakao jihād in the 1840s. This inaugurated a new era during which the Middle Casamance became a battleground between Islam and monarchy. This took the form of a three-sided armed conflict between the Mandinka, the French, and the Bainounk landowners. This armed conflict represents an inspiring model for apprehending the military jihād paradigm of Islamization, but it is still marginalized in the historical literature on Senegambia. The goal of the next chapter is to close this gap.

**CHAPTER 4**

# *Choosing between Death and Islam*

## Karantaba and the 1840s Pakao Jihãd

When the war on Mandouwari began, the tears and blood of the victims had crossed the river; the weapons were as numerous as dugout canoes; lost hats were as numerous as the water lilacs (*koubayo*) growing across Pakao; and children were crying because of the foods their mothers left in the kitchens while running to spare their lives.

—Mandinka epic song

The Pakao jihãd constitutes a striking case study for comprehending the military jihãd paradigm for the Islamization of Senegambia. By combining oral traditions and French archival sources this chapter provides the first full historical account of this jihãd that erupted in the Casamance in the 1840s. This was a time when the language for religious change shifted from the pacific coexistence that characterized the previous landlord paradigms to the use of physical violence against the Bainounk power centers. Scholars have noted the role of this jihãd in the institutionalization of Islam in Senegambia, but detailed historical studies of this movement are still lacking, including the most recent scholarship on Islamic revolutions in West Africa.[1] Anthropologist Matt Schaffer's ethnographic study on Mandinka Muslims is the only meaningful contribution to my knowledge of the Pakao jihãd.[2]

Unlike certain other jihãds in West Africa, the Pakao jihãd was not directed against the slave trade that sustained the local economies of the Middle Casamance well into the nineteenth century.[3] Nor was it led by Foula clerics although Mandinka leaders benefited from the military assistance of the theocratic state of Fouta Diallon. The Bainounk centers had long retained political privileges due to their old age and priority as landowners in the Middle Casamance. They seized this position of power to abuse the non-Muslim majority and the Muslim minority peasantries until the mid-nineteenth century when Muslims began to emerge as the dominant demographic group in the region. Though the jihād aimed at getting rid of these centers and their affiliates, it was never intended to replace them with a centralized state.

Besides offering conflicting poles of perspectives in conceptualizing the jihād, oral traditions and French sources each have specific shortcomings. According to the former, the jihād sought to liberate local farming communities from oppressive Soninké regimes.[4] Aided by their Foula allies, the Mandinka toppled these non-Muslim regimes, uprooted from their ancestral homelands people who refused Islamization, and forced them to start a new life elsewhere.[5] The latter paint a different picture by correlating the jihād with the Mandinka's jealousy of the French presence in the region. This Francophobia thus ignited the Mandinka's project to overthrow their Soninké overlords, to establish a new political order, and renegotiate the modalities of French colonial presence in the Middle Casamance on the Mandinka's own terms. In spite of these conflicting perspectives, it is possible to write a comprehensive history of the jihād by weaving together both types of sources.

The significance of the category of Soninké examined in this book changes with the religious or ethnic contexts. Where oral sources depict the populations singled out by the jihād as Bainounk, written documents identify them as Soninké. In reality, in the Middle Casamance, the label Soninké is traditionally used to distinguish between Muslims and non-Muslims. In Mandingo, Soninké designates individuals who rejected such core Islamic precepts as "praying" and "fasting," devoting themselves to "tapping and drinking palm wine," among other pre-Islamic beliefs. In the precolonial period, two distinct groups of Soninké existed in the region: non-Muslim Mandinka and the Bainounk landowners.

This chapter first documents the origins of the jihād, the tragic fall of Mandouwari (the capital of the Bainounk chiefdom of Pakao), and the generalization of the jihād that led to a radical shift in French colonial policy. French officials conceived of the jihād as a long-term threat to their commercial enterprises in Senegambia, given the European competition mentioned above. This became a serious French preoccupation in the decades following the erection of the fort in the late 1830s. Second, during this time Karantabans broke with their ancestral past, playing a preponderant role in the propaganda, prosecution, and settlement of the jihād. The chapter highlights the rationale behind this unprecedented political innovation. Third, the best way to conceptualize the jihād is by approaching it as a three-way conflict between

Mandinka Muslims, the French, and the Bainounk. By this time, Bainounk power had irreversibly diminished and was incapable of staving off either the Mandinka or the French, who moved on to become the dominant power players in the Middle Casamance.

## THE ORIGINS OF THE PAKAO JIHÃD

Jihãd, one of the most controversial topics in historical narratives on Islam, can be defined and interpreted in multiple ways, depending on the motivations and contexts. Its original meaning in Arabic is "struggling" or "striving" in the way of Allah (*jihad fi sabil allah*); but over time this has been understood to mean "holy war" in many regions of the world, including West Africa.[6] The Pakao jihãd falls in the category of *jihãd al-asghaar* (smaller jihad). One common denominator between the marabouts Tall in eastern Senegal, Fodio in northern Nigeria, and Ahmad Lobbo in Macina was to take up arms against African rulers who assaulted their emerging Muslim communities, but the historical contexts of these movements differed from one region to another.[7] These movements have recently been characterized as " jihãd from within," which implies that those who prosecuted them targeted other Muslim groups to end their unethical, non-Muslim practices.[8]

The Pakao jihãd was not part of the "jihãd from within" category, but it too targeted the Soninké regimes who had long oppressed the farming communities in the Middle Casamance. This prosecution was done *manu militari* in that Mandinka Muslims demanded that the Soninké regimes and their supporters choose between accepting Islam or facing punishment by death. As mentioned above, in the precolonial Bainounk homeland, Islam was tolerated as a minority religion, as in many other regions of Senegambia.[9] This continued until the first half of the nineteenth century when relations between the non-Muslim majority and the Muslim minority increasingly went sour. The changing demographics of the region, coupled with the rise of a new class of Soninké rulers for whom Islam was a real danger to the survival of their regimes played a key role in this process.[10]

Based on oral sources, nobody epitomized this negative change of demeanor more than a powerful, wealthy, intimidating monarch called Niadoumassani, who ruled over Pakao from his capital, Mandouwari. The jihãd, the "war of Mandouwari" or the "battle against Niadoumassani," implies that he embodied royal power abuses committed against local farming communities.[11] For example, the corn, millet, rice, cassava, and sweet potato grown by farmers enabled them to refill their granaries and participate in weekly markets.[12] The monarch suddenly initiated a radical change of policy, demanding that Muslim farmers pay him a form of tax on the harvest (*namoo*).[13] Muslim groups intimidated by this warning managed to meet this requirement at the end of every rainy season. Others rejected this taxation, arguing that earlier rulers like Bahoumba Daffé had endorsed the free settlement of clerics like Fodé Héraba in the Bainounk homeland.

Infuriated by this refusal, Niadoumassani encroached on the rights of recalcitrant Muslims, exposing them to daily humiliations. For instance, Muslim farmers who crossed Mandouwari while going to their fields were intercepted and "forced to drink wine," a proscription in Islam.[14] On the eve of key Islamic holidays, the monarch ordered the pillaging of Muslims' livestock.[15] Whenever a bad rainy season caused a terrible drought followed by hunger and starvation, the ruler's inner circle pillaged Muslims' cornfields with impunity, or deliberately "poured pig blood" into public wells to anger those fetching water. In some accounts these offenses are portrayed as "mutually inflicted wounds" that were accelerated by the increasing number of people living in this region during this time.[16] Others suggest that before the expansion of Islam, the Bainounk and Mandinka living side by side in the Pakao land area celebrated the circumcision rite of passage (*kouyamba*) together; these could never be held in the absence of Mandouwari's emissaries, but the opposite was true whenever these emissaries arrived first.[17]

In the Milo River valley region, Muslim immigrants often disturbed their Condé host communities, making loud calls to prayers at dawn. Many Condé groups coped with this unbearable situation by creating a new territory away from their original homeland.[18] The Bainounk reacted to this same annoyance by forbidding Muslims from reciting the opening chapter or *sura* of the Qur'an (*fatiha*) and from making calls to prayers (*waadanela*) that were loud enough to disturb non-Muslims.[19] Muslims who feared Niadoumassani's firepower swallowed their pride, only complaining behind closed doors. The decision to resolve this situation came from a brave Muslim cleric named Ibrahima Sylla for whom the only way to end these humiliations was to dismantle the Soninké regimes, beginning with Mandouwari where these anti-Islamic policies were crafted. Sylla was not among jihãd leaders who shared the honorable title of *almamy* in the wider Senegambia.[20]

Oral narratives suggest that religious and social considerations were the root causes of the jihãd, but the fact that it was prosecuted right after the

Figure 5. The French fort Pinet-Laprade built between 1838 and 1844 in Sédhiou. Source: (Photo by the author, October 2003.)

erection of the French fort proves that its economic motivations cannot be underestimated. In 1836, the French built their first fort in Karabane, a small, lush island located in the Lower Casamance.[21] They were quickly dissatisfied with this initial choice because sanitation problems and the lack of safety rendered life precarious on the island.[22] The French then established a second fort in the Middle Casamance to take advantage of the hospitable weather, luxurious and colorful vegetation, and fertile lands of this region.[23] Erected between 1837 and 1844 in Sédhiou, on the north bank of the river, the fort was strategically designed to be a political center and a gateway for the expansion of French commerce with the populations of southern Senegambia. "In the name of the French Republic," Commandant Henri Dagorne signed a treaty in which the Soninké ruler of Bakoum (Bodia Danfa) authorized him to purchase land measuring 250 meters in length and 100 in width.[24]

To adjust to the new economic context resulting from the transition from the illegitimate slave economy to legitimate trade, the French were already laying the groundwork for their ferocious accumulation of wealth in sub-Saharan Africa. Coined in many ways as *l'économie de traite* by Jean Dresch, this economic system consisted particularly during the second half of the nineteenth century of buying natural resources from the African peasant communities at extremely cheap prices. Like slaves and gum Arabic in the previous centuries, at this moment peanuts were becoming the defining crop of the French colonial economy in Senegal.[25] As we shall see below, in the Middle Casamance, the French targeted other valuable products, such as rubber, fabrics, cotton, and beeswax, using sophisticated methods of cheating at the expense of African farmers. By 1819, the French had already established a fort in Bakel on the left bank of the Senegal River. In the following decades, they sought to create a railway from the Casamance in the west to Bakel in the east in order to facilitate the transportation of these valuable products.[26]

Again, these transactions concerning the fort of Sédhiou intervened at a time when European powers were competing for commercial hegemony in southern Senegambia.[27] As indicated previously, Ziguinchor was already a Bainounk township where the Portuguese set up the first European trading post by the 1640s, whereas the British were working hard to solidify their power base in the Gambia River region.[28] One of French officials' primary concerns was to keep their contenders away from the Middle Casamance; they feared a potential Portuguese-British conspiracy that would dismantle the new fort due to its location halfway between The Gambia in the north and Guinea-Bissau in the south. This prompted French officials to sign additional treaties with the Soninké chiefs of Boudhié on the north bank and of Souna on the south bank. The treaties became effective on December 23, 1839, and August 2, 1840, respectively. In exchange for their complete commercial monopolization of the Boudhié land area, the French agreed to pay an annual tribute of 250 francs to Soninké rulers.[29]

By this time Pakao and the surrounding area were fast experiencing a demographic transition at the expense of the Bainounk landowners. Bocandé noted that shortly before the jihād in 1843 this region had already comprised nineteen Muslim villages and five non-Muslim villages, and that Muslims had already become the majority group in Balmadou and Souna on the south bank of the Casamance.[30] We have no idea about the ethnic and religious makeup of the other Bainounk chiefdoms. Though the Frenchman traveled within these areas many times for commercial purposes, he did not produce clear statistics to back up his assessments, basing his remarks only on his observations. However, in the period before 1843, he said, Islam had undeniably made a big leap forward in the Middle Casamance.[31] This breakthrough was partly due to the peaceful patterns of interfaith marriages, Muslim interlineage marriages, and Islamic education mentioned above. Oral narratives lend credence to Bocandé's observations, contending that on the eve of the jihãd many villages in the region had already been completely or partly Islamized, and that these changes sped the jihãd against the Soninké regimes.[32]

As time passed, the growing Muslim immigrants in the Middle Casamance characterized their Soninké political overlords as "drunkards" and "greedy kings," who were unfit to represent their interests, given their non-Muslim status. French officials at the fort likewise deplored the "greed" and excessive "drinking habit" of these rulers.[33] Simply put, from the beginning of the settlement of the fort in 1837 to the eruption of the jihãd in 1843, these negotiations did not consider the demographic change that was taking place in the region. This negligence was a critical element in paving the way for the prosecution of the jihãd.

From a French perspective, the jihãd somewhat aimed at determining whether Islam would become the official religion of the Middle Casamance, but social and religious motivations carried much less weight than political and economic ones. This explains why Mandinka's bitterness about French commercial prosperity animated the debates in French correspondence. The Mandinka failed to dissuade Soninké rulers from having more fruitful relations with the French. They then sought to overcome this setback by sabotaging the French presence in the region, waging jihãd on the Soninké regimes.[34] The Mandinka believed that the French would find it difficult to ignore their new status as the "new masters of the land" in Boudhié, the gravitational center of French commercial activities.[35]

In truth, the idea of waging a military jihãd predated the French presence in the Middle Casamance. According to Bocandé, some Mandinka Muslim immigrants to this region often waited until their numbers grew bigger to establish their own independent communities; they were forbidden from fortifying their new homeland; and they secretly armed themselves and awaited the best opportunity to subdue those who did not share their values.[36] Interestingly, Pakao's status as a "God-given Holy Land" or as "a divine blessing" for Muslims is a constant mention in Mandinka popular imagination. This old belief is validated by correlating it with the story of the "Seven Abdoul," and other holy men (*waliollou)* who were buried across Pakao.[37] The holiness of Pakao inspired Fodé Héraba and other "cultivators of Islam" to resettle in the Middle Casamance.[38] Other narratives also signal the cases of revered scholars who visited Pakao before the jihãd, including the Foula marabout El Hadji Oumar Tall; he is believed to have crisscrossed Pakao barefoot, out of respect for the holiness of the land. Since this momentous visit, the hut that sheltered the prestigious cleric and the tiny spot where he made his ablutions for prayers (*wudu*) near the river in Sédhiou have been transformed into sites of pilgrimage by some populations.[39] The cumulative effect of these old beliefs gave the Pakao jihãd an air of inevitability. When Mandinka Muslims began to outnumber the Soninké, they envisioned "holy war" as a pragmatic idea for them. All of this means that the creation of the fort was not the direct cause of the jihãd, but rather the accelerating factor of a revolution that had long been looming.

According to Syllaba and his entourage, because Mandouwari was wholly accountable for the mounting religious tensions in the Middle Casamance, the only solution was to make the Soninké accept Islam one way or another.[40] French archival sources are mute on the defining aspects of the jihãd, including the family background of Syllaba who is simply portrayed as a Muslim leader willing to becoming "king of Pakao." Given this shortcoming, I reconstructed the crucial phases of the jihad by historicizing what I describe as the epic of Syllaba. . In so doing, I interpreted the rich oral renditions portraying the epic as a chain of interconnected episodes that ended with the death of Syllaba in the aftermath of the jihãd.[41]

The first episode opened with Syllaba's birth, which probably occurred in the early nineteenth century in Oudoukar, one of the oldest townships in northern Pakao.[42] Anne Frances Leary defines ethnic identity by prioritizing the ancestral homeland over any other factors, and uses a more primordialist approach by painting Syllaba not as a Mandinka but as a Diakhanké.[43] In my view, the significance of ethnic identity should go beyond ancestral homeland and inheritance, without denying the importance of "descent-based attributes" in this process.

Syllaba's father, Boubacar Sylla, was an itinerant merchant-scholar who immigrated to Pakao from Boundou and was hosted by the Sylla clerics of Oudoukar in central Pakao. His mother, Diéynaba Kanté Cissé, was a Mandinka woman who belonged to the respected Cissé clerical lineage of Darsilamé.[44] She had long been crippled by a terrible foot injury that kept her from getting married unlike members of her generation. As a skilled specialist in pharmacopeia, Syllaba's father was hired to treat Diéynaba, combining Qur'anic verses and traditional medicine he brought with him from Boundou. After the successful treatment, the healer was supposed to be given two slaves (one man and one woman). However, after his initial nightly meditations and prayers (*istikhara*), Sylla realized that if he married his patient they would have a son whose glory would reverberate across the region.[45] So Sylla turned down his initial offer and chose to marry Diéynaba after his landlords in Oudoukar and Cissé clerics in Darsilamé made the appropriate arrangements through a chief negotiator (*silatamala*). Syllaba was born three years later in Oudoukar where his parents settled in accordance with the local rule of patrilocality.[46] As recommended by custom, after a lucrative business trip, Sylla's father tried to take his family to Boundou so that they could meet his relatives. His sudden death from natural causes in Niani County, Mali compelled Diéynaba and her son to reunite with her paternal brothers in Darsilamé.[47]

The second episode of the epic began with Syllaba's Qur'anic training, followed by his departure in search for superior knowledge abroad. His maternal uncles (*baring*) belonged to the *khadiri* order and were bright Qur'anic schoolteachers (*karamol*). They raised Syllaba according to Mandinka cultural norms, registered him in Qur'anic school at the age of seven, taught him to farm, and made him go through the usual male rites of passage, including circumcision.[48] Between the seventeenth and nineteenth centuries, some Wolof townships of northern Senegambia increasingly became outstanding citadels for the transmission of Qur'anic knowledge. Such famous jihãd leaders as Thierno Souleymane Bal and Abdoul Kader Kane of Fouta Tooro and Malick Sy of Boundou frequented these prestigious schools.[49] This was not the case of Mandinka men whose top destinations were rather Mauritania, and Fouta Diallon and Fouta Touba in Guinea, including Syllaba and one of his close friends, Diébatéba.[50] Precisely how old Syllaba was when he left Pakao and how long he stayed abroad are blind spots in oral narratives, but he was a middle-aged man when he returned home and called for jihãd.

The third episode was Syllaba's homecoming followed by his propaganda for war. Rallying Muslims around the banner of Islam was a painstaking work of persuasion. This began with Oudoukar where commoners first warmly welcomed Syllaba and helped him open a Qur'anic school. Using his personal charisma, Sylla began popularizing his project during *jumuah* when most dignitaries were present. Some immediately dismissed Sylla's audacious project as a political aberration, while others called him a "satanic" person who brought them "a shoe soiled with human remains."[51] By Mandinka cultural standards, this metaphor means causing chaos and destruction to one's own people through a self-inflicted wound.

Disgruntled by Syllaba's persistence, some individuals threatened to burn or desecrate his "satanic" books, or proposed to eliminate him physically for being a troublemaker. Villages like Sitaba and Kounkali campaigned against Syllaba, believing that given their proximity to Mandouwari, they would be the first targets of Niadoumassani's retaliation.[52] Culturally, a natural instinct for Mandinka who are rejected by their paternal family is to seek refuge with their maternal uncles. Syllaba adopted this conduct when he relocated from Oudoukar to Darsilamé, disregarding the offer by the populations of Mankonoba or Marandaw to shelter him, when he faced increasing death threats in Oudoukar. Syllaba knew that at this critical juncture the most powerful sources of religious authority in the region were Karantaba, Ndiama, and Dianaba, and that getting their support was a prerequisite for achieving popular support for the jihãd.[53] When Syllaba reiterated his intention to wage war in Darsilamé, his maternal uncles agreed to back up his plan only with the consent of the Dramé founding lineage. These latter agreed to endorse him only with the seal of approval of Karantaba, their ancestral homeland.[54]

Syllaba worked meticulously to overcome these predicaments, mending fences and sending countless diplomatic missions across the Mandinka country. When Karantabans heard the drum announcing a public event, they gathered around their spiritual leader, Fodé Sitokoto Dramé. During his speech, he cited some Qur'anic chapters and advocated for what he considered a "matter of death or survival for Muslims in the Middle Casamance." When leaders like Dramé and Diébatéba predicted a good outcome for the jihãd after long stretches of seclusion and meditation, the call for collective action inevitably gained popular support.[55]

The Pakao jihãd was part of the Soninke-marabout wars (*la guerre des marabouts*, in French) that swept West Africa between the eighteenth and nineteenth centuries, but no empirical evidence ties it to any previous model of proselytism.[56] While the Foula center of Timbo in Fouta Diallon was one of Syllaba's strongest supporters, nothing indicates that he was carrying out the political agenda of this theocratic state. This resembles the case of Ahmad Lobbo who acted independently in Macina, while seeking the support of Sokoto.[57] After persuading his fellow Muslims, Syllaba solicited military assistance from the Almamy Boubakar in Timbo, and got his wish thanks to his previous affiliation with Fouta Diallon.

According to one tradition collected by Schaffer, between 7,000 and 8,000 Foula warriors had entered Pakao on the eve of the jihãd to back up Syllaba's military efforts. Neither the oral narratives I collected, nor French archival documents corroborate these extremely impressive figures.[58] They rather suggest that Timbo sent hundreds of Foula warriors led by a military chief named Bakary Koing. Meat was the only diet of these superbly trained, motivated warriors who entered Pakao clandestinely to divert public attention. Syllaba was obligated to delay the jihãd for months so that he could meet this dietary restriction.[59] French sources depict Bakary Koing as a turbulent element who gathered many "bad elements" and responded to Syllaba's call, simply because Koing wanted to become "king" of the north bank of the Casamance. Whether Koing was a political dissident who took the path of self-imposed exile or an agent carrying out the orders of Fouta's *almamy* is unclear, but his military impact on the final outcome of the jihãd is clear in oral and written sources.[60]

From the outset Syllaba met with difficulty in mobilizing Muslims because of their widespread fear of Soninké retaliation; his war propaganda was first dismissed as as utopian due to rumor that some Mandinka leaders who "gave their word to Syllaba" were secretly planning to betray him in the end. This did not prevent Sylla from building a strong military coalition, repeating one of his favorite rallying cries: "Nothing is more honorable than dying in Islam's name."[61] This coalition comprised three regiments: the first Mandinka Muslim settlements and their offshoots; the old Bainounk townships whose populace converted to Islam over time; and Foula warriors who were recruited in Fouta Diallon. After selecting his first regiment of warriors among his own Qur'anic students, Syllaba challenged his fellow schoolteachers to do the same thing.[62] Once he became confident of his strong coalition, he automatically sent an ultimatum to Niadoumassani.

## THE TRAGIC FALL OF MANDOUWARI

The Mandinka are superstitious communities who firmly believe that such serious matters as land purchase, marriage, rites of passage, commercial transactions, and the building of new houses must be preceded by specific rituals designed to predict the outcome of these decisions.In examining the other critical episodes of Syllaba's epic, we see that waging war is no exception. The fourth phase of the epic was the prewar mystical preparations that involved invisible forces when the decision for war became public.[63] In Mandinka popular imagination, the jihãd was a litmus test for the survival of Islam in the Middle Casamance and beyond; and many mystical forces were needed to figure out "how the jihãd could be successfully prosecuted": istikhara, private sessions of Qur'anic recitation, the making of protective charms, animal sacrifices, and the hiring of talented diviners.[64] Prayers performed by Muslims before and during the assaults on Mandouwari were geared toward cursing the Soninké so that they would spread over time and space, like "the fruits or seeds falling from palm wine and palm oil trees."[65]

In the Mandinka camp two mystical revelations were imperative for the inevitability of Mandouwari's downfall. First, the jihãd would succeed only if one of Syllaba's "siblings" or "close relatives" was among the first Muslim warriors to perish. Syllaba was his parents' only child and his closest "sibling" was a man named Dabo who lived in Ndiama. They were not biological siblings but rather first cousins as their two mothers shared the same parents. Dabo, who did not mind dying for a noble cause, encouraged Syallaba to pursue his ambition. His only requirement before his death was that Mandinka holy men pray for the success of his descendants in return for his patriotism.[66]

Second, a successful jihãd required that holy water (*nasso*) be poured across Mandouwari before the military operations. Whether this came from Syllaba himself, a marabout in Fouta Djallon, or Fodé Sitokoto in Karantaba is a bone of contention in oral narratives. One account suggests that Karantaba's great marabout said: "Victory will come with ease and the battle should not be perilous. I have a secret weapon, a holy water; If someone succeeds without incident in pouring this water [in Mandouwari], we shall be victorious."[67] Other accounts recall that before the jihãd, diviners incentivized success by distributing holy water and talismans across the Mandinka country. Regardless of the originators of the holy water, this *nasso* was one of the most powerful "divine weapons" that made the Muslim victory possible.[68]

Syllaba was looking for a trustworthy person to carry out this risky mission whose failure or success would determine the outcome of the jihãd, and he chose a man called Djitté from his inner circle. He disguised himself as homeless, a beggar or a mentally challenged person wandering across Mandouwari, wearing rags from top to bottom.[69] The only equipment of this "sick man" was a bottle filled with holy water that contained a hole sealed with beeswax at the bottom. Metaphorically, Djitté had to "poison the spirits, souls, and minds of Mandouwarians" by pouring the *nasso* in the nine wells and public places (*bantang ba*) existing in Mandouwari at this time. As he moved throughout Mandouwari, some inhabitants ran away from him, while others made fun of "his mental state"; only women fetching water at public wells sympathized with Djitté, helping him refill his bottle.[70]

After accomplishing his mission, the "sick man" enthusiastically informed Syllaba, who sent Niadoumassani an ultimatum, asking him to choose between conversion to Islam or death. In the ruler's mindset, the fact that for years Syllaba had faced strong barriers to popular support for the jihād was grounded in the Mandinka's fear of his firepower. He did not consider how Syllaba surmounted this initial resistance after holding meetings of clarification with Mandinka elders. During this time, Bainounk children who wasted too much time while running errands for their parents were jokingly compared to Syllaba. This was a sarcastic way to remember his "procrastination" and his "lack of courage" in forming a winning coalition against Mandouwari.[71] Convinced that he had no valid reasons to take Syllaba seriously, Niadoumassani characterized him as an arrogant leader fighting a losing battle, and totally ignored his ultimatum. While Muslim leaders were looking for the right stimuli to boost the morale of their troops and formulate war tactics, the Soninké ruler invited his constituents to a public feast on the eve of the jihād.

Like their Muslim counterparts, Mandouwari's experts in divinatory practices worked night and day to bring about their own victory.[72] One reliable diviner foresaw "a monkey chasing a dog, and not the other way around, insinuating the imminence of a social revolution detrimental to the Bainounk." Niadoumassani labeled him a bad citizen and ordered his execution, condemning his "retrograde, unpatriotic attitude."[73] For Muslim elders, the indifference displayed by a monarch whose territory was on the verge of total demolition was the living proof that their mystical preparations were fruitful.[74] By contrast, blinded by his excessive confidence, Niadoumassani invited his subjects to a public feast so that they could celebrate his imminent victory. Many Mandouwarians were intoxicated when they returned home at the end of the night, giving Muslims the golden opportunity to exploit their collective weakness.[75]

The fort could have been a good source of supply for devastating weapons like firearms, cavalry, and heavy artillery, but it was under construction and poorly equipped, even for its own military protection at this moment. Muslims avoided the rainy season that lasted from the end of June to late September or early October. This would have been a bad time for recruiting warriors where farming was the foundation of local economic life; and where the heavy rains and the muddy terrain would have diminished Muslim warriors' ability to strike with efficiency and speed. Therefore, the first military assaults did not commence until March and April 1843 in the middle of the dry season, when the river was not too deep around Pakao. This enabled Muslims from both sides of the river to converge simultaneously on Mandouwari in central Pakao with limited risk.[76] Their chief military strategy was to surround Mandouwarians so that the they would not easily escape; throw straw on top of the huts and burn the village to the ground to physically weaken the populace; and finish them off with sticks, spears, arrows, iron bars, bows, and knives while they tried to escape. Some of these weapons are still hanging on some huts in Oudoukar and Darsilamé.[77]

Mandouwarians reacted to this unprecedented siege in four ways. Most hid in the cornfields and escaped the village once the Muslim assaults began.[78] The second group was those who fought with abnegation until they died heroically as martyrs on the battlefield. The third group was a minority of people who opted for suicide over captivity, including women and children between the ages of eight and seventeen who jumped into public wells. The fourth group was captives who were later liberated when they accepted Islam.[79] Again, there are no detailed statistics about the death toll resulting from the jihãd in French archival documents, which only acknowledge the occurrence of Soninké casualties. They nonetheless indicate that Muslim assaults claimed the lives of more than 400 people, including brave Karantaban warriors. These figures constitute a major loss by the standards of the Middle Casamance in the 1840s.[80] Because Karantaba was more populous than the other members of the coalition, it provided more soldiers, was the first to attack Mandouwari, and got the highest casualties. These losses reportedly came from the action of local slave warriors who bragged about themselves and challenged non-slave warriors to show the same manhood on the battlefield; or from Karantabans' decision to precipitate the assaults against Mandouwari, launching a series of initial battles that lasted only hours. After the jihãd, Muslims agreed to remedy this loss by replacing every dead Karantaban with two slaves: one man and one woman.[81]

Niadoumassani was hidden in a big hole under a silk cotton tree (fromager, French). When he was captured and refused to become Muslim by shaving his head, he was drowned to death in a nearby, small body of water, or a river tributary(*bolong*). The ruler's tragic death crushed the spirits of his toughest warriors and definitively ruined their chances to regroup.[82] The Muslim victory powerfully inspired oral performers across the Mandinka country. In praise poems, griots often recall the Soninké debacle in the following terms: "With the outbreak of the war on Mandouwari, the tears and blood of the victims had crossed the river; weapons mobilized were as numerous as dugout canoes; lost hats were as numerous as water lilacs (*koubayo*) growing across the Pakao; and children were crying because of the foods their mothers left in their kitchens while running for their lives."[83] This means the war on Mandouwari brought nothing but fear, chaos, and destruction to the Soninké. As a result of Mandouwari's fall, some Bainounk groups automatically accepted Islam and were disowned by others who rejected Islam and left the Pakao region.[84]

Reportedly, Syllaba refused his part of the war booty, arguing that Muslims' religious freedom was the driving force behind the jihãd, not economic profit. I agree with Schaffer that in oral narratives the correlation between the jihãd and enslavement is downplayed. I brought up this question during a private interview with an elder, who portrayed himself as half-Mandinka and half-Bainounk.[85] For him, the jihãd resulted in four categories of war captives: one group was sent to Bassaf, Ndiama, and Bissinki; a second group went to Darsilamé, Dioudoubou, and Bambadion; a third group went to Karantaba and Fouta Diallon; and the fourth group comprised orphan children who were adopted by some Muslim families in the Casamance.[86]

The plethora of bad charms buried in Mandouwari during the jihãd deeply worried Muslim leaders; they wanted to restrict the negative effects of these occult forces by dismissing this site as too cursed and too unfit for human settlement. Some villages that took part in the coalition were authorized to transform this empty space into farms where many crops are still grown today. Despite my best efforts of persuasion, informants declined to accompany me to this historic site so that I could take photographs, fearing that this gesture would breed chaos and destruction for their families.[87]

The last episode of Syllaba's epic corresponded with his death, but its exact date is unknown. Oral records persist that "this extremely brave warrior" died from natural causes about forty days after the storming of Mandouwari, meaning before the end of 1843 or several months after the assaults.[88] Neither Mandouwari's tragic fall nor Syllaba's death signaled the end of the jihãd; instead, these events motivated Muslims to extend their military operations from Pakao to the other chiefdoms in the Middle Casamance.[89]

## THE GENERALIZATION OF THE JIHÃD: SHIFT IN FRENCH POLICY

Muslims' initial decision to single out Mandouwari grew out of their calculated efforts to break the backbone of Bainounk power and cast doubt in the minds of the remaining Soninké communities.[90] Once this objective was achieved, the jihãd quickly spilled over into Souna and Balmadou on the south bank and into Boudhié on the north bank. Muslims conducted these new military operations by using the same tactic of surrounding and burning the Soninké townships to the ground. Those who deserted their houses as soon as they heard the arrival of Muslim forces facilitated these additional campaigns.[91]

These new operations affected the economic life of the fort so powerfully that French officials felt obligated to carve out a new policy in the Middle Casamance. Some clarifications are needed here to better contextualize the motivations of this urgent political move. The newness of the fort and its lack of a military arsenal were not the only reasons why political expediency dictated French officials' attitude when the jihād first broke out. They fully understood that it would be hard for them to achieve any commercial success in the region, without winning the confidence of the local populations, including respecting their customs and religious beliefs. Achieving this goal was difficult at the beginning because the French had little knowledge of the geography of Boudhié and the psychology of its populations. These weaknesses are highlighted in the reports sent in the 1830s and 1840s by the commandant of Gorée to the governor of Senegal.[92] By the time the fort was built, relationships between local populations were shaped by raids, land disputes, and the stealing of cattle. If they remained on the sidelines of these senseless feuds, the French thought, the belligerent groups would reciprocate, respecting and trusting them in their new establishment.[93] For these reasons, the exhibition of patience, neutrality, and moderation, not weakness, were central in the instructions the fort's authorities had to consider in their dealings with local populations.[94]

Moreover, the French thought that the search for economic profits was the rationale behind the jihād, but they never lost sight of its religious dimensions and were unable to predict the outcome, duration, and geographic scope of the conflict for some reasons.[95] First, in the 1840s, a lack of mutual trust hindered good relations between French agents and Soninké authorities, who threatened to reconsider the terms of the treaties they had previously signed with the French between 1838 and 1840; they lamented that the growing French prosperity did not result in an increase in the tribute payment due to them. Conversely, the French blamed Soninké rulers for their inability or unwillingness to create the level of protection required to keep their competitors away from the Middle Casamance.[96] Second, other populations shared the anti-French sentiment epitomized by the Mandinka. For instance, the Balante of Mangaroungou threatened to "welcome with sticks and other weapons" the French who entered their territory without their consent. The Diola of Samalite, Cadjinol, and Diémbéring questioned the legality of the French presence in the Lower Casamance, despite the treaties they had signed in 1828.[97] Third, in the first months of the jihãd the Muslim assaults were not directed at Sédhiou where the fort was located. Mindful of these uncertainties, the French concluded that siding with any of the conflicting parties would be a blind leap into the unknown, opting for a "wait and see" strategy.[98]

Some interesting parallels can be drawn between the Pakao jihãd and that prosecuted by the Foula cleric Maaba Diakhou Bâ (1809–67). During Maaba's jihãd in the Gambian kingdoms in the 1860s, British officials adopted a policy similar to that of the French in the Middle Casamance. Early British colonial rule in The Gambia was accompanied by the production and commercialization of groundnuts. The British viewed Maaba's course of action as a growing impediment to their commercial ambitions in this colony. Some governors sympathized with the Soninké regimes in the Badibu and Combo kingdoms, but the colonial office barred them from intervening militarily in favor of either party.[99] But in the Middle Casamance in mid-1843, when the Mandinka emerged as "the new masters of the land," they forced the Soninké to seek refuge at the fort, out of desperation. Others fled to remote regions like Fogny, a predominantly Diola region located to the west of the Soungrougrou River. This was the moment when the jihãd seriously became a three-dimensional conflict.[100]

On April 9, 1843, Muslim forces attacked the Soninké in Sandiniéri where they burned huts and killed numerous commoners.[101] In June 1843, another Muslim group departed from Karantaba and set fires in two Soninké villages in Souna; and the Foula invaded Mansakounda near Sédhiou, sparing only Muslim lives. In July, Foula warriors launched attacks against the Bainounk living on both sides of the Casamance; a number of Foula soldiers and a dozen Soninké perished in these battles. For commandant Hyacinthe Pelletier, these unsuccessful attacks greatly tarnished the Foula's prestige in this area.[102] Under Diébatéba's leadership, a regiment of Mandinka warriors from Dianaba targeted the Soninké of Kolibanta in Birassou, but they were pushed back toward Kandiénou.[103] When reporting on the political climate in Pakao and Boudhié between March and April 1843, Pelletier said: "The Soninké are no longer a factor. The marabouts have massacred many of them and the rest have accepted their domination. . . . The ruler of Boudhié is no longer significant and he is like the Sounaba [chief] in Sandiniéri who had already converted to Islam."[104]

Soninké groups on the north bank met the same tragic fate, beginning with Bakoum, whose ruler, Bodia Danfa, authorized the erection of the fort in Boudhié. In May 1843, Mandinka and Foula warriors synchronized their military operations against Bakoum. Simbé Diémé, the ruler of Bakoum at this time, was among the victims of the invasion that occurred when the populace celebrated a good harvest of palm wine.[105] Though the fort was not completely finished, Soninké fugitives desperately used it as a temporary refuge, taking advantage of its proximity to Bakoum. Women and children were among those captured in Bakoum.[106] Children, who became orphans as a consequence of these deadly attacks, were adopted by several Muslim families, while male and female captives were used in cotton fields.[107]

The only truce during the jihād was the period from July to September, when the heavy rainfalls caused real travel problems, and when widespread insecurity made farming problematic throughout the region. This resulted in an economic crisis due to a shortage of key staples like rice and millet. Public health deteriorated with the proliferation of malaria, yellow fever, smallpox, and some sexually transmitted diseases that affected civilians and soldiers.[108]

From the outset, French officials branded the jihād as useless religious warfare between "natives," but months later it turned out to be a serious blow to their commercial affairs. The interethnic tensions were both a curse and a blessing for the French: they generated economic instability while preventing the native communities from building a united anti-French front. When the French realized that the curse was fast outweighing the blessing, they opted for a new policy based on direct interventionism in the conflict. They precisely advocated for the use of military force, as shown in one of the long briefings sent to the governor of Senegal by the commandant of Gorée.[109] French archival letters acknowledge that the jihād was a real conundrum whose immediate resolution was indispensable, if the French were to become a powerful force in Senegambia. However, while military force was a popular view in French administrative correspondence, versatility, confusion, and hesitation combined to delay the methods and strategies that were needed to achieve this goal.

Several arguments explain these contradictions. For example, until 1843 the Muslim coalition had remained aloof from French economic interests, with the exception of few isolated incidents. In November 1843, Muslim leaders held a war council in Darsilamé after months of intensive military offensives that were only interrupted during the rainy season. Two crucial questions dominated the council's agenda: the compensation of Foula allies for their outstanding war efforts, and the transferability of taxes initially paid by the French from the Soninké to the Mandinka, "the new masters of the land." The council threatened to single out the fort militarily, if the French refused to meet its demands.[110]

Two crucial remarks should be made in relation to these two questions. First, oral narratives persist that Islamic solidarity was the rationale behind the Foula contribution to the jihãd. The Mandinka understood the efficacy of this military support and promised to compensate the Foula when they agreed to join forces in the name of Islam. When speaking about the war council, informants mentioned the case of many enslaved individuals sent from the Middle Casamance to Fouta Diallon.[111] Second, the importance given to the transferability of taxes validates the argument that economic gains cannot be totally ignored in the motivations of the jihãd.

In November 1843, Caternault, the commander of the fort, saw a causal link between the jihãd and the "state of economic stagnation" of the fort. For him, the same Muslim forces that had impressively built a far-flung coalition against the Soninké regimes could aggravate the already deplorable situation of the fort. Additionally, Caternault understood the imminence and inevitability of a military confrontation between the French and the Mandinka. He envisioned the planned council as a great opportunity to break the Muslim coalition by raising awareness of the irreconcilable disagreements between the Mandinka and the Foula on the applicability of the treaties signed in 1838. Caternault thought he could succeed by applying a policy of dividing and conquering, signing a convention of political neutrality with the Foula. This would deny the fort the right to shelter runaway Soninké targeted by Muslim offensives, but also forbid Foula warriors from intervening in any confrontations between the French and the Mandinka or other populations.[112] Caternault attempted to win over the most skeptical Mandinka leaders by convincing them of two critical things: the Foula had a "hidden agenda" and would never respect Mandinka economic interests, and the Mandinka had nothing to fear in case of a war with the Foula, because fighting in their own territory would give them a terrific advantage in terms of military recruitment.[113]

Unfortunately, Caternault's vision was not shared by some of his superiors like Pierre Thomas, the commandant of Gorée for whom the so-called convention was a restriction on French freedom at a time when French trade deserved supreme protection. Most importantly, he rejected Caternault's policy as a disservice to French economic interests in the Middle Casamance.[114] Around this time, French officials accused Bakari Koing of instigating the

Mandinka war council because of his "aspiration" to control the throne of Pakao. On November 28, 1843, Koing died in Darsilamé after falling from his horse shortly before the war council. French officials welcomed this news with a sigh of relief and hoped that Koing's death would ruin Syllaba's political ambition to "become king." Therefore, according to the French, Syllaba was still alive in November 1843.[115]

Despite being a big loss for Muslims, Koing's accidental death did not keep them from launching additional deadly assaults against the Soninké in the following years. In March 1845, Muslims in Pakao tightened the noose around the Bainounk of Bagnére, Bissary, and Dingwaré, killing numerous commoners.[116] The years 1845–50 were marked by a resurgence of anti-French sentiment expressed through multiple acts of sabotage that deliberately targeted French economic assets. For example, the populations of Dioudoubou pillaged dugout canoes loaded with merchandise belonging to European commercial houses (Griffon, Maurel and Prom, Monteillet, and Gasconi). In Bambadion, Mandina, and Karantaba, commoners ambushed caravans of goods passing near their territories; a dozen *laptops* (indigenous sailors) working for French commercial houses were killed whereas many others were wounded in these assaults.[117] Even some populations that were not directly involved in the jihād complicated this already unstable situation for the French. The Balante singularly orchestrated episodic raids against Europeans in the French quarter of Dagorne, where soldiers, French officials, and traders coexisted by 1848; these infringements were partly designed to take away as many animals as they could. On the north bank, the inhabitants of Ndiama and Saliguénié sabotaged European commercial houses ambushing their representatives.[118]

Over time, French authorities realized that these rising acts of vandalism were motivated not uniquely by an absence of concrete sanctions, but also a psychology that cast them as "unable to operate outside of the fort in Sédhiou."[119] In comparison, during Maaba's jihād in Niumi and Badibu, British governors were eager to see the end of the conflict and endorsed peace treaties between the belligerent Muslim and Soninké parties. As Charlotte Quinn notes, in the 1870s, some governors even pressured Soninké rulers to capitulate by becoming Muslims.[120] The French adopted a different position beginning with Captain Victor Roger who relied on physical violence when he commanded the fort in 1849. He accused the Soninké of being cumbersome individuals who caused nothing but liability for the French, while simultaneously seeking protection at the fort. Between April and June 1849, several

Figure 6. This cemetery was the site of former Pathiabor, one of the Bainounk capitals destroyed during the Pakao jihād. (Photo by the author, November 2003.)

pirogues loaded with trading goods destined for the fort were pillaged. Roger was beyond angry when he discovered that the Bainounk who had continuously sought French protection actively took part in these attacks.

Roger understood that collaborating with local communities without distinction was vital for French success in the Middle Casamance; but he was so displeased with the magnitude of these unpunished offenses that he made an unprecedented decision in the fort's history. In May 1849, Roger ordered punitive expeditions against the Bainounk, to expel them from Boudhié and dismantle their major settlements: Pathiabor and Bakoum.[121] His goal was to purge from the region all traces of Bainounk presence and then replace them with less troublesome individuals: the "Sarakholé." For the sake of transparency, let us recall that this group is referred to as "Sarakholé," but in terms of ethnicity and religion they are Soninké and Muslim, respectively. They had nothing to do with the Soninké or the non-Muslim populations targeted by the jihād.[122]

The propensity to categorize Africans was among the core features of European colonial knowledge. The French singularly tended to classify

African native communities by using dichotomies such as good-bad, right-wrong, peaceful-brutal, hospitable-hostile, and clean-dirty. But they drew a more favorable picture of the Sarakholé than the other populations in the Casamance, profiling them as industrious and potentially valuable business partners, given their hardworking spirit, loyalty, and friendship.[123] French officials also lauded the Sarakholé for their paramount role in making ships and working in the postal services on Gorée and Saint Louis Islands. François Manchuelle emphasizes the dynamism of these migrant workers in peanut farming in the region between The Gambia and the Rio Grande in Guinea-Bissau.[124] Kenneth Swindell and Alieu Jeng also highlight the prominence of "Serawoollies" in the Gambian groundnut trade system between the nineteenth and twentieth centuries.[125]

The permanent recruitment of a reliable, sedentary workforce was one of the toughest challenges the French faced, while trying to jump-start their commercial activities in the Middle Casamance. Due to the low population density of Boudhié, local inhabitants alone could not satisfy the growing labor opportunities provided by the fort in the 1840s and 1850s. To compensate for this deficit, the French recruited other migrant workers, including groups of Sarakholé men from the upper Senegal River region. These types of migrants are called *nawetaan*, a Wolof term for seasonal workers in search of farming opportunities during the rainy season (*nawet*), but who would return home during the dry season (*nor*). In the Middle Casamance, many Sarakholé followed the same pattern of settlement as in the Gambia River region.[126] They rented a portion of land from rich Mandinka landowners, paid them in heavy harvest taxes at the end of the season, made good profits by selling their products, and then returned home until the next season.[127]

The French also thought the presence of the Sarakholé in the Middle Casamance would be beneficial to them for other reasons: their peaceful attitude would make them a permanent source of manpower for French enterprises; given their foreign status, those who resettled near the French quarter would pose no threat to French interests such as claims of land ownership; and once they developed mutual trust with the Sarakholé, they would use them as a reservoir of soldiers in military confrontations with the Mandinka.[128] Meanwhile, the French deplored the fact that the Sarakholé who rented lands from the Mandinka allowed their landlords to accumulate substantial wealth, and they feared that growing patterns of intermarriage between the two groups could become another factor in rapprochement, leading to the Sarakholé's cultural assimilation into the predominant Mandinka groups.[129]

After weighing these advantages and inconveniences, the French supported the settlement of Sarakholé workers in Boudhié. By the 1850s, 770 individuals lived in Sédhiou, including some 114 Sarakholé who represented between 18 and 20 percent of the total population.[130] From 1855 to 1867, the Sarakholé collected between 200 and 260 baskets of groundnuts thanks to their strong work ethic.[131] Some European businessmen, impressed by these figures, supported definitive settlement of Sarakholé near the Dagorne quarter like Jules Rapet. This broker and partner with the Griffon House wanted the Sarakholé as a source of manpower for his company and welcomed them to Juleskounda, one of Sédhiou's smallest quarters, which was named after him.[132]

French efforts were unsuccessful because until the 1860s most Sarakholé workers preferred to travel back and forth between Boudhié and their native homeland. The deserted space created by the Bainounk's forced removal from Boudhié was ultimately occupied by the growing Mandinka communities. This was how Pathiabor became a cemetery where Muslims and non-Muslims still indiscriminately bury their dead.[133] Similarly, in the Upper Casamance, the nomad status of Foula cattle herders, the tense struggles between the nobles and slaves, and Molo's political exile to The Gambia were paramount factors in making the Fouladou a demographically instable French colony.[134] In The Gambia around the same time the British also sponsored the resettlement of pro-British communities (liberated Africans, runaway slaves, and landless refugees), hoping that they would help them accumulate wealth in this country.[135]

Captain Roger engineered another political reform whose timing was not accidental. By 1849, the fort was at the nadir of its popularity materialized by a resurgence of acts of sabotage happening almost simultaneously. Roger thought about refashioning the fort's public image at a time when the Middle Casamance was almost irresistibly falling into the orbit of Islam. In his view, a good tactical choice in this direction was to appoint a Mandinka Muslim scholar to a leadership position in Boudhié. Roger preferred somebody, who could be a trustworthy broker between the fort and the unwelcoming local communities, knowing that the powers of Soninké rulers were almost nonexistent.

On May 23, 1849, Roger signed a new treaty with a Muslim party led by the same Ndoura Kamara mentioned above. At this moment, he was a renowned schoolteacher and judge (*cadi*) who successfully mediated social disputes in Boudhié based on shariah.[136] The treaty that appointed Ndoura as "the supreme chief of Boudhié" permitted him to collect an annual tribute of 250 francs in recognition of his absolute loyalty to the French. He recognized the status of Boudhié as a French protectorate and served as a broker for the French.[137]

According to Leary, from 1849, when Ndoura was appointed "Boudhié's supreme chief," to 1864, when he died of smallpox, he "gained increasing personal powers."[138] French archival sources undermine this assertion, showing that Ndoura had quickly fallen from his pedestal, leading to his demotion to mere figurative chief of Boudhié. This downfall emanated from fatal mistakes committed by Ndoura during his tenure. For example, the Mandinka and the Bainounk both distrusted Ndoura because of his close relations with the French. He was not among clerics who supported the Muslim coalition against the Bainounk, partly because of his family ties with Bakoum where his wife, Yéri Danfa, resided. Instead, Ndoura sided with the French, who showered him with gifts when he recognized the new status of Boudhié, a political orientation that irritated the Bainounk landowners.[139] Ndoura sold a good portion of Boudhié's land to French businessmen, who consolidated their holdings at the expense of the Bainounk. Finally, Ndoura levied heavy taxes on Sarakholé workers, which angered the French who cherished them more than any other population in the Casamance.[140]

Given the magnitude of his "political gaffes" and "power abuses," French officials accused Ndoura of being more concerned with enjoying his personal power than serving as an intermediary between the fort and local populations. These contradictions can hardly be dissociated with the misleading nature of the 1849 treaty, including one paradoxical element: while designating Ndoura as the supreme chief of the entire Boudhié, the treaty considered Boudhié a French territory. In other words, territorial sovereignty across this region belonged exclusively to the French who appointed Ndoura.[141]

Whereas the Mandinka and the Bainounk separately strategized around the kind of punishments they thought Ndoura deserved, the French initiated new political measures that culminated in his dismissal. This began when Pierre Aumont, the commandant of Gorée, argued that Captain Roger's policies produced no valid remedy for the economic stalemate characterizing the fort. On June 1, 1849, Aumont sent a letter to Roger that denounced his counterperformances and ordered his replacement by Captain Jean Teissier. In the name of the French Republic, Teissier signed a new treaty with the "Republic of Boudhié" corroborating Ndoura's eviction and his replacement as Boudhié's chief by a man called Alaisanou.[142]

This same treaty proposed the repatriation of the Soninké who were expelled from their homeland by Captain Roger in 1849.[143] Teissier thought about facilitating this return by rebuilding the Bainounk villages of Bakoum, Patiabor, Badiari, and Bouno. Before acting Roger wanted the absolute guarantee that the returning populations would recognize Boudhié as a French territory, making no future claims of land ownership. The Soninké had no valid reason to trust either the Mandinka, who had persecuted them pitilessly since the beginning of the jihād, or the French, who arbitrarily sped up their forced removal from their ancestral homeland. Given their legitimate fear of additional persecution, the Soninké never returned home.[144] Finally, neither the treaty of May 1849 signed between Captain Roger and Ndoura, nor that of February 4, 1850, authorizing the Bainounk re-settlement in Boudhié, were implemented.

Afterwards, Teissier invited Ndoura to a meeting during which he clarified that the French were the "only masters of the land in Buje." He postulated that his administrative powers and legal authority enabled him to confiscate Ndoura's prerogatives, under the treaty of May 25, 1849. Moving from words to deeds, Teissier stripped Ndoura of his previous annual tribute, telling him that French officials alone were "entitled to deliver valid permits" for the purchase of land by local or foreign traders. Tessier then canceled the heavy taxes Sarakholé farmers were required to pay to their Mandinka landlords. Ndoura attempted to surmount these political measures and reestablish himself as Boudhié's leading authority, but to no avail.[145] Nonetheless, he was authorized to seek military protection or political asylum from the fort whenever his personal security was in jeopardy.[146] Ultimately, Governor Auguste Baudin disregarded the treaty of May 25, 1849, and that of February 4, 1850 never took effect, because the Soninké were already looking for ways to reinvent themselves elsewhere in Senegambia. Thus, French officials easily declared Boudhié as a French territory by right of conquest.[147]

With the fall of the Soninké regimes, the two remaining power players in the Middle Casamance were the Mandinka and the French colonial state. The French knew that the Mandinka would keep challenging their legal authority, and coped with this threat primarily by using military violence. Bocandé once requested punitive expeditions against local groups like the Kagnout who opposed French presence in the Lower Casamance. In March 1851, his wish was fulfilled when four ships and 135 troops assaulted the rebellious populations, forcing them to sign treaties recognizing French sovereignty in the Diola country.[148]

Impressed by this demonstration of power, Emile Pinet-Laprade (1822–69), the commandant of Gorée, convinced Governor Louis Faidherbe (1818–

89) to endorse the same procedure in the Middle Casamance. From Laprade's standpoint, military violence was the best way to convince belligerent groups like the Mandinka that the fort was indeed well prepared to retaliate outside of its base of operations in Sédhiou.[149] Following his request, in 1861, 50 ships, 300 infantrymen, 300 troops, and 60 artillerymen unexpectedly docked at Sédhiou and inflicted unprecedented military assaults on the populace.[150] The intense military operations and incomparable firepower used by the French on this occasion prompted Mandinka authorities to sign a merciless new treaty that guaranteed French sovereignty over the Pakao region. In the face of this weakness, the French erected more than twenty additional trading posts whose remains are still visible near the Casamance River. The fort's authorities equated these breakthroughs with a "provincial fair" (*foire provinciale*), or with a network of French markets in the Middle Casamance.[151]

The French dedicated the 1860s and 1870s to consolidating their position as the only colonial power in the region, with the creation of a postal service, a customs service, a bureau of accounting, and a maritime post, in addition to the preexisting fort. At this time, the leading trading houses in Sédhiou were Griffon, Malfilatre, Maurel, and Bocandé; they were engaged in fierce rivalries and remunerated their intermediaries in accordance with their public relations and marketing skills.[152] Using instruments like gourds and steel bars European businessmen exchanged African products, such as beeswax, wood, rubber, ivory, and peanuts, for guns, powder, cloths, beer and other attractive foreign products. Local farmers and traders often accused Europeans of intentionally using bad "systems of credits" and "sophisticated methods of cheating" in their commercial transactions.[153] This dissatisfaction reached a new level in 1861 when Governor Faidherbe approved the creation of a personal tax (*impôt personnel*). This exacerbated the conflicts of interest between European trading houses and their African "trading partners" who had continuously been the subject of economic exploitation.[154] Africans' verbal complaints, acts of sabotage, and negotiations did little to prevent the incorporation of the Middle Casamance into the expending French colonial empire.

The last three decades of the nineteenth century were partly marked by the sudden emergence of a new class of Muslim warriors from various backgrounds. Without downplaying their importance, these dynamics should not be viewed as a prolongation of the Pakao jihād because it was already won and these warriors acted alone. One warrior was Sounkai Yéri Kamara, Ndoura's son, who tried to replace his father as Boudhié's chief; he failed to achieve his goal because the French and African traders both refused to take him seriously, despite his determination.[155] Another warrior, Fodé Diombo Dramé of Bassaf, targeted a non-Muslim Foula group called Firdou, and tried to put a damper on the growing impact of French domination from his headquarters in Sandiniéri. Unable to carry out his goals and visions, Diombo was constrained to sign a peace treaty with Commandant Henri Canard which was mostly favorable to France.[156] The marabouts Ibrahima Ndiaye and Fodé Diéndé kept harassing the remaining Soninké fugitives and other populations who refused to become Muslims.[157] Some French officials blamed these warriors for being more committed to accumulating wealth through enslavement than with propagating Islam.[158]

If the militarism championed by this later generation of warriors greatly disrupted French colonial settlement in the Middle Casamance, no one typified this disruption more than the Diakhanké marabout Fodé Kaba Doumbouya (1818–1901). His fearless dedication to propagating Islam and defeating the Western presence in Senegambia annoyed several political actors in the Casamance. For example, Molo profiled Doumbouya as a dangerous rival and wanted to eliminate him so that he could increase his influence in the Upper Casamance. In the Middle Casamance, the Mandinka relegated Doumbouya to the rank of persona non grata largely because of his status as an outsider rooted in his Diakhanké and Tidjani identities.[159] In the Lower Casamance, Doumbouya's military expeditions pressured some Diola groups to seek refuge in neighboring Gambia. The marabout's growing sense of militarism inspired the British and French to suspend their rivalries and sign a mutually beneficial treaty to break Doumbouya's military machine definitively.[160] The brave marabout finally collapsed under the weight of his African and European enemies whose combined reactions put a damper on his extremely courageous political ambitions. By the time he signed a treaty with French governor Henri de Lamothe in May 1893, the aging marabout was already exhausted by his multifront battles. With Molo's complicity, the French profited from this weakness to launch the final military assaults that ended Doumbouya's life in March 1901.[161]

## CONCLUSION

In French sources, economic motivations overshadow any other considerations in explaining the origins of the jihād, because the accumulation of wealth was the primary motivation behind the French colonial presence in the Casamance. This explains why after the erection of the fort the French were looking for reliable individuals who could help them accumulate wealth, regardless of their religious and ethnic backgrounds. Only when the French realized that the jihād was running counter to their aspirations did they opt for the forced removal of the Soninké before annihilating Mandinka opposition through their incomparable firepower.

By contrast, oral sources tie the jihād to the need to liberate local farming communities from the abuses of the Bainounk centers. Well before the French and Mandinka knew a fort would be erected in the Middle Casamance, Mandinka Muslims were planning to subdue these centers whose representatives viewed Islam as a direct threat to their survival. The fact that these centers benefited from the new economic prosperity provided by the fort at a time when the region was irresistibly being incorporated into the Dar al-Islam irritated the Mandinka leadership. This negative sentiment unquestionably contributed to the outbreak of this jihād.[162]

The French claim that Syllaba and Koing shared the political agenda of becoming "king of Pakao" seems more based on suspicion than on fact. If this "shared hidden agenda" were true, it would likely have generated conflicts of interest between the Foula and the Mandinka whose sacred alliance assured the successful outcome of the jihād. Syllaba's "ambition" to create monarchy or a theocratic state is also highlighted in French sources. Turning this ambition into reality would have required new rules and regulations, a political capital, and a central authority. Even if Syllaba had lived longer, it would have been difficult for him to carry out his dream, considering the ways the Mandinka model of organization operated historically.

First, the jihād was fought and won not by Syllaba and his disciples alone, but by a coalition of Muslim forces; and the call for jihād generated widespread support only when it became clear that Syllaba's goal was not to end kingship so he could create a new one. This was what Mandinka informants meant when saying "Allah alone is king" (*allah kiling sotota*).[163] Second, Mandinka Muslims were kingless societies in which neither the *almamy* nor the *alkaly* could combine these two roles (with very few exceptions), let alone be elevated to the rank of king. Third, Dramé clerics of Darsilamé uncompromisingly considered Karantaba their decision-making center, ignoring their village's leading role in the jihād. Fourth, the Mandinka code of chronological presence classifies Syllaba's father as a latecomer who was welcomed, given a wife, and authorized to settle in the Middle Casamance; and in this social model wife-givers take precedence over wife-receivers.

To be sure, Foula's outstanding contribution to the jihād is beyond dispute in both oral and written sources, but contrary to the suspicion highlighted in French sources, in the post-jihād era no part of the Middle Casamance ever became a province of Fouta Diallon. Rather, the representatives of the Muslim coalition held a victory meeting in Karantaba: they proclaimed the Bainounk homeland as an "eternal part of the Dar al-Islam; they expressed their debt of gratitude to Syllaba and heaped praises upon him for his bravery, patriotism, and dedication to the cause of Islam; they elevated Syllaba to the rank of a national hero; and they posthumously rewarded him by supporting the attribution of the almamiyya in Darsilamé to his family. This honorable mission began with most of Syllaba's seven sons who obeyed the rule of male primogeniture.[164]

# Conclusion

While reevaluating the role of Islam in reshaping the course of West African history within these past few decades, scholars have mostly concentrated on the colonial and contemporary periods. Specialists of Senegambia on their part have prioritized the populations of the northern region in the period since the mid-nineteenth century. They have neglected to fully consider the original Mandinka Muslim townships of the Middle Casamance whose existence predates the advent colonial rule in Senegambia. Historians particularly can better reframe the conversations about the institutionalization of Islam in this region by taking into account the role of these much older communities in this process. My goal in this book has been to demonstrate that Karantaba's history represents a valid case study for helping us close this gap, using a long-term perspective on Islam.

The model of Islamic development emphasized in this book comprises four major chronological phases. First, as stated by George Brooks, "the privilege of marrying local women" played a role in incentivizing the settlement of highly skilled immigrants in many regions.[1] This includes the Middle Casamance where a class of prestigious Muslim clerics profited from their interfaith marriages with Bainounk women to obtain land grants that became the stepping-stones for the Dar-Islam in this region. This was the first phase of the landlord paradigm of Islamization. Second, after establishing their own homelands, Muslims relied on the strategies of inclusiveness and hospitality vis-à-vis other immigrants, as well as a tradition of interlineage marriage to consolidate the foundation of the emerging Dar al -Islam. This was the second phase of the landlord paradigm.

The third phase was the moment when the next generations of Muslims followed their forebears' recommendations by relocating from their new homelands to other regions in order to widen the borders of the Dar al-Islam, to the detriment of the preexisting Bainounk religion. This dispersal was followed by the establishment of Muslim offshoots with mosques and Qur'anic schools run by qualified members of the Muslim intelligentsia. This phase is consistent with Martin Klein's argument that "Islam eradicated the non-Muslim autocratic regimes in Africa not solely through the reliance on violent means, but also through the construction of mosques, Qur'anic schools, and the dissemination of Muslim scholars."[2]

For some reasons, no hermetically sealed boundaries really separated the Muslim and non-Muslim communities in the Middle Casamance: while the Bainounk landowners were willing to entice skilled immigrants, they were so mindful of their own safety that they forbade Muslims from surrounding their new concessions with fences; the erection of such boundaries would have been detrimental to Muslim clerics whose successful missionary work depended on the collaboration of local communities; the respect for local customary laws was a prerequisite for immigrants who wished to settle in the Bainounk homeland; and Muslims used specific sites for their own communities only with the consent of Bainounk authorities.[3] Nothing indicates that Muslims deliberately isolated themselves from non-Muslims to safeguard the authenticity of their faith. Instead, Muslims wanted to find adequate ways to introduce their customs and traditions to others, while preserving their original identity and keeping in contact with their non-Muslim neighbors.

Fourth, by the mid-nineteenth century, through peaceful means largely based on intermarriage and Islamic education, Muslims had already won over a growing number of non-Muslims in the Middle Casamance. This demographic change was among the factors that stimulated the military jihād paradigm of Islamization against the Soninké regimes that had dominated the region for generations. During the second half of the nineteenth century France sought to become a "Muslim power" (*puissance musulmane*) in Africa, colonizing as many Muslim populations as possible, at the expense of their British and Portuguese competitors. Africans reacted to this colonial ambition through accommodation, collaboration, or resistance, depending on the geographic and historical contexts.[4] The Mandinka obtained a bittersweet victory in the Middle Casamance: they defeated the Soninké regimes and their affiliates with the help of their Foula coreligionists and incorporated all the seven Bainounk chiefdoms into the Dar al-Islam. But despite their strong sense of patriotism the Mandinka did not prevent the French from accomplishing their goal thanks to their military superiority.

Following the lead of one of his professors, Jacques Ruffié, President

Léopold Sédar Senghor of Senegal (1960–80) liked to mention the importance of the cultural and biological hybridization (*métissage culturel et biologique*). Senghor said whenever and wherever two different population groups meet, even if they may often fight against one another, they will always end up getting mixed including through intermarriage.[5] This description fits the case of the Casamançais who can no longer be classified ethnically and linguistically, based exclusively on their first and last names. This is because geographic proximity, cross-cultural borrowings, and intermarriage have shaped and reshaped the relationships between the populations of the Casamance for multiple generations. For these reasons, human activities such as rice and cotton farming, pastoralism, life-cycle celebrations, weaving, the tapping of palm wine and palm oil, multilingualism, and Islamic education, to name but a few, are no longer the strongholds of any specific populations across the region.[6]

However, since their immigration to the Casamance groups like the Mandinka, Diola, Foula, and Balante have managed to survive ethnically and culturally in their new environment; and anybody who crisscrosses this region today will see specific townships, populations, languages, and rituals representing these four groups. It is increasingly difficult to formulate the same argument about Bainounk whose situation is almost sui generis in the history of ethnicity in the Casamance For example, both the agencies used by Mandinka and the Bainounk in their dealings with other populations prioritized geographic dispersal to serve their own best interests. This strategy led to a radically different outcome for these two groups. The Mandinka used dispersal to successfully introduce some of their major belief systems to neighboring populations. But the Bainounk conceived of dispersal as a defense mechanism to restrict their ethnic vulnerability, reinventing themselves in safer ecological niches. This unfortunately produced the opposite effect because in this process the dispersed Bainounk groups underwent a change of demographic status from being the majority across the Casamance to becoming the minority groups in the areas where they resettled.[7] This life-changing experience led to the assimilation of many Bainounk groups into other populations in the wider Senegambia. For this reason, today "the Bainounk languages are like small islands scattered across a sea of Diola and Mandinka populations";[8] and many populations who descended from the former Bainounk chiefdoms now call themselves ethnically Mandinka, Diola or Balante, and religiously Muslim due to their Mandinkization.

Many Casamançais now equate the name Bainounk with "ethnic extinction" or "backwardness," associating their foregone conclusion on the Masoboti curse. The Mandinka particularly have shifted from romanticizing intermarriage with the Bainounk in the past to criminalizing it in the present. Many confessed that while growing up their parents advised them to "avoid personal misfortune," by refusing intermarriage with the Bainounk. At the same time, a sizable number of Bainounk admitted that the biases and name callings resulting from the curse are the reasons why at one point in their lives they sought to escape belittling and ostracism, misleadingly portraying themselves as non-Bainounk.[9] Some believe the curse only haunted their communities for generations before vanishing over time, whereas others think that the curse is still affecting them in some ways. However, most Bainounk participants have completely demystified the curse as "obsolete" and "outdated"; they predicated their optimism on the successful life stories of many "sons and daughters of the Casamance" who descended partly or totally from the Bainounk.[10] What I found puzzling until the end of fieldwork is the mindset that still deflects legitimate criticisms of the Bainounk's downfall from the conquest of their homeland by other immigrant groups to "the self-inflicted wound" initiated by Masoboti.

The Mandinka spent a great deal of time congratulating their forebears on designating Karantaba as "the capital of Islam" when French colonization was making inroads in the Casamance. For them, this audacious gesture was a powerful reminder of the precedence of Islam symbolized by Karantaba's old mosque over French colonial rule represented by the Fort of Sédhiou.[11] Karantabans are proud of the fact that since the time of their founders their homeland has been a powerhouse for the training and recruitment of a multitude of Muslim scholars who still play leading Islamic roles in across Senegambia.[12] Every year, thousands of pilgrims from diverse backgrounds flock to Karantaba for the biggest Mandinka Muslim festival held in southern Senegambia.[13] Pilgrims bring with them food items and other objects as festival contributions and donations. They pray at the mosque, near water jars, under the taabo or other big trees, in the woods, and near the riverbank. Depending on the speakers, pilgrims believe the festival is a source of "healing and hope," a moment of direct "communion with God," or a true "spiritual salvation"; and if they are lucky enough to encounter the hidden "graveyards of the founding fathers," God will answer their prayers.[14]

One of the most popular beliefs associated with the festival is that a successful pilgrimage requires the reenactment of Fodé Héraba's spiritual journey, retracing his path across the Souna-Balmadou region. This wish can be fulfilled by entering Karantaba from the south bank of the river and by moving eastward from Bambadion where the holy man lived before creating his own village, and performing small prayers on a little rock near the river in Bambadion where the cleric did his ablutions before leading prayers. Other beliefs consist of sitting during the festival under the shade of the taabo, as did Fodé Héraba and his early companions, and extracting some leaves from the taabo to use as a source of spiritual blessing and healing for multiple purposes.[15]

That said, it would be misleading to indicate that Mandinka Muslims were exclusively responsible for the expansion of Islam in the Casamance over the past centuries. Many other scholars from different ethnic and linguistic backgrounds have actively participated in this process. Outstanding examples include Bidan clerics like Chérif Makhfouss Aidara (1855–1919), Chérif Sidou Aidara (1862–1942), and Chérif Younouss Aidara (1832–1917) who arrived in the Casamance between the last decades of the nineteenth hundreds and the early twentieth hundreds.[16] They peacefully settled in some areas like Dar Salam (corruption of Dar al-Islam) in the Lower Casamance, and Sibékouroto, Bagnére and Binako in the Middle Casamance.[17] These clerics' prestigious rank as Prophet Muhammad's descendants (*chérif*, deformation of *sharif*, Arabic) helped smooth the way for them as they sought to make long-lasting impacts mostly among the Diola, Balante, and Mandiago.[18] For instance, Chérif Makhfouss's ability to appeal to large crowds of followers derived from his mastery of the Qur'an and his ability to perform miracles.[19] He popularized Islam and "the jihâd of the word" (*jhiãd de la parole*, French) in several Diola districts like Combo and Fogny, like Shaykh Maas Khah and Cherno Momodou Jallow in The Gambia in the first half of the twentieth century.[20]

Bidan clerics' influence in the Casamance was somewhat slowed down by two crucial factors. First, as their Islamic expertise grew across this region, so did their antagonistic relationship with Mandinka scholars, with whom they were engaged in tense rivalries for the recruitment of disciples.[21] Second, the stability of these flourishing Bidan families was crippled by internal divisions partly due to their Sufi affiliations: Chérif Younouss belonged to the Tidjaniyya and was a close collaborator of Serigne Babacar Sy, the *caliphe général* of the Tidjaniyya (1922–57); and Chérif Sidou and Chérif Makhfouss were affiliated with the Khadiriyya and pledged allegiance to Cheikh Sadibou (1850–1917), their uncle and the Khadiri patron saint in Senegal. By the dawn of the twentieth century, French officials attempted to appease these "interlineage conflicts of competence" by reconciling the Bidan families.[22]

Another highly regarded group is Diakhanké scholars such as Fodé Kadiali and Héraba Diaby, who ran prestigious Qura'nic schools in Yacine in the second half of the nineteen century.[23] The best known was probably the venerated marabout Mbaal Fodé Diaby Gassama (1902–80) who lived in Marsassoum, a township located on the southwestern bank of the Soungrougrou. This full-fledged poet who belonged to the Maliki school was a brilliant expert in classical Arabic grammar. He welcomed to Marsassoum reserachers from Arabic countries like Egypt in the 1960s.[24] His eldest son, El Hadji Sidiyya Diaby, established himself in Taslima, a small village located near Diaroumé, in Sonkoudou. Taking advantage of the role of this whole area as a commercial hub helped Diaby promoted Qur'anic education after recruiting a good number of students from neighboring villages.[25] The same is true about the Foula of Médina Gounass since the 1930s when Thierno Mamadou Seydou Bâ (1900–80) created this holy village in the Upper Casamance. This is probably the only clerical township in contemporary Senegal where men and women are strictly prohibited from shaking hands in public.[26]

Based on scholar genealogies, Bidan, Diakhanké, and Foula clerics were undoubtedly devout "cultivators of Islam" between the Casamance and Guinea-Bissau: they taught local populations the Qur'an and hard work in farming; they sponsored the creation of mosques and Islamic communities; they converted numerous individuals to Islam; they mediated social disputes based on shariah; and the disciples and heirs of these "men of God" are still widely respected across this region for continuing their ancestral tradition of peaceful proselytism. But centuries before these missionary activities, which mostly happened in the course of the twentieth century, as in the case of many Islamic centers of northern Senegambia, older clerical townships aforementioned had set in motion this process of Islamization in the Casamance.

According to Fina Malang Faty of Simbandi Birassou, this began long before the "arrival of the white men" (*toubabo*). For this reason, he indicated, nobody should go to Karantaba unless they are prepared to say 'God is Great' (*allahou akbar*), because it towers above the other Qur'anic centers in the Casamance due to its centuries-old existence."[27] His colleague Fina Kéba Dakhaba classified Karantaba as "the equivalent of Pir and Kokki among the Wolof, Fouta Touba among the Diakhanké, and Boutilimit among the Moorish, or the destination of choice for men whose goal was to become qualified Muslim experts.[28] Chief Mansali of Bakoum said he heard his grandfather call Karantaba the "gateway of Islam in the Casamance," arguing that that its marabouts introduced Islam to a countless number of Bainounk and Balante families."[29]

In 2003, the Mandinka were thrilled to learn that the old mosque of Karantaba had been elevated to the rank of the national monuments in Senegal, alongside the shelter of Fodé Kaba Doumbouya in Médine and the Fort Pinet-Laprade in Sédhiou.[30] This decision, unprecedented in the history of Islam in the Casamance, testifies to Karantaba's pioneering role in sowing the seeds of Islam in southern Senegambia since its emergence in the seventeenth century. Considering their ages, the models of Islamic development they have championed for centuries, and their decisive contributions to the formation of Muslim experts up until the present time, it is safe to argue that Karantaba and the other original Mandinka settlements discussed in this book fully deserve more visibility in the historiography on Islam in Senegambia.[31]

# NOTES

## INTRODUCTION

1. For previous developments on Karantaba's history, see Aly Dramé, "Planting the Seeds of Islam: Karantaba, a Mandinka Muslim Center in the Casamance, Senegal," PhD diss., University of Illinois at Chicago, 2006.

2. The Maliki scholar Ibn Khaldun dates the appearance of Sufism to the time of the four Caliphs of Islam (632–61 CE. For more knowledge of the early history of Sufism, see A. J. Auberry, *Sufism* (London: Allen and Unwin, 1968).

3. In Islam, the turuq are considered the spiritual paths that lead worshippers to God. Since their emergence many centuries ago the turuq have used the major Sunni schools of jurisprudence (Hanbali, Shafi, Hanafi, and Maliki) as their source of inspiration.

4. Examples of miracles include but are not confined to curing diseases, ending drought, stimulating economic prosperity and healing infertility. Many Muslims view miracle performances as the concrete proof of their leaders' sainthood.

5. This spiritual guidance is referenced in Qur'anic chapters 5:32 and 17:57.

6. Every year, these Sufi devotional rituals mobilize millions of Muslims across the world, depending on their religious calendar.

7. Zachary Wright, "The Sufi Scholarship of Islamic West Africa," in *Jihad of the Pen: The Sufi Literature of West Africa*, ed. Rudolph Ware, Zachary Wright, and Amir Syed (Cairo: American University in Cairo Press, 2018), 1–24, and Rüdiger Seesemann, "Sufism in West Africa," *Religion Compass* 4, no. 10 (2010): 606–14.

8. David Robinson, *Paths of Accommodation: Muslim Societies and French Colonial Authorities in Senegal and Mauritania, 1880–1920* (Athens: Ohio University Press, 2000), 16–34.

9. Other important orders established during the second half of the nineteenth century are the Niasséniyya (a branch of the Tidjaniyya) founded by Cheikhou Abdoulaye Niasse and the Layéniyya by Seydina Limamou Laye. See Khadim Mbacké, *Sufism and Religious Brotherhoods in Senegal*, ed. John Hunwick, trans. Eric Ross (Princeton, NJ: Marcus Wiener Publishers, 2005).

10. For the majority of Senegambian Muslims this affiliation is the survival of a family heritage or the result of a doctrinal switch from one Islamic denomination to another. One popular saying in Senegambia is"if you do not have a wasila or a spiritual leader, then the *jinn* or satan will be your leader," implying the individual's risk of failure religiously.

11. This ephemeral movement is known in written sources as *toubnan*; see Boubacar Barry, *Senegambia and the Atlantic Slave Trade* (Cambridge: Cambridge University Press, 1998), 50–54.

12. Michael Gomez, *Pragmatism in the Age of the Jihad: The Precolonial State of Bundu* (Cambridge: Cambridge University Press, 1992); Charlotte Quinn, *Mandingo Kingdoms of Senegambia: Traditionalism, Islan and European Expansion* (Evanston, IL: Northwestern University Press, 1972); and David Robinson, *The Holy War of Umar Tal: The Western Sudan in the Mid-Nineteenth Century* (Oxford: Oxford University Press, 1985).

13. Mervyn Hiskett, *The Sword of Truth: Life and Time of Sheku Usamn Dan Fodio* (Evanston, IL: Northwestern University Press, 1994), and Barry, *Senegambia and the Atlantic Slave Trade*. For a newer interpretation of jihãd, including its broader implications in West Africa and beyond, see Paul Lovejoy, *Jihad in West Africa during the Age of Revolutions* (Athens: Ohio University Press, 2016).

14. Ousmane Oumar Kane, *Beyond Timbuktu: An Intellectual History of Muslims in West Africa* (Cambridge: Harvard University Press, 2016), 64–65.

15. Philip D. Curtin, "Jihad in West Africa: Early Phases and Inter-relations in Mauritania and Senegal," *Journal of African History* 12, no. 1 (1971): 11–24.

16. Arjan Post, "A Glimpse of Surface in the Circle of Ibn Taymiyya," *Journal of Sufi Studies* (2016): 156–87. He contends that some of Taymiyya's students and disciples were Sufi, and that Taymiyya himself shared some attributes with his contemporaries of scholars.

17. This brand of Islam is pejoratively called "Wahhabism" in western historiography. See Natana J. Delong-Bass, *Wahhabi Islam: From Revival and Reform to Global Jihad* (Oxford: Oxford University Press, 2004). Followers of this brand of Islam call it Salafism, including most of my students from the broader Middle East.

18. Shirk (*associationisme*, French) represents the greatest sin that will never be forgiven by God, as explained in Qur'anic chapter 4:48 and 4:116.

19. Delong-Bas, *Wahhabi Islam*. Speaking on the condition of anonymity, one Senegalese scholar I met in Maryland supported his Salafi argument, reiterating the significance of the Qur'anic chapter 112, which mentions God's uniqueness.

20. Bâ transmitted to his students the teaching methods and didactic tools he used in his early career. See Rudolph Ware III, *The Walking Qur'an: Islamic Education, Embodied Knowledge, and History in West Africa* (Chapel Hill: University of North Carolina Press, 2014), 203–4.

21. The decade 1950–60 saw the emergence of many anticolonial movements in

French West Africa. Touré is the son of the respected Tidjiani cleric Serigne Hady Touré, a close associate of Caliph Serigne Abdou Aziz Sy of Tivaouane. Mourid and Tidjiani men were among the student body who perfected their Qur'anic education under Serigne Hady's leadership in his home village. His son thought political independence could efficiently pave the way for religious independence in Senegal, allowing Muslims to practice their faith more freely. The journal *Réveil musulman* was one of the outlets he used while advocating for societal change in Senegal. See Muriel Gomez-Perez, "Un mouvement culturel vers l'indépendance : Le réformisme Musulman au Senegal (1956–1960)," in *Le Temps des Marabouts*, ed. David Robinson and Jean Louis Triaud (Paris: Karthala, 1997), 521–38.

22. Some members of the UCM left the organization, accusing their leaders of complicity with the Senegalese government. In 1978, they created the JIR (Community of God's Servants) in Thiés. See Idrissa Mané, "Les 'Ibadou' du Senegal: Logiques Religieuses, Logiques Identitaires," Thése de doctorat en éthnologie, Université de Pau, 2018, http://www.theses.fr/2018PAUU1049/document

23. While I was a student in Dakar, the arabisants were considered those who studied Arabic as opposed to French, although many of them were perfectly fluent in French. Members of the HAF have developed close ties with some Salafi groups in the Middle East, while those of the JIR are generally associated with powerful groups like the Ja'amat Tablikh in Pakistan.

24. Khadim Mbacké, "Le rôle du Mouvement réformiste dans le développement du Sénégal au vingtiéme siécle," *Africa* 57, no. 1 (2002): 87–101.

25. *Ibadou*, *arabisants*, and *alfalah* are still the generic terms used by the Senegalese public to refer to these Islamic reform groups, but the former is the most common expression. Qur'anic chapter 25:63 characterizes the *Ibadur rahman* as "slaves of God" who distinguish themselves through their peacefulness and modesty. For more developments on the places of worship of these groups, see Cleo Cantone, "The Shifting Space of Senegalese Mosques," in *New Perspectives on Islam in Senegal: Conversion, Migration, Wealth, Power and Femininity*, edited by Mamadou Diouf and Mara Leichtman (New York: Palgrave Macmillan, 2009), 51–69. Generally, male *ibadou* wear short pants and grow their beards, while women don hijab and avoid too many cosmetic products designed to enhance their physical look. However, many Senegalese Muslims who do not belong to these groups share the same lifestyle.

26. Gana Ndiaye, "Private Islamic Education in Africa," in *The Palgrave Handbook of Islam in Africa*, ed. Fallou Ngom, Mustapha H. Kurfi, and Toyin Falola (London: Palgrave Macmillan, 2020), 577–98.

27. I based this statement on my observations and conversations with Muslims, including friends, colleagues and relatives. In Sédhiou, for example, one of my fieldwork assistants said *ibadou* like her will always proudly consider their name a badge of honor, not an insult, regardless of what others may think about them.

28. These changes have increasingly captured my attention since the late 1980s.

Before that time, students in Dakar traveled by campus bus to attend the Friday congregational prayer (*jumuah*) in the nearby suburb of Mermoz. This continued until the completion of the campus mosque in the late 1980s. The college of imams who led the new mosque during their sermons levelled the heaviest criticisms against Sufi leaders and governmental officials, as well as "French neocolonialism." Many students praised these charismatic preachers for having the guts to indiscriminately speak truth to power in Senegal. In 2014, during a quick trip to Senegal I noticed additional breakthroughs made by these reform Islamic groups within the previous decade.

29. Roman Loimeier, "L'islam ne se vend pas: The Islamic Reform Groups and the State in Senegal," *Journal of Religion in Africa* 30, no. 2 (2000): 168–90.

30. Moriba Magassouba, *L'islam au Senegal: Demain les Mollah* (Paris: Karthala, 1985), 9–10.

31. This informant's identity is shielded upon his request. For more insights on these power struggles, see Timothy Furnish, "Sufi vs. Salafi: Winning Friends and Interdicting Enemies in Islamic Africa," *Rima Policy* 1 (April 2013).

32. George Brooks, *Landlords and Strangers: Ecology, Society, and Trade in West Africa, 1000–1630* (Boulder, CO: Westview Press, 1993).

33. Indeed, this sense of hospitality is a standard practice in sub-Saharan Africa.

34. Jean-Baptiste Labat, *Nouvelle Relation de l' Afrique Occidentale* (Paris: Pierre François Guichard, 1728), 338–58.

35. Lamin Sanneh, *Beyond Jihad: The Pacifist Tradition in West African Islam,* (Oxford: Oxford University Press, 2016), 80–91. In group interviews, many Mandinka elders used this jihãd analogy to explain how Fodé Héraba and his early companions cherished the prevalence of mutual peace and tolerance between Muslims and non-Muslims in the Casamance.

36. For example, Cheikh Amadou Bamba Mbacké, Cheikh Abdoulaye Niasse, Cheikh Bou Kounta, and Cheikhou Omar Tall.

37. Knut S. Vikor, "Sufi Brotherhoods in Africa," in *The History of Islam in Africa,* ed. Nehemia Levtzion and Randall L. Pouwels (Athens: Ohio University Press, 2000), 441–76. This model mirrors that used by Shaykh Usman Dan Fodio in northern Nigeria. See John Glover, *Sufism and Jihad in Modern Senegal: The Murid Order* (Rochester: University of Rochester Press, 2007), 49–53.

38. Ferdinand De Jong, *Masquerades of Modernity: Power and Secrecy in Casamance, Senegal* (Bloomington: Indiana University Press, 2007), 60; Robert Baum, "The Emergence of a Diola Christianity," *Africa* 60, no. 3 (1990): 370–98; and James Searing, "No Kings, No Lords, No Slaves: Ethnicity and Religion among the Sereer-Safèn of Western Bawol, 1700–1914," *Journal of African History* 43 (2002): 408. The Islamization of the Balantakounda also occurred at around the same time as in the Diola country. In the case of the Foulado kingdom in the Upper Casamance, see Adderrahmane Ngaïdé, *L'esclave, le colon et le marabout: Le Royaume Peul du Fuladu de 1867 á 1936* (Paris: L'Harmattan, 2012), 192.

39. One of the earliest proponents of this theory is French geographer Paul Pélissier in his *Les Paysans du Sénégal: Les civilisations agraires du Cayor à la Casamance* (Saint Yrieix: Imprimerie Fabrègue, 1966), 799–800. For additional accounts, see Olga F. Linares, *Power, Prayer and Production: The Jola of Casamance, Senegal* (Cambridge: Cambridge University Press, 1992), 204; Peter Mark, *A Cultural, Economic and Religious History of the Basse Casamance since 1500* (Stuttgart: Franz Steiner Verlag, 1985),100; De Jong, *Masquerades of Modernity*, 51–53; and Steven Thomson, "Revisiting 'Mandingization' in Coastal Gambia and Casamance (Senegal): Four Approaches to Ethnic Change," *African Studies Review* 54, no. 2 (2011): 95–121.

40. Group interviews, Sédhiou, December 13 and 14, 2003, and Brikama, December 18, 2003. Balante elders disliked the pace with which Mandinkization stimulated the disappearance of important aspects of their heritage, making them "relics of the past," to borrow from one balafon musician in Sédhiou.

41. Filidjiié Mané, interview, Sédhiou, October 7 and 17, 2003. For him, the balafon was the most powerful symbol of Balante cultural heritage, and no life-cycle celebration was complete without balafon music in the Balantakounda. Since the 1950s and 1960s, however, many Balante townships have adopted a totally different attitude. For example, their circumcision ceremony is now celebrated by imitating a Mandinka ritual called *diambadon* ("dance of leaves"). This is a public carnival during which the newly circumcised (*niansing*), their supervisors (*kintang*) and the crowd dance with a loud Mandinka musical instrument, *bobolong*, while moving from village to village throughout the day.

42. Thomson, "Revisiting 'Mandingization' in Coastal Gambia and Casamance (Senegal)," 51–53.

43. Linares, *Power, Prayer and Production*, 204.

44. The adoption of new ethnic attitudes is not necessarily a by-product of intentional efforts to undergo cultural assimilation by becoming Mandinka, for example. In some areas, Mandinkization emanated from a willingness to ameliorate the living conditions of the borrowing populations; but in others local populations saw Mandinkization as a good opportunity to integrate the political economy of the region, as in the case of some Diola groups in the Lower Casamance. See Linares, *Power, Prayer and Production*, 101.

45. The ethnic composition of northern Senegambia is dominated by the Wolof, Sérére, and Foula; but in the southern region they are among the minorities, except for important numbers of Foula in The Gambia and the Casamance.

46. I was among thousands of students who took Professor Barry's history courses in Dakar. During his lectures he sometimes criticized the arbitrary partition of Africa, blaming the French and British colonial powers. For Barry, any sustainable solutions for the negative repercussions of this partition must include the creation of a Greater Senegambia, including a system of large-scale regional integration for the benefits of all local populations. See Barry, *Senegambia and the Atlantic Slave Trade*.

47. As a result of Berlin Conference's resolutions, The Gambia became British while Senegal passed under French control.

48. The Sahel is the demarcation line between the desert and savanna ecological zones. Desertification continues to gain ground in this region due to a host of devastating ecological factors, including a shortage of rainfall. For a good study of sleeping sickness and its devastating impacts in Africa, see Kirk Hoppe, *Lords of the Flies: Sleeping Sickness Control in British East Africa, 1900–1960* (Westport, CT: Praeger, 2003).

49. Mungo Park, who visited southern Senegambia in the late eighteenth century, signaled the Mandinka's expertise in hunting elephants and other big game; he classified elephant's meat, skin, and ivory among the precious commodities at this moment. See Park, *Travels to the Interior Districts of Africa* (Durham: Duke University Press, 2000), 229–72.

50. Christian Roche *Histoire de la Casamance: Conquête et Résistance, 1850–1920* (Paris: Karthala, 1985), 308. The administrative map of Senegal has been subject to several modifications since the country's independence in 1960. The Casamance is now divided into three regions along ethnic lines implicitly: Ziguinchor for the Diola, Kolda for the Foula, and Sédhiou for the Mandinka.

51. Jean Girard, *Genése du Pouvoir Charismatique en Basse Casamance* (Dakar: I.F.A.N., 1969); Pélissier, *Les Paysans du Sénégal*; and Louis Thomas, *La Mort Africaine* (Paris: Payot, 1982). Thomas's study of death and funeral rites (*l'idéologie funéraire*) boosted his fame among Africanists. The Diola are the largest ethnic group in the Casamance; they have been the leading rice farming experts in Senegambia for many centuries; they have long resisted foreign institutions imposed on them; and they are responsible for the only national liberation movement existing in Senegal today.

52. Roche, *Histoire de la Casamance*. However, there has been some renewed interest in this direction since the 2010s. For some notable examples, see Robert M. Baum, *West Africa's Women of God: Alinesitoué and the Diola Prophetic Tradition (*Bloomington: Indiana University Press, 2016); and Aly Dramé, "From Bulsafay to Fodeyya: Qura'nic Education among Mandinka Muslims in Senegal," *Journal of Mande Studies13* (2014): 91–123. See also Christian Roche, *La Casamance Face à son Destin* (Paris: L'Harmattan, 2015). This is a quick summary of his previous book, with a strong emphasis on the contemporary period.

53. Ware, *The Walking Qur'an*; John Glover, *Sufism and Jihad in Modern Senegal: The Muris Order* (Rochester: University of Rochester Press, 2007); and Eric Ross, *Sufi City: Urban Designs and Archetypes in Tuba* (Rochester: University of Rochester Press, 2006).

54. Mamadou Diouf and Mara A. Leichtman, eds., *New Perspectives on Islam in Senegal: Conversion, Migration, Wealth, Power and Femininity* (New York: Palgrave Macmillan, 2009); Mamarame Seck, *Narratives as Muslim Practice in Senegal* (New York: Peter Lang, 2013); El Hadji Samba Diallo, *La Tijianiyya Sénégalaise: Les Métamorphoses des Modéles de Succession: Le Cas de la famille Sy de Tivaouane* (Paris: Publisud, 2010); and

Elisabeth Foster, *Faith in Empire: Religion, Politics, and Colonial Rule in French Senegal, 1880–1940* (Stanford: Stanford University Press, 2014).

55. Mara Leichtman, *Shi'i Cosmopolitanisms in Africa: Lebanese Migration and Religious Conversion in Senegal* (Bloomington: Indiana University Press, 2015); Zachary Valentine Wright, *Living Knowledge in West African Islam: The Sufi Community of Ibrahim Niasse* (Leiden: Brill, 2015); Fallou Ngom, *Muslims beyond The Arab World: The Odyssey of Ajami and the Muridiyya* (Oxford: Oxford University Press, 2016); Benjamin F. Soares, "New Muslim Public Figures in West Africa," in *Islamic Education in Africa: Writing Boards and Blackboards*, ed. Robert Launay (Bloomington: Indiana University Press, 2016), 268–84; and Cheikh A. M. Babou, "The Al-Azhar School Network: A Murid Experiment in Islamic Modernism," in *Islamic Education in Africa: Writing Boards and Blackboards*, ed. Robert Launay (Bloomington: Indiana University Press, 2016), 173–94.

56. Marloes Janson, *Islam, Youth and Modernity in the Gambia: The Tablighi Jama't* (Cambridge: Cambridge University Press, 2013); Assan Sarr, *Islam, Power and Dependency in the Gambia River Basin: The Politics of Land Control, 1790–1940* (Rochester: University of Rochester Press, 2016); Baum, *West Africa's Women of God*; Séga Séckou Sagna, *La Casamance, l'Islam et la France* (Paris: L'Harmattan, 2017); Kane, *Beyond Timbuktu*; and Sanneh, *Beyond Jihad*. In recent studies of Islam in West Africa only Assan Sarr has listed Karantaba among the Islamic centers in Senegambia. See Assan Sarr, "Islamic Philosophy in Africa," in *Palgrave Handbook of Islam in Africa*, ed. Fallou Ngom, Mustapha H. Kurfi, and Toyin Falola (Cham, Switzerland: Palgrave Macmillan, 2020), 270.

57. In the early 1880s, when Félix Cross was the president of the Chamber of Commerce on Gorée Island, he wanted to better protect the interests of French commerce, taking advantage of his power of persuasion and good writing skills. See Archives of the Republic of Senegal (ARS): Q 32, lettre de Cross au gouverneur du Sénégal, February 10, 1882.

58. ARS, lettre de Félix Cross au lieutenant-gouvernor Bayol, 6 Septembre, 1885, and ARS, 2 F4. See Roche, *Histoire de La Casamance*, 204–13.

59. This ajami literature is still underdocumented theme. This may partly be explained by the fact that European and Arab writers, who discovered this type of literature, did not fully grasp its meaning and disregarded it. For some decisive contributions see Moulaye Assane, "Ajami in Africa: The Use of Arabic Script in the Transcription of African Languages," in *The Meanings of Timbuktu*, ed. Souleymane Bachir Diagne and Shanil Jeppie (Dakar: CODESRIA/HSRC, 2008), 109–22; and for a fresher interpretation of this issue see Ngom, *Muslims beyond the Arab World*.

60. This type of Mandinka masking is the equivalent of what the Wolof call *Tiombogne*.

61. El Hadji Khadiry Barro, interview, Sédhiou, November 12, 2003.

62. A few accounts correlate Souané's unpredictable decision with the inability of

Dianaba's dignitaries to find a consensus on a reliable man who could replace him before his death.

63. Group interviews, Sédhiou, November 14 and 17, 2003.

64. El Hadji Manding, interview, Karantaba, September 25, 2003; Khadiry Barro, interview, Sédhiou, November 13, 2003. This project rapidly became a bone of contention between the inhabitants of the upper village (*santassou*) and the lower village (*doumassou*). Opponents feared that this reorganization would displace their Qur'anic schools, small prayer rooms, and ancestral homes; but in the end many recognized that this would make public life in Karantaba safer.

65. Interviews, Barro, Dramé, and Soly lineage elders, September 12 and October 7, 2003.

66. At times, El Hadji Manding invited some dignitaries from other lineages to these conversations so that they could be "witnesses of history." He later depicted his inclusive gesture as an old tradition in Karantaba.

67. Some critics have accused African oral experts of misrepresenting the past, intentionally using clichés, invented traditions, and other false renditions. For more nuanced re-interpretations of some of these criticisms, see Sarr, *Islam, Power and Dependency in the Gambia River Basin*, 36–58. See also David Conrad, *Sunjata, a West African Epic of the Mande Peoples* (Indianapolis: Hackett, 2004); Barbara Hoffman, *Griots at War: Conflict, Conciliation, and Caste in Mande* (Bloomington: Indiana University Press, 2000); Mark, *A Cultural, Economic and Religious History of the Basse Casamance since 1500*, 2.

68. Western nomenclature is riddled with derogatory terms and sweeping generalizations regarding sub-Saharan Africa and its populations, including "the heart of darkness," "the land of childhood," and the domain of "the primitive mind." See, for instance, Lucien Lévy-Bruhl, *How Natives Think* (Princeton: Princeton University Press, 2008). For him, Africans make judgments solely based on speculation and mythology, whereas Europeans enter into more logical and rational thinking. See also Frederik Hegel, *The Philosophy of History* (New York: Dover, 1985), 91–99.

69. When it comes to Senegambia, see Robert M. Baum, *Shrines of the Slave Trade: Diola Religion and Society in Pre-colonial Senegambia* (Oxford: Oxford University Press, 1999); Searing, "No Kings, No Lords, No Slaves;" and Mark, *A Cultural and Religious History of the Basse Casamance since 1500*.

70. There is still a scarcity of written sources on *diéliyya* (profession of *jeli*) and the *finayya* (profession of *fina*), but one significant contribution in this direction is noteworthy. See Marloes Janson, "We Are the Sauce on Top of the Rice," *Mande Studies* 8 (2006): 183–205.

## CHAPTER 1

1. Many individuals, Westerners and Africans alike, still wrongly characterize the populations of the Casamance as members of the same ethnic group. By discussing the

Bainounk, Balante. and Mandinka separately in this chapter, I will show some of the commonalities and differences among these populations.

2. See Dramé, "Planting the Seeds of Islam."

3. Baum, *Shines of the Slave Trade: Diola Religion and Society in Precolonial Senegambia* (Oxford: Oxford University Press,1999), 65. One explanation of the name Ziguinchor is "I came, they cry" (*cheguei choran*, Portuguese). This alludes to the enslavement of Bainounk people in the precolonial area. Another is that when the Portuguese arrived in the Casamance, the Bainounk escaped oppression, moving to safer areas: "There is no more place to go" (*asi nine core*). See Stephan Bühnen, "Place Names as an Historical Source: An Introduction with Examples from Southern Senegambia and Germany," *History of Africa* 19 (1992): 66. Amadou Fall said the name Bainounk probably originated from a Bainounk group called *iziguichor;* with the semantic evolution the *i* was abandoned and the name became *Ziguinchor*; and the Kabo of Djibélor were seemingly the first Bainounk clan who ruled the town. See Pape Cissokho, "Premier habitant de Casamance au Sénégal: Le Bainounk, le bienvéillant envers l'étranger," *Journal Societé*, September 13, 2015.

4. Doudou Camara, paper presented at the Journées Culturelles Mandingues *conference*, Sédhiou, November 1992.

5. Roche, *Histoire de la Casamance*, 21.

6. Jean Boulégue, "Aux Confins du Monde Malinké: Le Royaume du Kasa (Casamance)," paper presented at the Congrés on Mande Studies, London School of Oriental and African Studies, July 1972; Mark, "The Senegambian Horned Mask: History and Provenance," *Art Bulletin* 69, no. 4 (1987): 626–40, and Matt Schaffer, "Bound to Africa," *History of Africa* 32 (2005): 321–69.

7. Group interview, Sédhiou, September 13 and 14, 2003, and Bakoum, September 16, 2003. See John Bendor-Samuel and Rhonda L. Hartell, eds., *The Niger-Congo Languages* (Dallas, TX: University Press of America, 1989).

8. Alexander Cobbinah, "The Casamance as an Area of Intense Language Contact: The Case of the Baïnounk Gubaher," in "Multilingualism and Language Contact in West Africa," special issue, *Journal of Language Contact* 3 (2010): 175–202; and Friederike Lüpke, "Language and Identity in Flux: In Search of Baïnounk," in "Multilingualism and Language Contact in West Africa," special issue, *Journal of Language Contact* 3, no. 1 (2010): 155–74.

9. Group interviews, Bakoum, September 23; Diatouma, October 2; and Brikama, October 3, 2003.

10. In my discussion with elders in Bakoum, one of the oldest Bainounk communities in the Casamance, they testified that thanks to their ancestral blessings any "real" members of the Mansaly ruling class who fall from a palm tree would survive death. See group interview, Bakoum, November 23, 2003.

11. Mamadou Mansaly, Bakoum's village chief, interview, November 11, 2003; group interviews, Brikama, August 19, 2009, and Kaour, August 9, 2009.

12. Boulégue, "Aux Confins du Monde Malinké"; Mark, "Senegambian Horned Mask," and Schaffer, "Bound to Africa."

13. The Kaabounké for Kaabou, the Pakaoanké for Pakao, the Diakhanké for Diakha, and the Foutanké for Fouta, for instance.

14. Carlos Lopes, "Kaabu and Its Neighbors: A Historical and Territorial Interpretation of Conflicts," Journal of Mande Studies, 5 (2003): 113–26.

15. Aristide Vallon, "La Casamance, Dépendance du Senegal," *Revue Maritime et Coloniale* (Paris, 1862), 458. See also Boulégue's map of the Lower and Middle Casamance circa 1600.

16. Horton, "Stateless Societies in the History of West Africa," in *History of West Africa*, ed. J. F. Adeajayi and Michael Crowder (New York: Longman, 1985), 88; and John Thornton, "Ethnicity in Pre-colonial Africa," paper presented at the Mellon Sawyer Seminar on "Ethnicity in Africa: Historical, Comparative, and Contemporary Investigations," University of Michigan, Ann Arbor, December 2010.

17. This resembles the term *djolofin mansa* used in Mandinka popular traditions for the king of Djolof, but the appropriate term for ruler in this Wolof state is *bourba*.

18. As we shall see in chapter 4, because Boudhié was the site of the French fort in the Middle Casamance, Boudhié and its populations are more mentioned in French sources than the other Bainounk chiefdoms.

19. Boulégue, "Aux Confins du Monde Malinké."

20. De Lespinay, "Action sur le Territoire, Marqueurs Toponymiques et Enjeux Socio-Juridiques en Casamance (Senegal)," in *Noms et Renoms*, ed. Salih Akin (Rouen: Publications de L'Université de Rouen, 1999), 165–81.

21. Robert L. Carmeiro, "The Chiefdom: Precursor of the State," in *The Transition to Statehood in the New World*, ed. G. D. Jones and R. R. Kautz (Cambridge: Cambridge University Press, 1981), 37–79. Some informants used similar descriptions when explaining Bainounk model of organization. When analyzing the reproduction of African "traditional" societies, Igor Kopytoff and other authors have questioned the validity of the "tribal model," which conditioned the debates on the genesis of African societies for decades. Other experts have criticized these authors' own model, "the African internal frontier." See Igor Kopytoff, *The African Frontier: The Reproduction of Traditional African Societies* (Bloomington: Indiana University Press, 1987), and Allen M. Howard and Richard M. Shain, *The Spatial Factor in African History* (Brill: Brill Academic Publishers, 2005).

22. Boulégue, "Aux Confins du Monde Malinké."

23. Group interview, Sédhiou, October 29, 2003; see also Jacques Charpy, "Casamance et Sénégal au Temps de La Colonisation Française," in *Pour Comprendre la Casamance* (Dakar: Université Cheikh Anta Diop, 1994), 474–500.

24. Horton, "Stateless Societies in the History of West Africa," 1–116.

25. Sapir, *A Grammar of Diola-Fogny: A Language Spoken in the Basse Casamance Region of Senegal* (Cambridge: Cambridge University Press, 1965).

26. Mark, A Cultural, *Economic and Religious History of the Basse Casamance since 1500*, 85.

27. Baum, *Shrines of the Slave Trade*, 9–41.

28. Searing, "No Kings, No Lords, No Slaves," 407–29.

29. For more information on the *koumpo* and other popular masks in the Casamance, see Peter Mark, *The Wild Bull and the Sacred Forest: Forms, Meaning and Change in Senegambian Initiation Masks* (Cambridge: Cambridge University Press, 1992), and De Jong, *Masquerades of Modernity.*

30. Group interviews, Bakoum and Sédhiou, October 11 and 13, 2003, and December 7 and 17, 2003.

31. Francisco de Lemos Coelho, *Description of the Coast of Guinea (1684)*, trans. P. E. Hair, unpublished document (Liverpool: University of Liverpool, 1984). Informants formulated similar arguments in Sandiniéri, a small village located across the river from Sédhiou.

32. Sanoussy Diatta, interview, Sédhiou, November 10, 2003. He moved his family from his Bainounk village of Niamone to Sédhiou when he became a driver for the Senegalese administration in the 1970s.

33. Diatta, Sédhiou, September 11 and 12, 2003.

34. Group interview, September 17, 2003. One participant, Ibrahima Diatta (or Baay Niass), is one of Sanoussy's older children; he helped me schedule good interviews in the region.

35. Interview, Kaour, Moussa Sonko, Abdoulaye Mané, and Maimouna Manga, September 2 and 3, 2009.

36. The metaphysical and sociological significance of these old beliefs may vary from one African society to the next. See Gerald B. Gardner, *Witchcraft Today* (New York: Kensington Publishing, 2004); see also Adam Ashforth, *Madumo: A Man Bewitched* (Chicago: University of Chicago Press, 2000).

37. D'Alméda and Francisco de Lemos Coelho spoke about the practice of witchcraft in the Upper Guinea coast in the seventeenth and eighteenth centuries. See Walter Hawthorne (who quoted these authors), *From Africa to Brazil: Culture, Identity and an Atlantic Slave Trade (1600–1830)* (Cambridge: Cambridge University Press, 2010), 81–90. For another account on witchcraft in sub-Saharan Africa, see Gerrie Ter Haar, *Imagining Evil: Witchcraft Beliefs and Accusations in Contemporary Africa* (Trenton, NJ: Africa World Press, 2007). Senegambian groups like the Wolof, Diola, Sérére, and Mandinka call witches *demeu*, *ayla*, *onakohé*, and *bouha*, respectively.

38. This is much like the Diola rite called *casop*. See Baum, *Shrines of the Slave Trade*, 57.

39. African groups like the Mossi, Yoruba, and Sénoufo are also familiar with this practice. See Thomas, *La Mort Africaine*, 147–81. It is important to note the difference between this ritual and the postburial interrogation undergone by Muslims. In this latter situation some angels mandated by God ask the candidates specific questions about

their faith, which helps determine if they deserve to go to Heaven. See Qur'anic chapters, 56:88–89 and 92–93; and Leor Halevi, *Muhammad's Grave: Death Rites and the Making of Islamic Society* (New York: Columbia University Press, 2007).

40. Group interviews, Sédhiou and Brikama, September 29 and October 17 and 18, 2003, and Sanoussy, interview, Sédhiou, November 10, 2003. See also Le Prince, "Notes sur deux tribus de la Casamance," *Revue Coloniale* (Paris: Librairie Maritime et Coloniale, 1905), 595. He indicates that the Balante and Bainounk represent a branch of the Sarakholé, backing his assertion with no palpable evidence.

41. Le Prince, "Notes sur deux tribus de la Casamance," 594.

42. See Walter Hawthorne (who cited Balthasar Barreira), *Planting Rice and Harvesting Slaves: Transformations Along the Guinea-Bissau Coast, 1400–1900*), 94.

43. Group interviews in Sédhiou, November 11 and 29; Brikama, November 11; Bakoum, November 29; and Sandinieri, December 7 and 9, 2003.

44. The hiring of professional female mourners to weep at funerals for bereaved families still exists in some communities between the Casamance and Guinea-Bissau. Maimouna Manga, interviews, Kaour, November 11, 2008; Fina Fenda Faty, Sédhiou, October 17, 2003; and Ibrahima Diatta, Sédhiou, December 2, 2003.

45. Alexandre Lasnet, *Une Mission au Sénégal: Les Races du Sénégal, Sénégambie et Casamance* (Paris: Challamel, 1900), 175–188; and Lemos Coelho, *Description of the Coast of Guinea (1684)*. During the summer of 1994, my high school colleagues and I witnessed a similar ceremony in Kolda concerning a man who was half-Bainounk and half-Balante. One lady who attended the ceremony anonymously told me that this relatively wealthy man would be buried with palm wine, rice, and some of his belongings and that his widow(s) would remarry outside their husband's community. This shows that this practice has not completely disappeared in the Casamance; but it has lost considerable ground with the development of Islam and Christianity in the region.

46. Lamin Sanneh, *The Crown and The Turban: Muslims and West African Pluralism* (London: Routledge, 1996), 1–36, and Jack Goody, "Restricted Literacy in Northern Ghana," in *Literacy in Traditional Society*, ed. Goody (Cambridge: Cambridge University Press, 1975), 198–246.

47. For example, Hawthorne, *Planting Rice and Harvesting Slaves*, 93–94; and Walter Hawthorne, "Nourishing a Stateless Society during the Slave Trade: The Rise of Balanta Paddy Rice Production in Guinea-Bissau," *Journal of African History* 42, no. 1 (2001): 1–24.

48. Group interviews, Sédhiou, September 17, 2003; and Brikama, December 12, 2003.

49. The growing need to accommodate human settlements resulted in the dismantlement of these rice fields in the Middle Casamance.

50. El Hadji Manding, interview, September 30, 2003.

51. For additional insights on the role of farming in Bainounk societies, see De Lespinay, "Action sur le Territoire," 167–76. His Bainounk lexicon includes farming techniques in Senegambia.

52. Sylvian Golbéry, *Fragments d'un Voyage en Afrique*, book 2 (Paris: Libraires de la Nouvelle Société des Colonies Françaises, 1802), 2:396–98. Between 1785 and 1787, while working for Governor Stanislas De Boufflers in Senegambia, he contributed to the collection of French imperial knowledge. See Jenna Nigro, "Colonial Logics: Agricultural, Commercial and Moral Experiments in the Making of French Senegal, 1763–1870," PhD diss., University of Illinois at Chicago, 2013, 25–84.

53. These markets that still exist across Senegambia mobilize thousands of vendors and sellers from Senegal and neighboring countries. They are the ideal places to find calabashes, animal skins, horns, traditional medicines, and other valuable products that are difficult to obtain in daily markets. Thousands of traders regularly cross the borders between Senegal, Mali, The Gambia and Guinea-Bissau every week to participate in these lucrative transactions.

54. Group interviews, Karantaba, January 3, 2004, and Bakoum, January 4, 2004.

55. *Lançados* were the offspring of African women and Portuguese men. For more details on the dynamism of this category of traders see Peter Mark, *"Portuguese" Style and Luso-African Identity: Precolonial Senegambia, Sixteenth-Nineteenth Centuries* (Bloomington: Indiana University Press, 2002).

56. George Brooks, *Euro-Africans in Western Africa: Commerce, Social Status, Gender, and Religious Observance from the Sixteenth to the Eighteenth Century* (Athens: Ohio University Press, 2003), 44; Walter Rodney, *A History of the Upper Guinea-Coast, 1545–1800* (New York: Monthly Review Press, 1970), 1–38; Mark, *"Portuguese" Style and Luso-African Identity*. This Bainounk hospitality was a consistent reminder in interviews, Sédhiou, October 17, 2003.

57. Group interviews, Bakoum, November 13, 2003; Sandiniéri, November 13, 2003; Ndiama, November 22, 2003; and interview, Ibrahima K. Konté, interview, Dioudoubou, January 6, 2004.

58. Group interviews, Bakoum, November 13, 2003. Unfortunately, informants provided little details about Bainounk mystical practices on these occasions, but it is possible that these targeted individuals who engaged in such unlawful activities as theft.

59. Hawthorne, *Planting Rice and Harvesting Slaves*, 59–67; Brooks, *Landlords and Strangers*, 232–44; and for other developments on this issue see Mark, *"Portuguese" Style*.

60. Laurent Bérenger-Féraud, *Les Peuplades de la Sénégambie* (Paris: Ernest Leroux, 1879), 294.

61. Groups interviews, Bakoum, November 17, 2003; Sédhiou, December 6, 2003; Brikama, December 13, 2003; and Ziguinchor, January 1, 2004.

62. Fina Faty, interview, Sédhiou, October 11, 2003. For more details about Masoboti's dictatorial regime, including his attempts to re-organize the Bainounk militarily and economically, see Sagna, *La Casamance, l'islam et la France*, 45–50.

63. Mariama Diané and Khady Biaye, interview, Sinkére-Bainounk, November 28, 2003.

64. Diané and Biaye, interview. Among the Bainounk the color red traditionally symbolizes political power. Based on Wolof oral literature, Daouda Demba Fall ruled Kayor from 1640 to 1647, and was the cousin of the famous philosopher, Koch Barma Fall.

65. My students in Sédhiou were among the first who reminded me of the negative impacts of the Masoboti curse. However, only when Fina Fenda Faty and Diéli Lamine Kouyaté combined their oratory and musical skills to produce entertaining performances for me did I get a clear understanding of the significance of the curse. Interview, Sédhiou, November 6, 2003.

66. Diatta, interview, Sédhiou, November 3, 2003.

67. Roche, *Histoire de la Casamance*, 22.

68. Sékéné Mody Cissoko and Kaoussou Sambou, *Recueil des Traditions Orales des Mandingues de Gambie et de Casamance* (Niamey: CELHTO, 1974), 259; and Sarr, *Islam, Power and Dependency in The Gambia River Basin*, 50–51. He recalled one oral tradition according to which Masoboti's jurisdiction stretched from The Gambia to Guinea-Bissau.

69. Lemos Coelho, *Description of the Coast of Guinea*, as cited by Bühnen, "Place Names as an Historical Source."

70. Gerard Gaillard's introduction, *Colloquium on the Lower Guinean Coasts* (Lille: Université of Lille, 1997).

71. I was amazed by several Balante and Bainounk informants through their ability to weave together strong knowledge and eloquence while narrating history, despite their non-*diéli* and non-*fina* status.

72. This observation made by Malamine Djignaly was quickly endorsed by his peers. Group interview, Gonou, September 2, 2009.

73. Ansou Manga, Maimouna Manga, and Mousa Sonko, interview, Sinkére Bainounk, September 2, 2009.

74. Mamadou Mansala, Bakoum, October 24, 2003. Perhaps, despite the atrocities he committed, the Balante feared that the Bainounk might turn the whereabouts of his grave into a site of memory and pilgrimage.

75. Quinn, *Mandingo Kingdoms of Senegambia*, 29–52, and Donald Wright, *The World and a Very Small Place in Africa: A History of Globalization in Niumi, The Gambia* (New York: M. E. Sharpe, 1997).

76. Séga S. Sagna, "La Longue Marche de l'Islam en Casamance," *Lettres d'ivoire* 3(2007): 147–64.

77. For instance, Niamone, Affiniame, Enampor, Djibélor, and Tobor. See Baum, *Shrines of the Slave Trade*, 64–67. His study includes a map of Diola dialects and approximatively thirty Bainounk settlements in this area.

78. In Guinea-Bissau, this ethnonym is pronounced Balanta as opposed to Balante in Senegal. In the Francophone literature, two inspiring masters' theses are noteworthy. See Balla Moussa Sadio, "Les Balante de Gan-JAA (BIJAA N'Gan-JAA): Répartition

Spatiale, Organisation Sociale et Administrative, Evolution socio-culturelle et Politique: De l'éviction des Bainounk á la mise en place de l' Administration Coloniale, 1830–1899," Université Cheikh Anta Diop, Dakar, 2002; and Sény Sadio, "Le Peuple de Beeja ou Balante: Du Périple á la Sédentarisation," Université Cheikh Anta Diop, Dakar, 2006. In my judgement, this combined scholarship is a powerful background knowledge for those who would like to improve their historical knowledge of one of the most under-investigated ethnic groups in Senegambia.

79. Besides Hawthorne's study, see Marina Padrao Temudo, "From the Margins of the State to the Presidential Palace: The Balante Case in Guinea-Bissau," *African Studies Review* 52, no. 2 (September 2009): 47–67.

80. Geneviève Ndiaye Corréa, "Etude F.C.A. ou Balante: Dialecte *Ganja,*" *Annales de La faculté des Lettres et des Sciences Humaines* 3 (Dakar: Université Cheikh Anta Diop, 1973).

81. Ousmane Doua, interview, Sédhiou, October 27, 2003. See also Denis Creissels and Sékou Biaye, *La Balante Ganja: Phonologie, Morphosyntaxe et Liste Lexicale* (Dakar: I.F.A.N., 2016). Balante matriarchs and patriarchs lamented the considerable ground lost by Gandia to Mandingo in the Middle Casamance. For example, in Simbandi-Balante, Bidia Mission is the only quarter where Gandia is spoken daily, while in other quarters Wolof and Mandingo have almost superseded Gandia. For a recent discussion of the status of Gandia today, see Christina Thornell, *La Vitalité de la Langue Balant-ganja au Senegal* (Dallas, TX: SIL International, 2019). Using significant data through the participation-observation methodology, the UNESCO model of linguistic analysis and inspiring tables and maps, she showcases the evolution of Gandia in present-day Senegal.

82. Temudo, "From the Margins of the State to the Presidential Palace," 49–53.

83. Group interviews, Sédhiou and Bakoum, September 17 and 19, 2009.

84. Group interviews, Simbandi Birassou, October 31, 2003; and Brikama, October 31, 2003.

85. Roche, *Histoire de La Casamance,* 46–48.

86. Omar Kane, "Essai de Chronologie des Satigis au dix-huitiéme siècle," *Bulletin de l'Institut Fondamental d'Afrique Noire, Série B: Sciences humaines* 32, no. 3 (1970): 755–65.

87. Barry, *Senegambia and the Atlantic Slave Trade,* 8.

88. See Hawthorne (who cited Cornelia Giesing), *Planting Rice and Harvesting Slaves,* 28–29.

89. Sadio,"Les Balante de Gan-JAA (BIJAA- N'GAN-JAA," 35–42.

90. Filidjié and Doua, interview, Sédhiou, January 7 and 8, 2004.

91. Mané and Diatta, interview.

92. Group interview, Brikama, November 17, 2003.

93. Group interview, Brikama and Goudomp, December 1 and 9, 2003.

94. Mané, Sadio, Tamba, Manga, Biaye, and Diatta were among these patronyms.

95. Bérenger-Féraud, *Les Peuplades de La Sénégambie*, 299–306.

96. Omar Ba, "Le Royaume du Gabou," in "Colloque sur les Traditions Orales du Gabou," special issue, *Éthiopiques* (1980):25; Roche, *Histoire de La Casamance*, 25; and Hyacinthe Hecquard, "Rapport sur un Voyage dans la Casamance," *Revue coloniale* 6 (Paris, 1852), 409–32. This word loaned from Mandingo (*Balantakounda*) was possibly designed to make a clear political statement: the Balante wanted the Mandinka to recognize and respect the boundaries of their new homeland; or the Mandinka kept saying Balantakounda while referring to the Balante homeland until it became a popular designation across the Casamance.

97. Sadio, "Les Balante de Gan-JAA (BIJAA N'GAN-JAA)," 47-51. This is based on a tradition collected by Sadio on the territorial conquest of the Bainounk homeland by Balante warriors, but the name of this particular warrior is absent from my informants' recollections.

98. Group interviews, Mangaroungou and Brikama, November 17 and 19, 2003.

99. Group interview, Sédhiou, November 23 and 24. These offshoots include Bouno, Bambali, Dakhabanta, Mandina, Noumbasso, Namekounda, Boudhié-Samine, Frankounda, and Soumakounda in the Middle Casamance.

100. Balante elders, interview, Brikama, November 17, 2003, and Mangaroungou, October 11, 2003.

101. Sadio, "Les Balante de Gan-JAA (BIJAA N'GAN-JAA), 37-42; and group interview, Sédhiou, September 27, 2003. Erected in the middle of the forest, the cabaret was an exclusively male public square where elders met to resolve communal affairs, while playing music and drinking palm wine. This once sacred space, elders concurred, has now become a "relic of the past;" many blamed this setback on external dynamics, beginning with the spread of French colonial rule.

102. Séckou Diatta, interview, Sédhiou, December 12, 2003.

103. Ousmane D. Diatta, interview, Sédhiou, November 2, 2003.

104. Filidjié, interview, Sédhiou, November 17, 2003. This instrument, the equivalent of the Mandinka *bombolong,* was originally used as a tool of mass communication before being replaced by the balafon. See also Thiama Niaba, interview, Niafor, February 18, 2014. Because the balafon was historically "the node of Balante heritage," he said, no public rites could be complete without the inclusion of the balafon. This information came from a series of interviews I am currently conducting for a new project on the omnipresence of balafon music in Balante life-cycle celebrations.

105. Mambéna Mané, interview, Niafor, September 19, 2012.

106. Séckou Sadio, interview, Brikama, May 17, 2003; and Maimouna Manga, Sinkére-Bainounk, August 11, 2009.

107. This is the counterpart of the *homo kossi* among the Bainounk.

108. Lasnet, *Une Mission au Sénégal.*

109. For example, Mangaroungou, Kouniara, and Sandioum based on interview with Mambéna Mané, Niafor, September 19, 2012. He said most of his knowledge of this issue came from his mentor, Omar Koréto Danfa, who immigrated from Guinea-

Bissau to Simbandi Balante. Until his death in the early 1980s, Danfa was one of the best balafon makers, players, and instructors in Senegambia.

110. Anonymous informant, Sédhiou, October 13, 2003. During other rounds of interviews on balafon music some narrated the sad stories of their loved ones who unjustifiably lost their lives because of the tali. The narrators included two famous balafon experts, Thiama Niaba of Samine Balante, interview, February 18, 2014; and Mambéna Mané of Niafor, interview, September 19, 2012.

111. Mamadou Sarr, Sédhiou, January 3, 2004; see also Temudo, "From the Margins of the State to the Presidential Palace," 52. He spoke about an analogous antiwitchcraft ceremony called *fiery-yaab* in Guinea-Bissau in which organizers used a snake to detect evildoers such as witches.

112. Those who familiarized themselves with the ingredients necessary for making the poison, many informants said, easily learned how to make counterpoisons and subsequently save the lives of their loved ones.

113. Lasnet, *Une Mission au Sénégal*, 184. According to him, the Balante hired a non-Balante to administer the tali, hoping that he would be more neutral in his judgment given his outsider status; and this officer was paid in seed money or in material goods, but Lasnet does not specify his ethnic identity. The Balante considered this argument baseless, persisting that throughout this process his "oath taking" ceremony was an exclusively internal affair led by a knowledgeable Balante officer.

114. Hans Dieter Neuwinger, *African Ethnobotany* (London: Chapman and Hall, 1966), 305–9.

115. Roche, *Histoire de La Casamance*, 49–52. See also the report by a brilliant Diola interpreter and scholar, Tété Diédhiou, ARS, 2 G: 23–52; and Governor Maclaud's general report, ARS 136–381; and Baum, "Crimes of the Dream World: French Trials of Diola Witches in Colonial Senegal," *International Journal of African Historical Studies* 37, no. 2 (2004): 201–28.

116. De Jong, *Masquerades of Modernity*, 161.

117. Neuwinger, *African Ethnobotany* 305–9.

118. Roche, *Histoire de La Casamance*, 49. Group interviews, Simbandi Birassou, December 8, 2003, and Tanaff, January 3, 2004.

119. Group interview, Sédhiou, December 6, 2003.

120. In the early 1990s, I witnessed on many occasions lavish funeral ceremonies in the Casamance for people from various ethnic and religious backgrounds. Many well-off people across this region have long felt the need to hide their wealth from others to restrict the risks of evildoing arising from jealousy. Funeral ceremonies are therefore the best moments to gauge how wealthy people were in real life.

121. Hecquard, "Rapport sur un voyage dans la Casamance," 409–32; and Bérenger-Féraud, *Les Peuplades de La Sénégambie*, 285–311; and group interviews, Sédhiou and Brikama, November 11 and 15, 2003. This does not mean that raiding was nonexistent in non-Balante communities.

122. Lasnet, *Une Mission au Sénégal*, 179–83. A Manodji man called Paolo (whose

last name I no longer remember) was the first who talked to me about raiding. He was my next-door neighbor in Sédhiou where he was particularly famous among youth thanks to his successful abortion practices through Balante traditional medicine.

123. Hecquard, " Rapport sur un Voyage dans la Casamance,"420. See also Amadou Mapathé Diagne, "Contribution á l'étude des coutumes des Balante de Sédhiou," *Bulletin de l'Enseignement de l A.O.F.* 83 (April–May 1933): 137–49.

124. Group interview, Brikama, January 4, 2004.

125. Temudo, "From the Margins of the State to the Presidential Palace," 53. He alludes to the recruitment of Balante warriors during the national liberation movement against Portuguese colonial rule in the 1970s in Guinea-Bissau. This shows that raiding as a marker of male identity has not completely disappeared in this country.

126. Hawthorne, *Planting Rice and Harvesting Slaves*, 129.

127. Mark, *"Portuguese" Style and Luso-African Identity*, 114–43.

128. Group interviews, Sédhiou, September 17, 2003, and Brikama, December 12, 2003.

129. Pélissier, *Les Paysans du Senegal*, 593; group interviews, Brikama, November 11, 2003, and Simbandi Balante, November 16, 2003.

130. Group interview, Sédhiou December 21, 2003.

131. For a new analysis of other core dimensions of Balante cultural belief systems see Aly Dramé, "Life-Cyle Celebrations: The Balafon among the Balante of Senegal" (*International Journal of African Historical Studies* (forthcoming).

132. Balante popular imagination metaphorically depicts these warriors as "hyenas, antelopes and buffaloes," and as soldiers though their ability to mystically leave their "souls and minds with their wives at home" before joining the battlefield.

133. Interview, Ibrahima Mané, Sédhiou, November 17, 2009; and group interview, Goudomp, September 11, 2003.

134. Brooks, *Euro-Africans in Western Africa*, 37–67.

135. Proper Cultru, "Le Faux d'un Historien," *La Quinzaine Coloniale* (Paris, 1910): 399–402; and Labat, *Nouvelle Relation de l' Afrique Occidentale*.

136. Cultru, *Premier Voyage du Sieur La Courbe in 1685* (Paris: Libraires de la Société des Colonies Françaises, 1913), 252–58.

137. Brue helped establish some French forts like that of Galam in 1699. See Ibrahima Seck, "The Relationships between Saint Louis, Its Hinterlands, and Colonial Louisiana," trans. Joanna E. Burnett, in *French Colonial Louisiana and the Atlantic World*, ed. Bradley G. Bond (Baton Rouge: Louisiana State University Press, 2005), 266–67; and Abdoulaye Bathily, "The Land of Gold," *Journal of African History* 32, no. 3 (1991), 522–23.

138. Duran, *Voyage au Sénégal ou Mémoires Historiques, Philosophiques et Politiques sur les Découvertes, les Etablissements et le Commerce des Européens dans les Mers de L' Océan Atlantique* (Paris: Henri Agasse, 1802), 105–6.

139. Duran, *Voyage au Sénégal ou Mémoires Historiques*, 105–6.

140. Mané, interview, Sédhiou, November 27, 2003.

141. Mandinka Muslims particularly were unwelcome to the Balantakounda up until the time the last Balante canton chiefs were appointed by French officials in the mid-twentieth century. See Pelissier, *Les Paysans du Senegal*,5 93.

142. Doua, interview, Sédhiou, October 23 and 24, 2003.

143. Cornelia Giesing and Valentin Vydrine, *Ta:rikh Mandinka de Bijini (Guinee-Bissau)* (Leiden: Brill, 2007); and Mark, *"Portuguese" Style and Luso-African Identity*, 22. They cite Hawthorne for whom some Bissau-Guineans intentionally intermarried with their Mandinka neighbors to acquire a more hybridized identity, being not completely Balante or Mandinka. This means that the Balante did not always react to ideas of intermarriage with the Mandinka in the same manner.

144. The Gambia is the only country across Senegambia where the Mandinka are still the largest ethnic group.

145. Makhtar Diouf, *Le Sénégal: Les Ethnies et la Nation; La Répartition des Ethnies et les Chiffres du Recencement de 1988* (Dakar: Nouvelles Editions Africaines, 1988).

146. Madina Ly-Tall, "Quelques Précisions sur les Relations entre l'empire du Mali et le Gabou," in "Colloque sur les Traditions Orales du Gabou," special issue, *Éthiopiques* (1980): 124–27.*

147. According to oral historian Lansana Mané, cited by Niane, Soundiata and Tiramakha were cousins through their lineages' cross-cousin marriages: Sogolon, Soundiata's mother, came from Tiramakha's lineage, and the Keita to which Soundiata belonged gave one of their daughters to the Traoré's lineage. See Niane, *Histoire des Mandingues de l Ouest*, 9. See also Sarr, *Islam, Power and Dependency in the Gambia River Basin*, 36–44.

148. Donald Wright (who cited Alvise Da Mosta), *The World and a Very Small Place in Africa* (New York: M.E. Sharpe, 1997), 75.

149. James Searing, *West African Slavery and Atlantic Commerce: The Senegal River Valley, 1700–1860* (Cambridge: Cambridge University Press, 1993), 47. Regarding the antiquity, distribution, and typology of horses in Africa, see Jack Goody, *Technology, Tradition and the State in West Africa* (Oxford: Oxford University Press, 1971); and Humphrey Fisher, "The Horse in the Central Sudan II," *Journal of African History* 14 (1972): 355–79.

150. Robin Law, *The Horse in West Africa History* (Oxford: Oxford University Press, 1980), 10–12.

151. The Ferlo or *zone silvo-pastorale* is largely populated by Foula farmers and pastoralists who still face tough challenges, including a Sahelian climate, a deficit of rainfall, and growing desertification.

152. Ndiadiane Ndiaye was the founder of Djolof, the most powerful state in Senegambia between the thirteenth century and the 1550s. Djolof extended its jurisdiction over neighboring kingdoms such as Sine, Saloum, Bawol, Walo, and Kayor. See Boulégue, *Le Grand Jolof: XIII-XVI siecle* (Paris: Karthala, 1987; Mamadou Diouf, *Le Kajoor au XIX siècle: Pouvoir Ceddo et Conquête Coloniale* (Paris: Karthala, 1990), 31–39; and Searing, *West African Slavery and Atlantic Commerce*, 10–18.

153. This is a rendition by Wa Kamissoko during the First International Colloquium

of Bamako held from January 22 to February 1, 1975. See Jan Jansen, *Epopée, Histoire et Societé* (Paris: Karthala, 1987).

154. Djibril T. Niane translated a performance by Diéli Mamadou Kouyaté entitled *Soundiata ou l'Epopée Mandingue* (Paris: Karthala, 1960). Though scholars have questioned the validity of Niane's "authentic" version since the 1960s, there are still conflicting stylistic approaches on the thematic and chronological ambiguities of the epic. See Ralph A. Austen, *In Search of Sunjata* (Bloomington: Indiana University Press, 1999); John William Johnson, *The Epic of Son-Jara* (Bloomington: Indiana University Press, 2003); and Gordon Innes, *Sunjata: The Three Mandinka Versions* (London: Routledge, 2001).

155. The Gambia River region was the site of most of these offshoots: Combo, Kantor, and Fogny on the south bank, and Badibu, Wuli, and Niumi on the north bank. See Quinn, *Mandingo Kingdoms of Senegambia*. The name Kaabou is spelled in multiple ways, including Gabou, Kabu, and Ngabu.

156. Ly-Tall, "Quelques Précisions sur les Relations entre l'empire du Mali et le Gabou," in "Colloque sur les Traditions Orales du Gabou," special issue, *Ethiopiques* (1980): 124–27; and Teixeira Da Mosta, "Les Relations de l'Ancien Cabou avec quelques Etats voisins," in "Colloque sur les Traditions Orales du Gabou," special issue, *Éthiopiques* (1980): 149–67.*

157. The Mande studies conference held in London in July 1972 and the International Colloquium on Kaabou's oral traditions in Dakar in 1980.

158. Djibril T. Niane, *Histoire des Mandingues de l'Ouest* (Paris: Karthala, 1989), and Yves Person, "Les problémes de l'histoire du Gaabu," in "Colloque sur les Traditions Orales du Gabou," special issue, *Éthiopiques* (1980): 67.

159. Boulégue, "Aux Confins du Monde Malinké."

160. While it is difficult to conceptualize Kaabou chronologically, we can distinguish at least two important sequences in its history. For a good analysis, see Nouha Cissé, "La Fin du Kaabu et le Débuts du Royaume du Fuladu," *Mémoire de maîtrise* (Dakar: Université Cheikh Anta Diop, 1978).

161. Brooks, *Western Africa to C/1860 A.D.: A Provisional Historical Schema Based on Climate Periods*, Indiana University African Studies program, Working Paper Series 1 (Bloomington: Indiana University, 1985), 97–126; and George Brooks, "Ecological Perspectives on Mande Population Movements, Commercial Networks and Resettlement Patterns from the Atlantic Wet Phase (ca. 5500–2500 B.C) to the Present," *History in Africa* 16 (1989): 23–40. See also Sharon E. Nicholson, "Climatic Variations in the Sahel during the Past Five Centuries," *Journal of Arid Environments* 1, no. 1 (1978): 3–24.

162. Quinn, *The Mandingo Kingdoms of Senegambia*, 10–11.

163. Harold Courlander, *A Treasury of African Folklore* (New York: First Marlowe and Company, 1996).

164. Lilyan Kesteloot, "Les Mandingues de Casamance : Kankurang, Castes et Kora," in *Pour Comprendre la Casamance: Chronique d'une Intégration Contrastée*, edited by

Francois-George Barbier-Wiesser (Paris: Karthala, 1994), 98–117; and Cissoko, *Recueil des Traditions Orales de la Gambie et de la Casamance, 193.*

165. Group interviews, Sédhiou, December 23 and 24, 2003, and January 6, 2004. For more information on the relationhip between Kaabou and Sine and Saloum, see R. P. Gravrand, "Le Gabou dans les traditions orales Sereer et Guelwar," in "Colloque sur les Traditions Orales du Gabou," special issue, *Éthiopiques* (1980):: 40–59;* and Birame Ngom, *La Question Guélwar et l'Histoire du Siin: Mémoire de Diplôme d'études Approfondies* (Dakar: Université Cheikh Anta Diop, 1987); and Abdoulaye S. Diop, "L'impact de la Civilisation Mandingue au Sénégal," *Bulletin de l'Institut Fondamental d'Afrique Noire, Série B: Sciences humaines* 40, no. 4 (1978): 689–707.

166. Group interview, Sédhiou, September 11, 2003.

167. Group interview, Sédhiou, December 3 and 4, 2003.

168. Group interview, December 6 and 8, 2003.

169. Djiéli Sérifo Kouyaté, interview, Bounkiling, January 6, 2004.

170. Barry, *Senegambia and the Atlantic Slave Trade*, 16.

171. Gravrand, "Le Gabou dans les traditions orales Sereer et Guelwar," 40–59; and Mbaye Guéye, "Les Guélowares et le Sine," *Ethiopiques* 28 (1981).

172. Searing, *West African Slavery and Atlantic Commerce*, 1–26.

173. Group interview, Mansakounda, Sédhiou, October 28, 2003.

174. Mandinka life-cycle celebrations included the little and big circumcisions (*kouyanding* and *kouyamba*). These rituals historically lasted some three months during which the circumcised (*gniansou*) absorbed a wealth of knowledge which they could share with no other individual. During this ceremony, a venerated mask (*kankourang)* protected the circumcised and their supervisors (*kintang*). The man behind this mask transformed himself into a scary "invisible force" whose noise reverberated throughout the night. He carried with him two sharp swords (*fanhoo*) to punish those who disobeyed his orders and protected the circumcision camp against any looming evil forces. The product used to make this mask came from the bark of a tree called *faara*.

175. De Jong, *Masquerades of Modernity*, 35. For him, the *afan gureng* are selected among Diola male elders but the religious and social impacts of these forests considerably diminished because the Islamization of the Lower Casamance.

176. Baum, *Shrines of the Slave Trade*, 53; and Nianga Gouléle, a famous healer of abdominal diseases with Diola traditional medicine. Interview, Bignona, December 6, 7, and 8, 1992.

177. Mori Kéba, interview, Chicago, August 9, 2005.

178. For more details on the *tiéddo*'s lifestyles, see Barry, *Senegambia and the Atlantic Slave Trade*, 81–93, and James Searing, *"God Alone Is King": Islam and Emancipation in Senegal; The Wolof Kingdoms of Kajoor and Bawol, 1859–1914* (Portsmouth, NH: Heinemann, 2002), 4–118.

179. Carlos Lopes, "Kaabu and Its Neighbors."

180. Golbéry, *Fragments d'un Voyage en Afrique: Fait dans les années 1785 , 86 et 87*

*dans les Contrées occidentales de ce continent,* book 2 (Paris: Libraires de la Nouvelle Societé des Colonies Françaises, 1802), 252. Group interviews, Sédhiou, October 31, 2003; Simbandi Birassou, September 13, 2003; and Bakoum, September 27, 2003; and interview, Fina Fenda Faty, Mansakounda, December 11, 2003.

181. Provinces like Souna and Pakao are mentioned in the oral traditions on this issue.

182. Cissoko, "De l'Organisation Politique du Gabu," *communication* (Dakar: Ethiopiques, 1980), 28.

183. Group interviews, Karantaba, January 6, 2004; Sédhiou (Mansakounda and Morikounda), December 1 and 2; and Bakoum, December 9, 2003.

184. Niane, *Histoire des Mandingues de L'Ouest,* 111–22. For additional insights on the repercussions of the slave trade, see Walter Hawthorne, *Planting Rice and Harvesting Slaves: Transformations along the Guinea-Bissau Coast, 1400–1900* (Portsmouth, NH: Heinemann, 2003). See also Walter Rodney, *A History of the Upper Guinea Coast, 1545–1800* (New York: Monthly Review, 1980); and Fina Fenda Faty, Sédhiou, October 11 and 12, 2003. He explained the causal link between both the rise and fall of Kaabou to the rise and fall of the slave trade in the Casamance.

185. Group interview, Bakoum, October 18 and 18, 2003.

186. Cissoko, "Premier Habitant de Casamance au Sénégal," 80; and Teixeira Da Mosta, "Les Relations de l'Ancien Cabou avec quelques Etats voisins." 155–59.

187. Group interview, Bakoum. This enslavement did not seem to have affected many of the Foula of noble origins (*rimbé*). The primarily enslaved group (*maccoubé*) led by Alpha Molo Baldé profited from the *tourouban kélo* ("the war that ended the clan") that weakened Kaabou to successfully revolt against the mansaya. So, they created the short-lived Fouladou kingdom in the Upper Casamance between 1867 and 1881. See Ngaïdé, *L'esclave, le colon et la marabout,* 42 and 51–56, and Cissé, "La Fin du Kaabu et les Débuts du Royaume du Fuladu." For another insightful analysis, see Alpha Oumarou Ba, "Islam and Emancipation: Fuladu Fulani in the Kaabu Empire," in *Palgrave Handbook of Islam in Africa,* edited by Fallou Ngom, Mustapha H. Kurfi, and Toyin Folola (London: Palgrave Macmillan, 2020), 117–31.

188. Both griots and ordinary citizens emphasized these long-standing power abuses committed against the Foula and other vulnerable populations by Kaabou's officials.

189. Ibrahima K. Konté, interview, Sédhiou, October 29, 2003; and Ngaïdé, *L'esclave, le colon et le marabout,* 53–56. He metaphorically depicted the Foula as the "food of the Mandinka," alluding to their intense economic exploitation Kaabou's officials.

190. Kouyaté, interview, June 12, 2001. The profound mutations that reshaped the lives of the Foula pastoralists of the Upper Casamance partly emanated from their centuries-long domination by the Mandinka. See Abderahmane Ngaïdé , "Domination politique et Influences socioculturelles des mandingues sur les Peuls du Fuladu (Kolda-Senegal)," in Peuls et Mandingues: Dialectique des constructions identitaires, eds. Mirjam Bruijn and Han van Dijk (Paris: Karthala, 1997), 147–64.

191. Hawthorne, *Planting Rice and Harvesting Slaves*; and Rodney, *History of the Upper Guinea Coast.*

192. For more about the role of Fouta Diallon in the transformations undergone by the the southern Rivers region see Thierno Diallo, *Les Institutions Politiques du Fouta-Djallon au XIXè siécle* (Dakar: Université Cheikh Anta Diop, 1972).

193. Barry, *Senegambia and the Atlantic Slave Trade*, 159–76; Diallo, *Les Institutions Politiques du Fouta- Djallon.*

194. Yves Person, "Les Problémes de l'histoire du Gabou," in "Colloque sur les Traditions Orales du Gabou," special issue, *Éthiopiques* (1980): 60–71;* and See Niane, *Histoire des Mandingues de l'ouest*, 49. These Muslim quarters are called *morikounda* in Mandingo. Group interview, Sédhiou, October 17 and 18, 2003.

195. Group interviews, Tanaff, September 13, 2003, and January 7 and 9, 2004. Tanaff is a commercial hub located near the Senegal–Guinea-Bissau border. Interviewers included people whose families originated in Kaabou. Some formulated this argument while criticizing what Sana Faty called "the mansaya's complex of superiority."

196. Fina Fenda Faty, Sédhiou, Dec 7, 2003.

197. Niane, *Histoire des Mandingues de L'ouest*, 155–56. Group interviews in Bakoum and Karantaba, in September 14 and December 11, confirmed his assessment.

198. Group interview, Sédhiou, Nov 17, 2003.

199. Kouyaté, interview, Chicago, June 12, 2001. French archival documents corroborate his assessment. Chapter 4 will emphasize how, for example, the French came to dominate the regional economy of the Middle Casamance following the treaties they signed with Bainounk authorities.

200. Kouyaté, interview, June 12, 2001. For him, we shouldn't lose sight of the fact that decades before the dramatic developments, only a handful of Kaabounké provinces had maintained absolute loyalty to Kansala.

201. This remarkable exhibition of dignity and honor by Kaabounké women resembles another one that happened decades earlier in northwestern Senegambia. Wolof oral records recall that, by March 7, 1807, while men were away from home in the Waalo-Waalo village of Nder, women avoided enslavement in extremis by Mauritanian slave raiders by committing suicide through self-immolation.

202. Kouyaté interview; Fina Kéba Dakhaba, interview, Simbandi Birassou, June 20, 2003; and Fina Fenda Faty, interview, Sédhiou, November 6, 2003. See also Cissé, "La Fin du Kaabu et le Débuts du Royaume du Fuladu."

203. The consensus among prolific storytellers like Kouyaté is that Kaabounké diviners who investigated the outcome of the war kept telling Dianké Waly and his entourage that Foula warriors were still "in their lands." For them, this was a misleading statement because "in their lands" meant that while traveling from Guinea to Kaabou over months Foula soldiers brought with them sandbags, which they used during the night as pillows. So, this confusion between Foula's "sandbags" and "homeland" plunged the Kaabounké in a state of general panic when they heard that Foula soldiers had suddenly taken Kan-

sala by storm. For a fresher version of this watershed moment in Kaabou's story, see Cornelia Giesing and Denis Creissels, *Les Mémoires de Mala Galisa sur le Royaume Confédéré du Kaabu,* (Leiden: Brill, 2017), 14.

204. Lasnet, *Un Mission au Sénégal,* 152. When studying the diversification of humans in Senegambia, Lasnet highlighted the commonalities between the Balante and the Bainounk. But without providing any concrete evidence, he concluded that these two populations should be classified under the same ethnic category. See also Linares, *Power, Prayer and Production,* 85–89, and Baum, *Shrines of the Slave Trade,* 63–68.

205. In Senegal, the most popular term for hospitality, *téranga,* comes from the dominant Wolof language, but the Mandinka, the Balante, and the Diola of Casa call it *bounia, kinwala adiadié, and kawalenak diak,* respectively.

206. Lasnet, *Un Mission au Sénégal,* 182.

207. I did not conduct fieldwork among the Diola. I heard such stories from Diola people whose families had resettled in the Sédhiou land area generations ago. This included one anonymous schoolteacher who originated in Oussouye in the Lower Casamance. For him, Diola elders instinctively wanted to know if the newcomers were trustworthy; and "once they passed this trust test" everything else became easy for the newcomers in terms of social integration into Diola society.

## CHAPTER 2

1. Christopher Fyfe and V. R. Dorjahn, "Landlord and Stranger: Change in Tenancy Relations in Sierra Leone," *Journal of African History* 3, no. 3 (1962): 391–97; Rodney, *History of the Upper Guinea Coast*; Bruce L. Mouser, "Landlords and Strangers: A Process of Accommodation," *International Journal of African Historical Studies* 8, no. 3 (1975): 425–40; and for more developments see Brooks, *Landlords and Strangers.*

2. Wright, *The World and a Very Small Place in Africa.* For additional accounts. see Pamela J. Kea, *Land, Labour and Entrustment: West African Female Farmers and the Politics of Difference* (Leiden: Brill, 2010), 1–26; Linares, *Power, Prayer and Production,* 151–53; and Sarr, *Islam, Power, and Dependency,* 33–83.

3. Robert Horton, "On the Rationality of Conversion: Part 1," *Africa* 45, no. 3 (1975): 219–35; and "On the Rationality of Conversion: Part 2," *Africa* 45, no. 4 1979): 373–99.

4. Humphrey Fisher, "Dreams and Conversion in Black Africa," in *Conversion to Islam,* ed. Nehemia Levtzion (London: Holmes and Meier, 1979), 217–35; and "The Juggernaut's Apologia: Conversion to Islam in Black Africa," *Africa* 55, no. 2 (1985): 153–73. Fisher's model resembles the paradigm elaborated by J. Spencer Trimingham, who also perceived Islamization as a three-stage process (infiltration, conversion, and assimilation) in the transition from "traditional religion" to Islam in West Africa. But contrary to Fisher, Trimingham says Africans only entered history with conversion. See J. Spencer Trimingham, *Islam in West Africa* (Oxford: Oxford University Press, 1959), 33–46.

5. See, for example, James Searing, "The Greater Jihad and Conversion: Sereer Interpretations of Sufi Islam in Senegal," in *New Perspectives on Islam in Senegal: Conversion, Migration, Wealth, Power, and Femininity*, edited by Mamadou Diouf and Mara Leichtman (New York: Palgrave Macmillan, 2009), 91–110, and Searing, "Conversion to Islam," 73–94; and Aly Dramé, "Migration, Marriage and Ethnicity: The Early Development of Islam in Precolonial Middle Casamance," in *New Perspectives on Islam in Senegal*, 169–88. For newer interpretations, see Brendan Carmody, ed., *Religious Conversion: An African Perspective* (Lusaka: Gadsden Publishers, 2015). Core aspects of the Horton-Fisher exchanges are used in this volume as starting points for reexamining new models of conversion; and James N. Nnoruga, "Fisher's Historical Approach to Religious Change in Igboland," *African Journal of Multidisplinary Research* 15, no. 1 (2020): 72–85. Perhaps Horton's death in 2019 will motivate scholars to revisit his legacy, including his heated debate with Fisher. For example, see Nimi Wariboko, "Robin W. G. Horton (1932–2019): His Life and Work," *Journal of the International African Institute* 90, no. 4 (2020): 822–30.

6. Madina Ly-Tall, Sedou Camara, and Bouna Diouara, *L'Histoire du Mandé d' aprés Jeli Kanku Madu Jabetyé de Kela* (Bamako, Mali: Association SCOA pour la recherche scientifique en Afrique noire, 1987).

7. Philip Curtin, *Economic Change in Pre-colonial Africa: Senegambia in the Era of the Slave Trade* (Madison: University of Wisconsin, 1975), 59–91; Robert Launay, *Beyond the Stream: Islam and Society in a West African Town* (Berkley: University of California Press, 1992), 49–76; Robert Griffeth, "The Dyula Impact on the Peoples of the West Volta Region," in *Papers on the Manding*, ed. Carleton T. Hodge (Bloomington: Indiana University Press, 1971), 166–81; and Wright, *The World and A Very Small Place in Africa*, 65–94. See also Brooks, "A Provisional Historical Schema for Western Africa."

8. Ivor Wilks, "The Juula and the Expansion of Islam into the Forest," in *The History of Islam in Africa*, ed. Nehemia Levtzion and Randall L. Pouwels (Athens: Ohio University Press, 2000), 95.

9. Thomas C. Hunter, "The Development of an Islamic Tradition of Learning among the Jahanka of West Africa," PhD diss., University of Chicago, 1977; Lamin Sanneh, *The Jahanke Muslim Clerics: A Religious and Historical Study of Islam in Senegambia* (New York: University Press of America, 1989), 1–3; and A. A. Batran, "The Kunta, Sidi al-Mukhtar al-Kunti, and the Office of Shaykh al-Tariqa'l-Qadiriyya," in *The Cultivators of Islam*, vol. 1, ed. John Ralph Willis (London: Frank Cass, 1979), 13–46.

10. Nehemia Levtzion, "Islam in the Bilad al-Sudan to 1800," in *History of Islam in Africa*, ed. Levtzion and Randall L. Pouwels (Athens: Ohio University Press, 2000), 68.

11. Group interviews, Karantaba, November 17, and Sédhiou, November 17; and Almamy Fossar Souané, interview, Sédhiou, September 13, 2003.

12. John R. Willis, "Introduction: Diffusion of Islam," *Studies in West African Islamic History*, vol. 1, *The Cultivators of Islam* (England: Frank Cass, 1979), 1–39.

13. Sanneh, *Beyond Jihad*, 46–48; and Ware, *The Walking Qur'an*, 85–86.

14. For some examples see Ware, *The Walking Qur'an*, 96–99.

15. Ware, *The Walking Qur'an*, 96–99.

16. Sanneh, *Beyond Jihad*. He provides some interesting examples on this issue.

17. Group interviews, Karantaba, October 3, 2003; Sédhiou, October 17, 2003; and El Hadji Manding, interview, Karantaba, October 22, 2003. Mandinka clerics deplored these natural disasters that have disrupted their families for generations. Schaffer said Omar Sylla of Darsilamé was the first who told him about the manuscript in the 1970s, but he first saw an eleven-page manuscript in 1972 in Babadi where the "original copy" was kept, according to Schaffer's informants. In his view, the sanctity of this document was probably the reason why the copy he saw was placed inside a Qur'anic copy. See Matt Schaffer, "'Pakao Book': An Introduction to Pakao Expansion and Social Structure by Virtue of an Indigenous Manuscript," in *African Languages* 1 (1975): 96–123. In other villages, I saw similar copies of the book with different pages and writing styles that are also considered "original copies;" but some informants clarified that these unfinished copies came from the original manuscript. It is hard to imagine that the *Pakao al-qurano* was initially an eleven-page document, because the old copy I saw in Karantaba was by far more voluminous. When it comes to the other African manuscripts I have mentioned above, scholars have expressed divergent opinions regarding their chronology, originality, real authors, and historicity. See Ivor Wilks, Nehemia Levtzion, and Bruce Haight, *Chronicles from Gonja: A Tradition of West African Muslim Historiography* (Cambridge: Cambridge University Press, 1987); John Hunwick, "A Historical Whodunit: The So-Called 'Kano Chronicle' and Its Place in the Historiography of Kano," *History of Africa* 21 (1994): 127–46; Christopher Wise, *Ta'rikh al-Fattash: Timbuktu Chronicles 1493–1599*, trans. from Arabic by al Hajj Mahmud Kati, ed. Wise (Trenton, NJ: Africa World Press, 2011); and Hunwick, *Timbuktu and the Songhay Empire. Al-Sadis'Tar'rikh al-sudan Down to 1613 and Contemporary Documents* (Leiden: Brill, 2003).

18. Levtzion, "Merchants vs. Scholars and Clerics in West Africa: Differential and Complementary Roles," in *Rural and Urban Islam in West Africa*, ed. Levtzion and Humphrey Fisher (London: Lynne Rienner, 1987), 36.

19. Group interview, Karantaba, October 2, 2003.

20. Hunwick, *Timbuktu and the Songhay Empire*; Catherine Coquery-Vidrovitch, *The History of African Cities South of the Sahara: From the Origins to Colonization*, trans. Mary Baker (Princeton, NJ: Markus Wiener Publishers, 2005), 109–12; and Joseph Ki Zerbo, *Histoire Générale de l'Afrique* (Paris: Hatier, 1986), 149–50. See also James C. McCann, "Climate and Causation in African History," *International Journal of African Historical Studies* 32, no. 2 (1999): 261–70. For him, Timbuktu's demographic boom in the 1590s was partly sparked by climate change and its implications. See Ousmane. O. Kane, *Beyond Timbuktu: An Intellectual History of Muslim West Africa* (Harvard: Harvard University Press, 2016), 21–40.

21. Zachary V. Wright, "The Islamic Intellectual Tradition of Sudanic Africa, with Analysis of a Fifteenth-Century Timbuktu Manuscript," in *The Palgrave Handbook of Islam in Africa*, ed. Fallou Ngom, Mustapha H. Kurfy, and Toyin Falola (London: Palgrave Macmillan, 2020).

22. Lansiné Kaba, "The Pen, the Sword, and the Crown: Islam and Revolution in Songhay Reconsidered, 1464–1493," *Journal of African History* 25, no. 3 (1984): 241–56.

23. Roche, *Histoire de La Casamance*, 54. See also Emily L. Osborn, *Our New Husbands Are Here: Households, Gender, and Politics in a West African State from the Slave Trade to Colonial Rule* (Athens: Ohio University Press, 2011), 44 and 68. Osborn did not make this argument, but it is possible that these immigrants too were already fluent Sarakholé speakers by the time they arrived in Eastern Guinea.

24. Mbacké, *Sufism and Religious Brotherhoods in Senegal*, 39. For Mbacké, Cheikh Amadou Bamba was initiated to the Khadiriyya by his father, Mame Mor Anta Sally. Taking the *wird* is the ritual that renders official people's adherence to a specific Sufi order. The general norm among Senegambian Muslims had long been to make this move as people got older, but now many do so at much younger ages.

25. This mountain located outside of Saudi Arabia is the place where Prophet Muhammad received through archangel Gabriel the divine Revelation to introduce Islam to humanity.

26. Almamy Barro, interview, Karantaba, September 29, 2001, and Fenda Faty, Sédhiou, November 6, 2003.

27. Group interview, Fodékounda, the ancestral house of the Dramé lineage of Karantaba, October 23, 2003.

28. Charles Monteil, *Les Kassonké: Monographie d'une Peuplade du Soudan Français* (Paris: Ernest Leroux, 1915), 353–404. See also Labat, *Nouvelle relation de l'Afrique Occidentale*, 347–53. He mentions the fierce resistance "Brue" encountered while trying to build a trading center in Daramane. Some of the commercial entrepots created by the French in this region did not last long partly because of the local resistance led by the Bathily lineage and other powerful aristocratic groups in Galam at this time. See Abdoulaye Bathily, *Les Portes de L'or: Le Royaume du Galam (Sénégal) de L'ère Musulmane au Temps des Négriers (8th–18th)* (Paris: L'Harmattan, 1989). For a fresher re-evaluation of the colonial encounter between the French and the populations of Galam, see Makhroufi Ousmane Traoré, *Slavery, Resistance and Identity in Early Modern West Africa: The Ethnic-State of Gajaaga* (Cambridge: Cambridge University Press, 2023).

29. They were Harounaba Dramé of Dioudoubou and Dianko Tanko of Koling, both old Bainounk townships. Group interviews with elders, Karantaba, September 22 and 23, 2003.

30. A group of six Mandinka elders led by Mansani Dramé, Diatouma's village chief, November 11, 2003.

31. Ross, *Sufi City*, 28. His analysis includes the involvement of "common tropes of religious significance" (animals, divine inspiration, trees, and years) in the formation of Muslim communities. When religious persecutions compelled Prophet Muhammad (570–632 CE) and his followers (*muhajirrin*) to migrate from Mecca to Yathrib (Medina), they were warmly welcomed by Yathrib's populace (*hansar*). Mandinka traditions suggest that during these painful experiences (*fitna*), God was testing Fodé Héraba's piety, as in the case of many Muslim clerics. For instance, Mourid sources formulate

a similar argument when explaining Cheikh Amadou Bamba's deportation to the Central African Republic of Gabon. The same is true for the Layénne fishermen of the Cap Vert peninsula. As devout followers of Seydina Limamou Laye (1843–1909), they have created a sacred geography, using Mecca and Medina and the Prophetic personal odyssey as models of worship. See John Glover, "The Prophet Muhammad Reincarnated and His Son, Jesus: Re-centering Islam among the Layenne of Senegal," *Journal of Historical Geography* 42 (2013): 24–35.

32. Group interview, Bambadion, October 12, 2003.

33. See Goody (who cited Hunwick), "The Impact of Islamic Writing on the Oral Cultures of West Africa," *Cahier D études Africaines* 11, no. 43 (1971): 455–66.

34. Boubacar Dabo, interview, Bambadion, December 6, 2003.

35. Ware, The *Walking Qur'an*, 99. André Alvarés D'Alméda in the 1580s and Balthasar Barreira in 1608 made mention of the opening of new Qur'anic schools in Senegambia. See also Ware, *The Walking Qur'an*, 96.

36. Robinson, *The Holy War of Umar Tal*, 128–33. After the relationship between the ruler and the marabout deteriorated beyond repair, this latter prosecuted a military jihād in this area in the 1850s.

37. Group interview, Karantaba, October 13, 2003.

38. Group interview, Bambadion, October 17 and 18, 2003.

39. El Hadj Kémo Demba, interview, Sédhiou, December 3, 2003, and Kéba Dahaba, interview, Simbandi Birassou, December 10, 2003. Group interviews, Yoro Touré, interview, Ndiama, September 12, 2001; Chief Almamy Fossar Souané, interview, Sandiniéri, October 24, 2003; and Chief Mansani Dramé, interview, Diatouma, November 11, 2003. In Diatouma and Sandiniéri elders exhibited some Arabic documents (translated into French) containing the names of the Seven Abdoul. Chief Souané testified that these documents, which belonged to his ancestors, are hard to get, but I found similar copies in Karantaba.

40. Interview, Karantaba, September 23, 2003. The taabo is botanically classified as *cola kordifolia*. See Matt Schaffer, *Djinns, Stars and Warriors: Mandinka Legends from Pakao, Senegal* (Leiden: Brill, 2003), 5. Group interviews, Yoro Touré, interview, Ndiama, September 12, 2001; Chief Almamy Fossar Souané, interview, Sandiniéri, October 24, 2003; and Chief Mansani Dramé, interview, Diatouma, November 11, 2003.

41. Group interview, Bounkiling, January 10, 2004.

42. El Hadji Manding and Sékouba Diba, interview, Karantaba, November 7 and 8, 2003; and Khadiry Barro, Sédhiou, October 22, 2001. After more than 400 years of existence the taabo sadly collapsed in 2003 or 2004, shortly after I departed the Middle Casamance. Local authorities agreed to leave its debris in its initial place, out of respect for the taabo's antiquity. I was later told that a little taabo is slowly germinating under the original one and will probably be its "legitimate replacement," to Karantabans' greatest delight.

43. One of my first interviews on Islam in Southern Senegal was with the griot Mori

Kéba, Chicago, June 12, 2001. See also Sékouba Diba, interview, Karantaba, November 13, 2003; Almamy Fossar Souané, interview, Sandiniéri, October 24, 2003; Karamo Dinding Cissé, interview, Kounayan, October 13, 2003; and Filidjié, interview, Sédhiou, November 3, 2003.

44. Kouyaté, interview; Sékouba Diba, Karantaba, November 13, 2003; Almamy Fossar Souané, interview, Sandiniéri, October 24, 2003; Karamo Dinding Cissé, interview, Kounayan, October 13, 2003; and Filidjié, interview, Sédhiou, November 3, 2003.

45. Group interview with elders, Karantaba, October 24, 2003.

46. El Hadji Manding, interview.

47. Hunwick, *Timbuktu and the Songhay Empire. Al-Sa'dis Ta' rikh al sudan down to 1613 and Contemporary Documents* (Leiden: Brill, 2003), 218–32; Ki Zerbo, *Histoire Générale de l'Afrique*, 197–200; and Paul Lovejoy, *Transformations of Slavery: A History of Slavery in Africa* (Cambridge: Cambridge University Press, 2000), 31. For additional information on Ahmed Baba's activities in Marrakech from 1594 and 1608, see Kane, *Beyond Timbuktu*, 100–101.

48. Roche, *Histoire de La Casamance*, 54. See also Sagna (who confirmed Roche's statement in several ways), *La Casamance, L'Islam et La France.*

49. Almamy Fossar Souané, *Les Manding de la Moyenne Casamance* (Dakar : Université de Dakar, 1988), 15.

50. Niane, *Histoire des Mandingues de l'Ouest*, 121–22.

51. The generations are Fodé Héraba Dramé, Sambaya Koumba Barro Dramé, Fodé Bakari Dramé, Fodé El Hadji Dramé, Fonémouna Dramé, Mamadou Lamine Sitokoto Dramé, and Fodé Almamy Dramé.

52. See, for instance, J. D. Y. Peel, *Christianity, Islam, and Orisa-Religion: Three Traditions in Comparison and Interaction* (Oakland: University of California Press, 2015). Other important themes highlighted in this new scholarship include overlapping religious practices, Pentecostalism, correlations between conversion and negotiation, and correlations between globalization and conversion. See, for example, Abdulkader Tayob, *Islam in South Africa: Mosques, Imams, and Sermons* (Gainesville: University of Florida Press, 1999), 96–101. For newer perspectives on these issues, see Viera Pawlikova-Vilhanova, "Islam and Christianity in Africa," in *Palgrave Handbook of Islam in Africa*, ed. Fallou Ngom, Mustapha H. Kurfy, and Toyin Falola (Cham, Switzerland: Palgrave Macmillan, 2020), 237–44; and Jason Bruner and David Dmitri Hurlbut, eds., *Religious Conversion in Africa* (Basel: MDPI, 2020).

53. Diouf and Leichtman, *New Perspectives on Islam in Senegal*, 1–14. This volume resulted from two panels Leichtman and I put together at the African Studies Association conference held in November 2006 in San Francisco, California.

54. See the following chapters in *New Perspectives on Islam in Senegal: Conversion, Migration, Wealth, Power and Femininity*, ed. Mamadou Diouf and Mara Leitchman (New York: Palgrave Macmillan, 2009): Mara A. Leichtman, "The Authentication of a Discursive Islam," 111–38; James Searing, "The Greater Jihad and Conversion: Sereer

Interpretations of Sufi Islam in Senegal," 91–110; Marloes Janson, "Searching for God: Young Gambians' Conversion to the *Tabligh Jama'at*," 139–68. For a groundbreaking analysis of conversion to Islam focusing on a poorly understood minority group in Senegal, see Mara A. Leichtman, *Shi'i Cosmopolitanisms in Africa: Lebanese Migration and Religious Conversion in Senegal* (Bloomington: Indiana University Press, 2015).

55. Aly Dramé, "Migration, Marriage and Ethnicity: The Early Development of Islam in Precolonial Middle Casamance," in *New Perspectives on Islam: Conversion, Migration, Wealth, Power and Femininity*, ed. Mamadou Diouf and Mara Leitchman (New York: Palgrave Macmillan, 2009), 169–88.

56. Claude Levi-Strauss, *Les Structures Elementaires de la Parentée* [Elementary structures of kinship] (Paris: Presses Universitaires de France, 1949). For a criticism of this worldview, see Francis Korn, *Elementary Structures Reconsidered: Levi-Strauss on Kinship* (Berkeley: University of California Press, 1973). See also Gary Ferraro, *Cultural Anthropology: An Applied Perspective*, 7th ed. (Belmont, CA: Tomson Learning, 2008), 208.

57. Qur'anic chapter 5:5. Even non-Muslim brides must receive a dowry (*mahr*, Arabic).

58. Qur'anic chapters, 2:221; and 5:5. These verses do not suggest that conversion can be achieved violently.

59. For a similar case, see Osborn, *Our New Husbands Are Here*, 43–44.

60. Chief Fossar Souané, interview, Sandiniéri, October 23, 2003.

61. Levtzion, "Islam in the Bilad al-Sudan," 63–91, and David Robinson, *Muslim Societies in African History* (Cambridge: Cambridge University Press, 2004), 124–38.

62. Nehemia Levtzion and Jay Spaulding's short introduction, *Medieval West Africa* (Princeton, NJ: Markus Wiener Publishers, 2007), and Ki Zerbo, *Histoire Générale de l'Afrique*, 106.

63. This trip intervened shortly after the Prophet Muhammad received his divine Revelation. This group of refugees included Usman Ibn Affan who served later as Islam's third caliph (644–56 CE), and Rokhiyya, the prophet's daughter and caliph Usman's wife.

64. Ware, The *Walking Qur'an*, 85–86; Ki Zerbo, *Histoire Générale de l'Afrique*, 11; and Levtzion and Spaudling, *Medieval West Africa*, 9–22.

65. One anonymous informant is a direct descendent of Serigne Matar Ndoumbé Diop, who created the prestigious village school of Kokki in the province of Ndiambour, in what is now the region of Louga. For him, his ancestor inherited the land concession where he established his Qur'anic school from Meissa Tenda Dior Fall, the *damel* of Kayor in the early eighteenth century. His description resembles the case of Serigne Khaly Amar Fall noted above.

66. Searing, *God Alone Is King*, 21–24; Glover, *Sufism and Jihad in Modern Senegal*, 42; and Cheikh A. M. Babou, *Fighting the Greater Jihad: Amadou Bamba and the Founding of the Muridiyya of Senegal, 1853–1913* (Athens: Ohio University Press, 2007),

24–28. In Wolof, *serigne lamb* means "marabout of the drum" and *lew* is an adjective that signifies "legitimate" or "legal." *Lew can also be translated as a* portion of land freely given to somebody. One anonymous informant, a direct descendant of Cheikh Abdoulaye Niass, told me that his ancestor established himself in the quarter of Léona (it is legal, Wolof) in Kaolack thanks to a lew from French colonial officials in Senegal.

67. Yaya Wane, *Les Toucouleur du Fouta Tooro (Senegal): Stratéfication Sociale et Structure familiale* (Dakar: I.F.A.N., 1966). The same observation is valid for Haussaland when King Yayi ruled Kano from 1349 to 1385; Koumasi in Ghana during the 1800s when Muslims befriended King Osei Bonsu; and the Nilotic Sudan where similar donations helped clerics known as *fuqara*. See R. S. O'Fahey, "Islam, State, and Society in Dar Fur," in *Conversion to Islam*, ed. Nehemia Levtzion (New York: Holmes and Meier, 1979), 189–206.

68. El Hadji Manding, interview, Karantaba, October 23, 2003; Boubacar Dabo, interview, Bambadion, December 6, 2003; and Mansani Dramé, interview, Diatouma, October 25, 2003. Yassa Tounkara, Némouna Diakoumba, and Diakoumba Barro were among Fodé Heraba's wives. Diakoumba belonged to the Barro lineage founded by Fodé Barro discussed in chapter 3.

69. This strategy of enticement was characterized as a widespread practice in the Bainounk country in interviews in Sédhiou, November 11, 2003; Bakoum, November 12, 2003; and Karantaba, November 29 and 30, 2003. El Hadji Manding, interview, Karantaba, October 23, 2003. A similar example is Muslim Haussa traders/scholars who immigrated to northern Ghana; they too performed "religious services" for some local chiefs who later became Muslims. See Stephen Owohaene-Acheampong and Charles Prempeh, "Contemporary Zongo Communities in Accra Interfaith Marriages: The Case of Muslims and Christians in Accra," *African Studies Quarterly* 19, no. 1 (2020): 23–40.

70. Sanneh, *Beyond Jihad*, 8–9; Ware, *The Walking Qur'an*, 96–98. See also Robinson, *Muslim Societies in African History*, 124–38.

71. Mauro Nobili, "Reinterpreting the Role of Muslims in the West African Middle Ages," *Journal of African History* 61, no. 3 (2021), 26–27. His model applies essentially to the political formations of medieval Western Soudan, like Mali and Songhay. For more information on the interactions between religious experts and African rulers in precolonial Africa, see Susan K. McIntosh, *Beyond Chiefdoms: Pathways to Complexity in Africa* (Cambridge: Cambridge University Press, 2005).

72. Group interviews, Karantaba, November 17, 2003, and Bakoum, November 21, 2003.

73. Group interviews, Karantaba, September 29, 2003, and Bakoum, October 3, 2003.

74. Sarr, *Islam, Power and Dependency in the Gambia River Basin*, 76. See also Adell Patton, "An Islamic Frontier Polity: The Niger Mountains of Northern Nigeria, 1846–1902," in *The African Frontier: The Reproduction of Traditional African Societies*, ed. Igor Kopytoff (Bloomington: Indiana University Press, 1987), 195–213. Some Haussa clerics

(*mallams*) rejected a taxation system imposed on them by the Sokoto Caliphate in the 1800s and avoided retaliation by resettling in northern Nigeria. They created a Muslim state in this region after winning the confidence of local populations.

75. Sarr, *Islam, Power and Dependency in the Gambia River Basin*, 84–109. When re-evaluating the multifold importance of land, he shows the persistence of such old beliefs in The Gambia.

76. Group interviews, Bakoum, December 10, 2003; Dioudoubou, December 10, 2003; and Sédhiou, December 16, 2003.

77. For Bainounk informants, this was a litmus test that applied to most Muslim clerics in the Middle Casamance.

78. El Hadji Khadiry Barro, interview, Sédhiou, October 17 and 23, 2003. See also Ware, *The Walking Qur'an*, 97–98. He explains this mutually advantageous "spatial marginality" while discussing this "kind of quarantine" in Senegambia.

79. Group interview, Bambadion, September 29, 2003. I kept this informant's name confidential at her request.

80. Boubacar Dabo, interview, Bambadion, December 6, 2003.

81. Group interview, Sédhiou, October 29, 2006.

82. Qur'anic chapter 49:13 explains that God intentionally divided humankind into various tribes and nations for them to know one another; and that Muslims can befriend non-Muslims who do not chase them away or fight them because of their faith. See Qur'anic chapter 60:8. These include individuals with political power (*al-mulk*) like statesmen and kings. The *khutbah,* the equivalent of the speech given by the pastor at church on Sunday, is a remnant of a tradition initiated by Prophet Muhammad.

83. Group interviews, Karantaba, December 11, 2003, and Bambadion, December 13, 2003.

84. Dabo, interview, Sédhiou, December 7, 2003. This is the biggest Muslim festival known in Wolof as *gamou,* held between The Gambia and Guinea-Bissau. Since the 1990s, I have attended on many occasions this festival. I will come back to the importance of this event while concluding the book.

85. Brooks, *Landlords and Strangers*, 37–67.

86. See the description of the signares by Michel Adanson cited by Searing, *West African Slavery*, 93–98, and Brooks, "The Signares of Saint Louis and Goreé: Women Entrepreneurs in Eighteenth-Century Senegal," in *Women in Africa*, ed. Nancy J. Hafkin and Edna G. Bay (Stanford: Stanford University Press, 1976), 19–44.

87. For example, see Francis Moore, *Travels into the Inland Parts of Africa* (London: Kingle Edition, 1738), 30–50.

88. Osborn, *Our New Husbands Are Here*, 26 and 50–56. She argues that a chief warrior married his daughter to Kaba Laye whose lineage ruled Kankan in eastern Guinea.

89. Group interviews, Sédhiou, November 17, Karantaba, November 21, and Bakoum, December 1, 2003.

90. Denise Semley, "Kétu Identities: Islam, Gender, and French Colonialism in West Africa, 1850s–1860s," PhD diss., history, Northwestern University, 2002, 97–98, and 116–17. As Semley notes, interfaith marriage in this region was a stepping-stone in incorporating Muslim immigrants into local populations in the nineteenth century. This is strikingly similar to the instances of Mandinka Muslims in the Middle Casamance.

91. Schaffer, "An Introduction to Pakao Expansion and Social Structure by Virtue of an Indigenous Manuscript."

92. For example, in the Soundiata epic, while Soundiata is the central character, some women like his mother (Sogolon), the first wife (Sassouma), and his half-sister (Nana Triban) played a key role in the accomplishment of his destiny. While collecting oral data, I noticed the same "omission" emphasized by Schaffer.

93. Interestingly, throughout fieldwork, one of my assistants kept reminding me to never share this information with others. When I asked him to define his personal identity now, he simply responded by saying "Mandinka of course."

94. Ansoumana and Moulaye Dramé, interview, Dioudoubou, August 9, 2009. At the time of my interviews, the direct descendants of Harounaba assumed the roles of village chief and imam, respectively.

95. Ansoumana and Moulaye Dramé, interview.

96. Chief Mansani Dramé, Diatouma, November 11, 2003; Ansoumana Biaye, interview, Sandiniéri, October 23, 2003; Fina Manlang Fenda Faty, interview, Sédhiou, November 6, 2003; and Kambo Konté and Tamartha Djité, interview, Dioudoubou, March 5, 2009.

97. Mousokéba Souané and Tooribaly Cissé, interview, Dioudoubou, August 19, 2009. I heard this metaphor many times from some anonymous matriarchs in Dioudoubou, September 22, 2003.

98. Ibrahima Kékoye Konté, Sédhiou, November 23, 2003.

99. Group interview, Dioudoubou, January 3, 2004.

100. Younouss Dabo and Bourama Mané, interview, Sédhiou, August 18, 2009.

101. Nano Kombo, interview, Dioudoubou, August 17, 2009.

102. Mankawali and Bambara Fanné were probably among these men.

103. Diané Dabo and Mariama Cissé Konté, interview, Ndiama, August 13, 2009; El Hadji Fondalo Seydi and Nimbaly Dabo, interview, Ndiama, August 13 and 14, 2009.

104. Elders, group interview, Ndiama, December 10 and 11, 2003. In Ndiama's early history, they said, the *salalinko* was the tree under which warriors got dressed for war, while the *kabanla batan* was the tree under which they undressed after war.

105. Nembali Dabo, interview, Sédhiou, September 17, 2009. See also El Hadji Bassirou Seydi. For him, the wives of Ndiama's founder included Aissatou Diao and Rokhiyatou Diallo, but both were Muslims before their marriages.

106. Group interview, Ndiama, September 12, 2001. According to Yoro Touré, the name Ndiama means "peace," a reminder of the Bainounk's willingness to welcome others to their homeland. But others said Ndiama is a deformation of *dianatul muslimin in Arabic*, implying here the birth of a new Muslim community.

107. "Two rainy seasons" is another way of saying two years.

108. Dikily Seydi and Ismaila Koma.

109. Malang Koussa Koma, Ibrahima Souané, El Hadji Bécaye Souané, interview, Dianaba, September 1, 2009. The prefix *ba* stands for greatness in Mandingo, but here it is used to make a distinction between two townships (for example, Dianaba (th*e big diana*) and a much younger community called Diana Malari. This also refers to a highly educated individual in a praiseworthy manner (for example, Harounaba, Fodé Héraba, Syllaba, or Mousoba). Souané was Dikily's uncle whose affinities with Koma stem from their common passion for big game hunting. See Schaffer, *Djinns, Stars and Warriors*, 158–59. This version mentions no Bainounk leader who played a role in creating the village.

110. Dionsaba Cissé, interview, Dianaba, September 3, 2009, and Fodé Alamamy Fossar Souané, interview, Sédhiou, October 31, 2003. For him, Basso Badjinka was the wife of Boukaryding Souané of Dianaba.

111. Group interviews, Bakoum, November 11, 2003; Karantaba, November 17, 2003; and Sédhiou, November 23 and 24, 2003. Boubacar Souané, interview, Dianaba, February 10, 2018.

112. The baobab, one the biggest species of trees in the savanna woodland, is the national symbol of Senegal. Besides its great nutritional values, this tree has traditionally served as a powerful source of spiritual healing and connection with occult forces and ancestral spirits in many African societies. Regarding Senegambia, see Assane Seck, "La Moyenne Casamance:Etude de Géographie Physique," *Revue de Géographie Alpine* 43, no. 4 (1955): 707–55.

113. Boubacar Cissé, interview, Kounayan, November 2, 2003; Chief Mamadou Mansaly, interview, Bakoum, October 20, 2003 ; group interview, Sédhiou, December 2, 2003. Ndoura and Yéri Danfa gave birth to Sounkari Yéri Kamara, who fought against the French in Boudhié after his father's death. One oral account describes Ndoura ethnically as a Bainounk from Guinea-Bissau; he was naturalized as a Mandinka Muslim before joining his "uncle" Bodia Danfa in Boudhié; and Ndoura's wife was either Danfa's daughter or one of his relatives. See Sagna, *La Casamance, l'Islam et la France*, 185–86.

114. In popular imagination the name Sédhiou came from *nsinadié or* "we will see" in Mandingo, but the invitation to settle is also plausible.

115. Group interviews with small batches of women, Sédhiou, October 26 and 29, 2003; and Charlotte Sarr, interview Sédhiou, October 24, 2003.

116. The brides' age, physical look, previous matrimonial status and social rank all played a role in determining the amount of the bride-wealth. Given the patrilineal and patriarchal nature of Mandinka and Bainounk societies, male authorities began the negotiations before informing their families and neighbors. The man selected as the chief negotiator is called *silatamala* in Mandingo. This gift (*mahr*, Arabic) is mentioned several times in the Qur'an. See, for example, Qur'anic chapters 4:4, 19, 20, and 60:10, 11. This must be paid to both Muslim and non-Muslim brides.

117. For a fresh interpretation of the place of marriage and other social institutions in Mandinka cultural heritage, see Lamine Touré, "Etudes des Valeurs chez les Manding de Casamance (au sud du Senegal): Enquête Réalisée á partir des Chants," Thése de doctorat, Université Assane Seck (Ziguinchor), 2022. Concentrating mostly on the modern period, Touré discusses the importance of specific songs in the transmission of human knowledge among the Mandinka of Senegambia.

118. Qur'anic chapters 37:35 and 48:29.

119. Group interviews, Bakoum, Sédhiou, and Karantaba, December 7, 9, and 11, 2003. This (*shahada*) consists of saying "there is no God but God, and Muhammad is the messenger of God."

120. Nato Konta and Tida Cissé, interview, Dianaba, October 24, 2003.

121. Today, many people's names in the Casamance are corruptions of Arabic names: for example, Khady or Kadya (Khadija), Roki (Rokiyatou), Mariétou (Marie), Awa (Hawa), Fatoumata or Fatou (Fatima), and Diarra (Hajarra) for women and girls; and Séni (Al-Hussein), Sana or Lansana (Al-Hasan), Bakari (Abou Bakr), and Mamodou (Mohammad) for men and boys. Group interviews, Bakoum, November 17, 2003; Karantaba, November 27, 2003, and Sédhiou, November 29, 2003.

122. Group interviews, elders, Sédhiou, September 30; Bakoum, September 30; and Dioudoubou, October 2, 2003.

123. Group interviews, and Fina Fenda Faty, Sédhiou, October 17, 2003; group interviews, Bambadion, November 2; and Bakoum, November 3, 2003.

124. Depending on the interlocutors, "bad blood" means in this context people who no longer deserve to be considered "real" Bainounk, who must be executed, or who betrayed their communities through their unforgivable bad deeds.

125. Diatta, interview, September 9, 2003.

126. Marc David Baer, "History and Religious Conversion," in *The Oxford Handbook of Religious Conversion*, ed. Lewis R. Rambo and Charles E. Farhadian (Oxford: Oxford University Press, 2014), 25–47.

127. Lucie G. Colvin, "The Shaykh's Men: Religion and Power in Senegambian Islam," in *Rural and Urban Islam in West Africa*, ed. Nehemia Levtzion and Humphrey J. Fisher (Boulder, CO: Lynne Rienner, 1987), 55–65.

128. Roche, *Histoire de La Casamance*, 54.

129. Sarr, *Islam, Power and Dependency in the Gambia River Basin*, 66.

## CHAPTER 3

1. Isaac Schapera, "Marriage of Near Kin among the Tswana," *Africa* 27, no. 2 (1957): 139–59.

2. One good example is the Ewe-speaking communities on the Upper Slave Coast where patterns of intermarriage existed between Ewe women and "ethnic outsiders" between the seventeenth and nineteenth centuries. Because sometimes intermarriage

led to a loss of land when local women passed their properties to their sons outside their kins, "ethnic insiders" sought to resolve this situation by prioritizing "interward marriages" (*tasavinyruivisro*). See Sandra E. Green, *Gender, Ethnicity and Social Change on the Upper Slave Coast* (Portsmouth, NH: Heinemann, 2009), 1–47. For additional interpretations, see Mary F. Smith, *Baba of Kano: A Woman of the Muslim Hausa* (New Haven: Yale University Press, 1954). One of the defense mechanisms used by Senegambian groups like the Sérére-saféne in western Bawol consisted of closing off their homeland to suspicious strangers or refusing intermarriage with them. See Searing, "Conversion to Islam: Military Recruitment and generational Conflict in a Sereer-Safen Village (Bandia), 1920–38" *Journal of African History* 44 (2003): 73–94. Besides the act of becoming Muslim followed by the adoption of a new worldview, he argues, local populations viewed conversion as a threat to "local configurations of power, kingship and inheritance."

3. Tal Tamari, "The Development of Caste Systems in West Africa," *Journal of African History* 32 (1991): 221–50. Intermarriage is commonplace the Islamic world partly because shariah tolerates affine ties among some but not all close kin members. For some explanations of this issue, see Qur'anic chapters 4:22–24 and 33:50.

4. Before the development of Islam in the Casamance Bainounk belief systems included a similar practice locally known as *djibé silla.*

5. This is to say that no Islamic pillar is more important than the testimony of faith. Believing in God is the pre-condition of worship God, as referenced in the Qur'an. See, for example, chapter 2:39.

6. Kémo Soly, interview, Karantaba, October 23–24, 2003.

7. Group interview, Karantaba, October 29, 2003.

8. El Hadji Khadiry Barro, interview, Juleskounda, Sédhiou, October 23, 2003.

9. Qur'anic chapter 2:256, which says "there is no compulsion as a method of Islamic conversion because every occurrence on earth is predetermined by God." The brothers Karamo Dinding and Boubacar Cissé repeated this passage during my interview with them in Kounayan, November 4, 2003.

10. El Hadji Manding and Kémo Soly, interview, Karantaba, October 23, 2003.

11. As Launay notes, despite their minority status, Dioula migrants reshaped the lives of the Sénoufo and other acephalous communities in precolonial Kohorgo. Besides the risk of violating one sacred rule of Souwaré's teachings (the need to collaborate with non-Muslims), he adds, in the seventeenth century non-Muslims outnumbered Muslim immigrants by ten to one; and this may have been a disincentive for waging military jihād against non-Muslims. See Launay, *Beyond the Stream,* 77–103.

12. Malang Fenda Faty, interview, Sédhiou, November 6, 2003.

13. Kopytoff, *The African Frontier*, 7–18.

14. El Hadji Manding, Karantaba, October 11, 2003.

15. Schaffer, *Djinns, Stars and Warriors*, 131.

16. Launay, *Beyond the Stream*, 80; and Sanneh, *Jahanke Muslim Clerics,* 1–12.

17. Wilks, "The Juula and the Expansion of Islam into the Forest," 94–98. Among the perpetuators of Souwaré's legacy were Mouhammad Dougouri in Ivory Coast, Mouhammad Bouni in Mafourrou, and El Hadji Youssouf in The Gambia. See Wilks, "The Transmission of Islamic Learning in the Western Sudan," in *Literacy in Traditional Societies*, ed. Jack Goody (Cambridge: Cambridge University Press, 1975), 162–97; and Sanneh, Beyond Jihad, 86. His list includes clerics like Salla Kébé, Bamba Wagué, and Fa Abdoulahi Maréga.

18. Group interviews, Karantaba, October 23, 2003; and interview with Mori Kéba Kouyaté, Chicago, June 12, 2001.

19. While Fodé Héraba was affiliated with the Khadiriyya and the Maliki school, he never disregarded the importance of the other schools of jurisprudence in terms of educating Muslims.

20. Mansani Dramé, interview, Diatouma, October 16, 2003; Fodé Almamy Fossar Souané, interview, Sédhiou, December 6, 2003; and group interview, Fodékounda, the ancestral home of the Dramé lineage in Karantaba.

21. Group interviews, Karantaba, October 23 and 24, 2003.

22. Kéba Dakhaba, interview, Simbandi Birassou, December 10, 2003.

23. Jack Goody, *The Social Organization of the Lo Wiili* (Oxford: Oxford University Press, 1967), 37. In the precolonial period, Goody indicates, humans played a more appealing role than land in African economic systems, particularly in issues related to the productivity of land. For some conflicting approaches, see Jeffrey Herbst, *States and Power in Africa: Contemporary Lessons in Authority and Control* (Princeton: Princeton University Press, 2000), 11; John Thornton, *Africa and Africans in the Making of the Atlantic World* (Cambridge: Cambridge University Press, 1998), 72–97.

24. Kopytoff, *The African Frontier*, 53–60.

25. Concerning West Africa, see Sarr, *Islam, Power and Dependency in the Gambia River Basin*. For different analyses of this issue, see Sara Berry, *Chiefs Know Their Boundaries: Essays on Property, Power and the Past in Asante, 1896–1996* (Portsmouth, NH: Heinemann, 2001); Carola Lentz, *Land, Mobility and Belonging in West Africa* (Bloomington: Indiana University Press, 2013); and Kea, *Land, Labour and Entrustment*. See also Aly Dramé's review of *Islam, Power and Dependency in the Gambia River Basin: Politics of Land Control, 1790–1940*, by Assan Sarr, *International Journal of African Historical Study* 50 (2017).

26. Dramé, review of *Islam, Power and Dependency in the Gambia River Basin*, 6.

27. See, for example, Sarr, *Islam, Power and Dependency in the Gambia River Basin*.

28. This code guided the progression of oral historians while they explained the genesis of Muslim settlements in the region. For them, the question of knowing who came first, second, or third generated inter-lineage tensions, as in many other human communities. However, these tensions did not derive from misconceptions or ignorance of "the chronology of presence," but from deliberate efforts by powerful hamlets to impose their will on others.

29. Group interview with elders, Sédhiou, October 25, 2003.

30. For a similar case, see Lentz, *Land, Mobility and Belonging in West Africa*, 28–81.

31. Schaffer, "A Study of a Social Process among a Mandinko People of the Senegambia," Ph.D. Diss (Oxford: University of Oxford, 1976), 302.

32. In the seventeenth century, Badibu was still largely populated by non-Muslims. See Quinn, *Mandingo Kingdoms of Senegambia*, 29–52.

33. This is the official version of the Diba lineage narrated by Sékouba Diba, interview, Karantaba, November 13, 2003; and Kébouté Diba, interview, Karantaba, September 29, 2001.

34. This is the official version of the Dramé ruling family. Mamadou Doudou Dramé, interview, Sédhiou, November 10, 2003; and Balla Dramé, interview, Darsilamé, November 16, 2003.

35. Filidjié Mané, interview, Sédhiou, November 27, 2003; Bainounk chief Mamadu Mansaly, interview, Bakoum, October 20, 2003; Fina Malang Fenda Faty, interview, Sédhiou, November 6, 2003; Diéli Mori Kéba Kouyaté, interview, Chicago, June 12, 2001; Almamy Fossar Souané, interview, Sandiniéri, October 24, 2003; Kémo Soly, interview, Karantaba, October 23, 2003; and El Hadji Khadiry Barro, November 29, 2003.

36. Sékouba Diba, interview, Karantaba, November 13, 2003; and Kébouté Diba, interview, Karantaba, September 29, 2001.

37. Based on oral testimonies, Fodé Moussa Soly was greatly admired across the Souna-Balmadou region thanks to his wisdom and mastery of the Qur'an. One of his accomplishments was to mystically save one day Fodé Héraba's daughter from a crocodile attack, which considerably reinforced Soly's status as a man of God.

38. Fakéba Soly, interview, Karantaba, November 7, 2003; and El Hadji Manding and Kémo Soly, interview, Karantaba, December 8, 2003.

39. Almamy Barro, interview, Barrokounda, Karantaba, September 29, 2001; and El Hadji Khadiry Barro, Sédhiou, November 29, 2003. See also Sanneh, *Beyond Jihad*, 196. He posits that when the cleric Fodé Amar Sylla moved from Touba in Guinea to Pakao, the marabout Ousmane Kaba offered him his daughter in marriage before Danso clerics hosted him in The Gambia. Sanneh does not mention when this relation occurred, but this yields evidence that these marriage alliances were not confined to Karantaba in the Middle Casamance.

40. Not surprisingly, many Mandinka believe that Fodé Héraba and his companions probably followed the example of the Prophet Muhammad with his four Rightly Guided Caliphs (*saabbah*). Aisha, his youngest wife, was the daughter of Abu Bakr Al-Saddikh, the first caliph of Islam (632–34 CE); and Hasfa, the daughter of Umar Ibn Khatab, the second caliph of Islam (634–44 CE), was also married to the Prophet. The Prophet gave his daughter, Fatima, to Ali Ibn Abu Thalib, his first cousin and the fourth

caliph (656–61 CE). The Prophet also married his daughter, Rokhiyya, to Usman Ibn Affan, the third caliph of Islam (644–56 CE), and when Rokhiyya died he gave him one of his other daughters, Umu Kalsum. Similar marital practices existed in many West African regions. If we focus on northern Senegambia, for instance, some of Cheikh Amadou Bamba's and El Hadji Malick Sy's daughters were married to their closest associates (*mukhadam*, Arabic). Sokhna Faty Diakhaté, mother to the former Mourid caliph Serigne Saliou Mbacké (1915–2007), is the daughter of Serigne Amadou Asta Diakhaté of Kayor. Sokhna Rokhaya Ndiaye, mother to the Tidjani caliph Serigne Babacar Sy (1885–1957), is the daughter of Serigne Aly Boye Ndiaye whose family befriended El Haji Malick Sy when he moved to Saint Louis from Gaya by 1880.

41. Fyfe and Dorjahn, "Landlord and Stranger," 396–97.

42. *Kounda* means family or lineage in Mandingo and Diakhanké.

43. Sanneh, *The Jakhanke Muslim Clerics: A Religious and Historical Study of Islam in Senegambia* (New York: University Press of America, 1989), 38.

44. Robert Launay, *Traders without Trade: Responses to Changes in Two Dyula Communities* (Cambridge: Cambridge University Press, 1982), 48–54; and Esther Goody, *Contexts of Kinship: An Essay in the Family Sociology of the Gonja of Northern Ghana* (Cambridge: Cambridge University Press, 1973).

45. Souané, "Histoire des Manding de la Moyenne Casamance," 26.

46. Bérenger-Féraud, *Les Peuplades de la Sénégambie*, 209; Hecquard, "Rapport sur un Voyage," 123–36; and Park, *Travels in the Interior Districts of Africa*, 76–96.

47. Park, *Travels in the Interior Districts of Africa*, 79.

48. Mindful of the sacredness of the almamiyya, the Mandinka strongly believe that the talented carpenter selected to make the almamy doko must also be a pious Muslim.

49. In Kounayan, the descendants of Fodé Koutama Cissé told me that their rejection of the alkaliyya was rooted in their hatred for anything looking like greed and royalty. So, they let their Kanté and Souané neighbors assume this function and kept the almamiyya for themselves. In Ndiama, the descendants of the village's founder have long monopolized the *alkaliyya* and his nephew's offspring, Daffé, take the *almamiyya*. Townships like Bambadion, Dioudoubou and Sandiniéri adopted the Karantaba model.

50. El Hadji Manding, interview, Karantaba, October 23, 2003. I noticed his frequent use of the historic present while elaborating on the importance of this old rule.

51. Sékouba Diba and his fellow lineage members, interviews, Karantaba, November 13, 2003.

52. Diba, interview, November 13, 2003. On this occasion, like El Hadji Manding before him, Diba sought to include other clerics, but they were away from homes.

53. El Hadji Karamba Soly, Solykounda, interview, Karantaba, September 29, 2000, and El Hadji Manding and Kémo Soly, October 23, 2003.

54. Representatives from other kabilas formulated the same remarks.

55. My first informant on this issue was El Hadji Karamba Soly, a Qur'anic school-

teacher, on September 29, 2001. El Hadji Manding, Kémo Soly, repeated this statement in group interview, Karantaba, October 23, 2003.

56. Souané, "Histoire des Manding de la Moyenne Casamance," 33.

57. Kémo Soly Sakho, interview, Karantaba, September 29, 2001; and El Hadji Manding, interview, Karantaba, October 23, 2003.

58. Abdou Kounta Djité, group interview, Sédhiou, October 12, 2003. This famous saxophonist was among the musicians who created the U.C.A.S. Jazz Band of Sédhiou in 1959; he remained with the band until his death at the age of 76. Because the Dramé and Djité are *sanos*, he liked to make fun of me whenever we saw each other in town.

59. Matt Schaffer, *Mandinko: The Ethnography of a West African Holy Land* (Waveland, IL: Prospect Heights Press, 1980).

60. This is based on my own observations during fieldwork.

61. This was the response given by the chief when his grandson asked him about power sharing in the late 1980s. See Souané, "Histoire des Manding de la Moyenne Casamance," 33.

62. Many male participants men came from polygynous households.

63. Almamy Fossar Souané, a schoolteacher, interview, Sédhiou, October 24, 2003; and Fina Malang Fenda Faty, interview, Sédhiou, November 6, 2003.

64. Souané, "Histoire des Manding de la Moyenne Casamance," 24–25.

65. Mamadou Sarr, Sarrkounda, Sédhiou, October 17, 2003.

66. Group interview, Sédhiou, October 17, 2003.

67. This popular verse included in the second and longest Qur'anic chapter (*al-baqara*). Millions of Muslims recite it daily as a protection against all sorts of dangers.

68. Because poverty was the defining characteristic of life at this moment, seldom could people afford enough clothes to cover all their body parts. Perhaps this layout was designed to avoid the exposure of people's private parts during prayer sessions.

69. Ross, *Sufi City*, 212–15.

70. According to Caliph Usman, who pieced together the Qur'an, the Prophet once said that "whoever builds a mosque for Allah [God]), Allah will build a house like it for them in Paradise." This is based on a hadith reported by Imam Sahil Bukhari. The mosque (*masjid*) is mentioned more than twenty times in the Qur'an. As stated in the Qur'an, no place on earth is closer to God than mosques; mosques are houses of God; and mosques belong to God alone. See Qur'anic chapters 72:18, 9:18, and 24:36.

71. El Hadji Kémo Soly, interview, November 17, 2003.

72. Almamy Barro, interview, Karantaba, November 21, 2001; and Almamy Fossar Souané, interview, Sandiniéri, October 29, 2003.

73. Group interview, Karantaba, October 11, 2003.

74. As time passed, Muslims began to hold other crucial events at the mosque: funeral services, weeding ceremonies, distribution of charity and zakat, and conflict resolution, for instance.

75. El Hadji Manding, interview, Karantaba, November 17, 2003.

76. Fakéba Soly, interview, Solykounda, Karantaba, October 10, 2003.

77. Fakéba Soly, Solykounda. In the 2000s, he expertly commanded one of the most famous Qur'anic schools in the Souna-Balmadou.

78. Group interview, Ndiama, September 17, 2003; Ibrahima Mané, interview, Sédhiou, August 13, 2003; and Faty, interview, Sédhiou, October 29, 2003.

79. Imam Demba, interview, Sédhiou, December 4, 2003. Before his death around the age of ninety-five, he enjoyed tremendous prestige for accomplishing the pilgrimage on foot in 1953. The imam gave me valuable advice on proper manners for interacting with his fellow elders.

80. I noticed the persistence of this tradition in the 1990s in the greater Sédhiou region while attending funerals.

81. Boubacar Cissé, interview, Kounanya, November 2, 2003; and El Hadji Manding, Karantaba, October 23, 2003. This resembles "the individualized nature of instruction" examined by Tal Tamari who follows Roger Santerre's and Louis Brenner's lead on this question. See Tal Tamari, "Styles of Islamic Education: Perspectives from Mali, Guinea, and The Gambia," in *Islamic Education in Africa: Writing Boards and Blackboards*, ed. Robert Launay (Bloomington: Indiana University Press, 2016), 30.

82. Karamo Soly, interview, Karantaba, September 13, 2001.

83. Group interview, Sédhiou, October 29.

84. Group interview with clerics, Karantaba, November 17 and 18, 2003; and Qur'anic students, interview, Karantaba, November 17 and 18, 2003.

85. The Mandinka consider the smoke rising to the sky from the *karanta-dimba* a powerful tool for communicating with God. Mori Kéba Kouyaté, interview, Chicago, June 7, 2001; Karamo Dinding Cissé, interview, Kounayan, October 3, 2003; and Ibrahima Touré, interview, Karantaba, December 8, 2003. Kouyaté grew up in the 1960s in Bounkiling, a small village located in Sonkoudou. He volunteered that across the Middle Casamance firewood was so highly valued that young Qur'anic students who returned home from the farms without their bundles of wood were severely punished.

86. Group of women, interview, Sédhiou, September 30, 2003; and Mariama Diané and Khady Biaye, interview, Kaur, October 17 and 18, 2008. According to another group of anonymous women, because in the early Mandinka society girls got married between the ages of thirteen and fifteen, their level of Qur'anic knowledge rarely went beyond "knowing God" (*allah long*). Both girls and women were only expected to possess the rudimentary knowledge necessary for following the basic recommendations of shariah: praying, fasting, body purification, and educating children. And up until the present time, homemaking skills, obedience to male authority, and the bearing of children were and are still the defining features of good female citizenship in the Mandinka society. Women unanimously characterized this discrimination as a reflection of the male-dominated nature of Mandinka Islam.

87. Group interview, Sédhiou, December 2, 2003. Female informants mentioned the correlation between cooking food and obtaining ink, while explaining women's contribution to this educational process.

88. The origins of this technique of harvesting ink are obscure in scholarly genealogies, but some other Muslim groups inside and outside of Senegal are acquainted with this same technique. In the Wolof country, for example, the harvesting of ink is called *soss daa*. For some developments see Geert Mommersterg, "Learning the Word of God: The Primitive City of Timbuktu," *Saudi Aramco Magazine* 42, no. 5 (1991): 2–11. Some Foula groups use a wet corncob to harvest ink, but a wet piece of cloth is their most popular technique.

89. Group interview with elders, Sédhiou, December 17 and 18, 2003.

90. Abdoulaye Cissé, interview, Sédhiou, November 11, 2009. This school administrator who was my student dedicated a considerable amount of his time, helping me schedule and carry out interviews almost everywhere.

91. El Hadji Manding, interview, Karantaba, oct 18, 2003; and group interview, Sédhiou, Oct 17, 2003.

92. Group interviews, Karantaba and Ndiama, September 27 and 29, 2003.

93. Imam Demba, Sédhiou, December 7, 2003. He characterized this type of exchange as a nice way to strengthen relations between graduating students and their teachers.

94. Fina Fenda Faty, interview, Sédhiou, December 10, 2003. Most Qur'anic teachers I interviewed had more than one wife. See also Marcel Decressac-Villagrand, *Souvenirs du Senegal: Lettre sur la Gambie et La Casamance* (Guéret: Imprimerie P. Amiault, 1890), 243.

95. Interviews, Chief Mansani Dramé, Diatouma, November 11, 2003; and Fina Kéba Dakhaba, Birassou, January 10, 2004. The Diakhanké and the Swahili are among African groups who have long been familiar with this ritual; they call this coronation *naw mili* and *kilemba*, respectively. See Loimeier, " L' islam ne se vend pas," 171; and Sanneh, *Beyond Jihad*, 156-57.

96. Group interviews, Sédhiou, Karantaba, and Diatouma, November 17, 19, and 23, 2003.

97. Group interview, Karantaba, October 29, 2003.

98. Sanneh, *Jahanke Muslim Clerics,* 156. The Wolof and Foula say *kala nala* and *fildé alfa*, respectively, when congratulating someone on a great achievement.

99. Cheikh Bou Kounta inherited a land concession from Damel Samba Laobé Fall, where he settled the holy city of Ndiassane in 1884. See Ross, *Sufi City*, 140. This antiquity partly explains why the Khadiriyya may still be the dominant Sufi order in the Casamance, without downplaying the breakthroughs by the Mouridiyya and Tidjaniyya in the past decades.

100. Almamy Fodé Fossar Souané, Sedhiou, October 22, 2003.

101. For example, on December 3, 2003 in Fodékunda I met a graduate student from Guinea-Bissau, Ibrahima Touré. He first studied under Fodé Almamy Dramé before switching to his son, El Hadji Manding, following his original teacher's death in the 1990s.

102. Many Mandinka who shared this worldview refused to make their sentiment public. To better apprehend the Mandinka Qur'anic school system, see Aly Dramé, "From Bulsafay to Fodeyya: Qur'anic Education among Mandinka Muslims in Senegal,"*Journal of Mande Studies*, 13 (2014): 91–123.

103. For instance, this is called *kal* or *gamou* among the Wolof in Senegal, *sanakou* among the Foula in Guinea, *sanankouyya* among the Bambara in Mali, and *eguregu* among some Igbo groups in eastern Nigeria.

104. See Marcel Griaule, "L'alliance cathartique," *Africa* 18, no. 4 (1948): 242–58. He describes the specific case of the *mongou* between the Bozo and Dogon in the Niger River region. For another interpretation, see A. R. Radcliffe, "On Joking Relationships," *Africa: Journal of International African Institute* 13, no. 3 (1940): 195–210.

105. For the wider Senegambia, see, for example, Katherine Ann Wiley, "Joking Market Women: Critiquing and Negotiating Gender and Social Hierarchy in Kankossa, Mauritania," *Africa* 84, no. 1 (2014): 101–18. She highlights the case of the once enslaved Haratin women and market venders who use it as a tool for negotiating their social reintegration in Mauritania; Etienne Smith, "La Nation par le côté: Politique des Cousinages au Senegal," *Cahier d'études Africaines* 46, no. 184 (2006): 907–65; Etienne Smith and Cécile Canut, "Pactes, Alliances et Plaisanteries," *Cahier d'études Africaines* 46, no. 184 (2006): 687–754; and Ferdinand De Jong, "A Joking Nation: Conflict Resolution in Senegal (Casamance)," *Canadian Journal of African Studies* 39, no. 2 (2005): 389–413.

106. The same remark applies to northern Senegambia. Throughout my adult life, I have bantered with my Cissé, Touré, Mandiang, and Djitté *sanos* in the Casamance; and my Kébé, Sakho, and Samb *kaals* in Dakar and Rufisque.

107. Among Senegambians, joking relationships can be intraethnic, as in the cases linking Diop-Ndiaye and Seck-Samb among the Wolof; Ba-Diallo among the Foula, who sarcastically "accuse" each other of being too fond of beans; and Touré-Cissé-Dramé among the Mandinka. Joking relationships can also involve people from distinct ethnic identities, as in the case of the Sérére and the Diola. Oral tradition recalls that their female ancestors were sisters who one day lost track of each other while traveling together on the river during a rough high tide. When their dugout canoes broke and split into two pieces, the older sister (probably Diambone) landed in the Sine region where the Sérére now live; and the younger sister (probably Aguéne) found herself on the shores of the Diola country in the Lower Casamance. This sad event generated a joking relationship between the two groups, demanding that their members never harm each other, given their common ancestry. While grading the baccalaureate exams together in the summer of 1994, some of my Diola and Sérére colleagues profited from our breaks to jokingly recall this old common tradition. See Saliou Sambou, *La Lègende d' Aguéne et de Diambone* (Dakar: Niamagne Editions, 2005).

108. Mori Kéba Kouyaté, interview, Chicago, October 11, 2001. He described sanoyya as a multinational institution and explained its widespread use across the Mande world

in West Africa, before using his own experience as a salient example. Kouyaté, a bard, musician, and storyteller, was part of a scene in which "tradition" took precedence over "modernity." While visiting the capital of Mali (Bamako) probably in 1982, he was in a state of urgency and urinated on the walls of the National Assembly. Bayo was the patronym of the Republican guard who caught him committing this serious offense. When Kouyaté exhibited his identity card, Bayo realized that they were *sano*, warned him to never commit this offense again, and let him go home. Without the power of sanoyya, Kouyaté concluded, he would have gone to prison or been forced to pay a heavy fine.

109. Group interviews, Karantaba, November 13, 2001, and October 17, 2003; and group interview, small group of Karantabans living in Sédhiou, December 3 and 4, 2003.

110. Group interviews, Karantaba, October 2 and 3, 2001; and Kémo Soly, interview, Karantaba, August 17, 2001.

111. El Hadjii Khadiry Barro, interview, Sédhiou, November 2, 2003.

112. Group interviews, Sédhiou, December 3, 2003. See also Sanneh, *Beyond Jihad*, 111. He mentions a similar situation in which "family bonds" and "professional solidarity" were part of the expected outcomes of Muslim intermarriages.

113. These consanguineous relationships are not part of the forbidden marriages highlighted in Qur'anic chapters 22–24 and 33:50. In numerous polygynous households I noticed that at least one wife was the product of cross-cousin marriage. One old practice in Senegambia consists of urging one's relatives or friends to marry their maternal and paternal cousins, calling these "your legitimate wife or husband." And a popular banter among groups like the Wolof is to ask an outsider who "stole" your female cousin (your legitimate wife) through marriage to give you a punitive damage (*takkou deune*). In Karantaba, the offspring of those who shared biological parents, like members of the Dramé and Sakho kabilas, were excluded from these alliances.

114. Kémo Soly and El Hadji Manding, interview, Fodékounda, Karantaba, November 29, 2003.

115. Group interviews, Sédhiou, December 7, 2004; Bakoum, October 23, 2003; Bambadion, September 30, 2003; and Ndiama, November 8, 2003. Among these are the Dramé-Samaté and Sylla-Cissé in Darsilamé, Dramé-Dabo and Seydi-Daffé in Ndiama, Kamara-Seydi-Touré-Dramé and Cissé-Ndiaye-Dabo in Dianaba, Barro-Gassama and Dabo-Seydi in Saliguénié, Soly-Konté and Dramé-Mané in Dioudoubou, and Mané-Dramé and Mansaly-Sadio in Koling.

116. Almamy Fossar Souané, interview, Sédhiou, December 10 and 11, 2003. When I met him on one occasion at Mapathé Diagne Middle School, this bright educator and administrator passionately told me that any additional interviews on my part in other old Islamic centers like Ndiama, Saliguénié, Mankonoba, Dianaba, and Darsilamé would inevitabbly lead to the same conclusion.

117. Mousokéba Souané, interview, Dioudoubou, August 19, 2009; and Biaye, interview, Sinkére Bainounk, October 4 and 5, 2009. This is one of the few places where the populace is still fluent in their Bainounk mother tongue. Biaye and Maimouna Manga

did a good job in explaining some linguistic correspondences between the Bainounk and Mandingo.

118. The most famous centers are in Yoff for the Layénnes, Touba for the Mourids, Ndiassane for the Khadirs, Tivaouane for the Tidjanes, and Medina Bay for the Niassénes. Millions of people profit from the festivals held annually in these towns to make pious visits to these holy sites.

119. Two good examples are Arfang Nembali Sita, Fodé Almamy Dramé, and Kaoussou Soly. Contrary to Sita, who died at a young age, Dramé and Soly sojourned in Saudi Arabia for ten and twenty-eight years, respectively. Their fame increased by leaps and bounds when they returned home after performing the pilgrimage. See Matt Schaffer, *Mandinko,* 39.

120. I noticed these patterns of behavior by observing pilgrims during the festivals in Karantaba.

121. Mamadou Mansaly, interview, Bakoum, November 17, 2003; Mamadou D. Dramé, interview, Sédhiou, November 23, 2003; Karamo Dinding Cissé, interview, Kounayan, October 3, 2003; and group interview, Sédhiou, October 31 and November 1, 2003.

122. Barro, interview, Sédhiou November 17, 2003.

123. Barro, interview. His ancestor's name is Arfang Nimbali Kansaba Dramé.

124. El Hadji Dramé, interview.

125. Group interview, Sédhiou, October 24, 2000; and Imam Kémo Demba, interview, Mansankounda, Sédhiou, October 11 and 12, 2003. See also Osborn, *Our New Husbands Are Here*, 28–31. I recorded a few scholar genealogies that suggest that in some cases the dispersal of clerics was triggered by deafening rivalries among male siblings or political unrest.

126. Group interview. Almamy Fodé Fossar Souané, Sédhiou, October 17, 2003.

127. Group interviews, Karantaba, September 29, 2003; Sédhiou, December 2, 2003; Diatouma, December 4, 2003; and Fossar Souané, Sandiniéri, December 11, 2003.

128. El Hadji Manding, Karantaba, December 2, 2003.

129. For more insights on Bocandé's report, see Gabriel Debrien, "Bertrand Bocandé (1812–81): Un Nantais de Casamance," *Bulletin de l'Institut Fondamental d'Afrique Noire, Série B: Sciences humaines* 16 (1970): 440–98.

130. Boudhié-Karantaba was a tiny village located in the wider Sédhiou area, not too far away from Boulock, a district known for its important lumber mill resources. My students from Boulock said their village was destroyed by a series of wildfires in the 1900s. See also Seck, "La Moyenne Casamance." His fieldnotes include these devastating fires.

131. Karantaba elders, Karantaba, October 23, 2003; and Balla Dramé, interview, Darsilamé, November 16, 2003.

132. Following his acceptance of Islam, Sanoba adopted the Dramé patronym. In reality, it was not infrequent to see new Muslim converts adopt various Islamically known first and last names in the Casamance, not only the Dramé patronym.

133. They were Malan Niara Dramé, Sisao Demba, Bourama Seydi, and Bakaoba Dramé. Group interview, Wandifa Dramé, Khady Cissé, Fatoumata Dabo, and Nani Djitté, Sédhiou, August 13, 2003.

134. Group Interview, elders, Diatouma, August 18 and 19, 2003.

135. Mansali Dramé and Sana Seydi, interview, Diatouma, November 12, 2003.

136. El Hadji Manding, interview, Karantaba, Oct 3, 2003.

137. J. M. Gray, *A History of The Gambia* (Cambridge: Cambridge University Press, 1940), 290 and 446.

138. Ibrahima Touré, interview, Karantaba, December 8, 2003. Touré, who called me his *sano*, was already a graduate student when I first encountered him in 2003, but he stayed in Karantaba instead of returning to his native Guinea-Bissau. He later told me he was undergoing soul searching while acquiring superior knowledge from his spiritual guides.

139. Group interview, Ndiama, December 11, 2003. The categorization of many African clerics in the most uncharitable terms was part of European colonial psychology, as typified by the writings of Paul Marty, the main ideologue of the French colonial state. In the case of Senegalese clerics by Marty, for example, see his voluminous study, *Etudes sur l' Islam au Sénégal: Les doctrines et les institutions, tome 2* (Paris: Ernest Leroux, 1917. See also Sanneh, *Beyond Jihad*, 199. He portrays Kadiali as one of the heirs of the Diakhanké tradition of teaching and community building in Senegambia. Established in the 1890s, Bagadadji is a corruption of Baghdad, Iraq. Ndiama's other offshoots include Diaroumé, Souaké, Kandiankou, Madina Daffé, Bassaf, and Manconto. Villages like Diopkounda, Kamakounda, Bantandian, Diana Malari, and Koursiyya descended from Dianaba. Imam El Hadjii Bassirou Seydi, Ndiama, interview, February 5, 2018.

140. Group interviews, Karantaba, Darsilamé, and Diatouma, October 29 and November 11 and 13, 2003. If we consider the oldest communities that have maintained religious ties with Karantaba, Bambadion is the only one where both powers are now monopolized by a single lineage, namely Chief Daffé's descendants

141. Group interview, Sédhiou, Nov 2, 2003.

142. Almamy Fodé Fossar Souané, interview, September 12, 2003.

143. Paul Marty, "Les Mandingues, Element Islamisé de la Casamance," *Revue du Monde Musulman* 31 (Paris, 1915): 443–68.

144. For more insights on these educational trips, see Ibrahima Baba Kaké, *Combats pour l'Afrique* (Paris: Présence Africaine, 1965); and Marty, "Les Mandingues, Element Islamisé de la Casamance." These study abroad programs diminished over time, with the spread of Qur'anic knowledge followed by the proliferation of scholars. That said, *fodéyya* may well be a dead religious institution in the Mandinka country. Between 2003 and 2004, I counted about 100 *fodé* who were all already dead by the time I began fieldwork. Karantaba has the biggest number of *fodé*, with a total of forty-seven men, Fodé Almamy Dramé being the last man to be crowned in 1957. In comparison, in Dianaba, the last man to obtain this coronation was Fodé Malang Siré Souané in 1962, and in

Badougha, it was Fodé Bankhaly Kagny in 1964. Central in explaining this setback is the fact that since the early 1960s, the educational landscape of the Casamance has slowly but continuously been modified by the spread of the Francophone school system, to the detriment of the pre-existing Qur'anic school model. My ongoing research on the spiritual legacy of Karantaba in Senegambia will shed light on the place of fodéyya in the Mandinka country today.

145. Barro, interview, Sédhiou, September 23, 2003; and El Hadji Manding, interview, Karantaba, December 11, 2003.

146. Lentz, *Land, Mobility and Belonging*, 40.

147. Griffeth, "The Dyula Impact on the Peoples of the West Volta Region."

148. Anne Frances Leary, "Islam, Politics, and Colonialism. A Political History of Islam in the Casamance Region of Senegal, 1850–1914," PhD diss., Northwestern University, 1974, 212.

149. For a better conceptualization of Diola's overall attitude toward strangers, see Baum, *Shrines of the Slave Trade*; and Roche, *Histoire de La Casamance*, 28–46 and 267–94.

150. Mark, *A Cultural, Economic and Religious History of the Basse Casamance*, 95–115.

151. Bertrand E. Bocandé, "Notes sur La Guinée Portugaise ou Sénégambie Méridionale," *Bulletin de La Société de Géographie* 12 (1849): 57–93; and De Jong, *Masquarades of Modernity*, 52–62. For him, the lifestyle of Diola groups who accepted Islam included the Muslim dress code, and this form of Mandinkization was a contamination of Diola identity.

152. Hecquard, *Voyage sur la Côte et dans l'interieur de L'Afrique Occidentale* (Paris: Bénard et Compagnie, 1855), 134.

153. The same is true for many African regions where Muslims and non-Muslims lived in separate towns. For instance, nothing in the reports by Arab authors concludes that these groups were entirely separated from one another in pre-Almoravid Ghana; religious and ethnic intermingling, not total quarantine, was a central element in framing the relationship between Muslims and non-Muslims.

## CHAPTER 4

1. For some recent studies, see Fulera Issaka-Toure, "Interpretations of Jihād in Africa: A Historical Overview," in *The Palgrave Handbook of Islam in Africa*, ed. Fallou Ngom, Mustapha H. Kurfi, and Toyin Falola (London: Palgrave Macmillan, 2020), 77–92; and Amir Syed, "Between Jihād and History: Reconceptualizing the Islamic Revolutions of West Africa," in *The Palgrave Handbook of Islam in Africa*, ed. Fallou Ngom, Mustapha H. Kurfi, and Toyin Falola (London: Palgrave Macmillan, 2020), 93–116.

2. Matt Schaffer, "A Study of Social Process among the Mandinko People of the Senegambia," PhD diss., University of Oxford, 1976; and Schaffer, *Mandinko*; and Leary,

"Islam, Politics and Colonialism. A Political history of Islam in the Casamance Region of Senegal, 1850-1914" PhD diss. (Evanston: Northwestern University, 1974), 95 and 103–4.

3. For newer perspectives on these revolutions, see, for example, Amir Syed, "*Between Jihād and History: Reconceptualizing the Islamic Revolutions of West Africa," in Palgrave Handbook of Islam in Africa*, eds. Fallou Ngom, Mustapha H. Kurfy, and Toyin Falola (Cham, Switzerland: Palgrave Macmillan, 2020), 93–94; and Syed, "Al-Hajji Umar Tal and the Realm of the Written: Mastery, Mobility and Islamic Authority in Nineteenth-Century West Africa," PhD diss., University of Michigan, 2017.

4. Group interviews, Ndiama, September 12, 2001; Karantaba, October 23, 2003; and Diatouma, November 11, 2003.

5. Ibrahima K. Konté, interview, Dioudoubou, May 5, 2005.

6. Some Qur'anic chapters and *ahadith* reported by prominent scholars like Al Bukhari, Abou Hurairah, and Sahl Bin Saad emphasize the meaning, legal doctrines, conditions, and justifications of jihād. Scholars distinguish two major kinds of jihād: the greater jihād (*jihad al-akbar*) and the smaller one (*jihad al-asghaar*). See, for example, Qur'anic chapters 9:36 and 41; 2:216; 61:10–13; and 4:95–96. For more developments, see Michael Bonner, *Jihad in Islamic History* (Princeton: Princeton University Press, 2008).

7. *Syed, Between Jihād and History*, 102–4.

8. Fulera Issaka-Toure, "Interpretations of Jihād in Africa: A Historical Overview," in *The Palgrave Handbook of Islam in Africa*, ed. Fallou Ngom, Mustapha H. Kurfi, and Toyin Falola (London: Palgrave Macmillan, 2020), 80.

9. Almamy F. Souané, interview, Sandiniéri, October 24, 2003; Boubacar Dabo, interview, Bambadion, December 6, 2003; and Konté, interview, Sédhiou, May 2, 2005.

10. El Hadji Kémo Demba, interview, Sonkoudou, December 3, 2003; and group interviews, Sédhiou, October 24, 2003.

11. Group interviews, Kounayan, November 2, 2003; and Sédhiou, October 23 and 26, 2003.

12. Group interviews, Karantaba and Sédhiou, October 23 and November 3, 2003. See also Jacques Faulquier, *Les Français en Casamance de 1826 à 1854: Mémoire de diplôme d'études supérieures* (Dakar: Université Cheikh Anta Diop, 1966), 25.

13. Souané, "Les Manding de La Moyenne Casamance," 53. Mori Kéba Lamine Cissé and Youssouf Corta, interview, Sédhiou, November 20, 2003. For example, in Birassou, the term *naamo* also means tax.

14. Almamy Fossar Souané, interview, Sandiniéri, October 24, 2003.

15. Baana saalo, the equivalent *eid-al adha* in Arabic, occurs in the Muslim calendar during the hajj in Mecca. According to Islamic tradition, God once ordered Prophet Abraham to sacrifice his own son Ismael, as an act of loyalty to God, but before he executed this painful order God had already replaced Ismael with a sheep. This is the reason why during the month of hajj *(dhu al-hijjah)*, Muslims who can afford it slaughter a sheep, as a remembrance of this emotional event.

16. Group interviews, Karantaba, September 10, and Sédhiou, October 3, 2003.

17. Schaffer, *Djinns, Stars and Warriors*, 69.

18. Osborn, *Our New Husbands Are Here.*

19. Karamo Dinding Cissé, interview, Kounayan, October 31, 2003. These calls (*azan*) are one of shariah's recommendations and occur five times during the day.

20. In Mandinka oral sources, his only nickname is "Syllaba" or Sylla the Great.

21. Initially, the Portuguese liked this island surrounded by mangrove swamps, but the mosquitoes that populated this whole area forced them to relocate to Ziguinchor by 1645. In the 1860s they conceded Karabane to the French who had to pay the Kagnout landowners an annual tribute of 196 francs.

22. The Portuguese nicknamed Karabane the island of the mosquitoes (*ilia dos mosquitos*) because it was infested by mosquitoes, which cause malaria.

23. The purchase of Karabane resulted from a treaty signed on January 22, 1836 by French commandant Louis Malavois with Kagnout's village chief. For the clauses of this transaction see Faulquier, *Les Français en Casamance de 1826 á 1854, 39.*

24. Archives de la République du Sénégal (ARS), 1 G 14: mission de Dagorne en Casamance; cession à la France de terrains à Seju, 1838.

25. For more insights on this system of intense economic exploitation, see Bernard Founou-Tchuigoua, *Fondements de l' économie de Traite au Sénégal: La surexploitation d'une colonie, 1880–1960* (Paris: Silex Editions, 1981)

26. This project was part of the treaty signed in 1883 between the French and King Moussa Molo of Fouladou. See Ngaïdé, *L'esclave, le colon et le marabout*, 120–25. The French used Molo in their conquest of the Upper Casamance, but his project never became reality.

27. Barry, *Senegambia and the Atlantic Slave Trade*, 217–22.

28. Bertrand J. Bocandé, Debrien Gabriel, and Saint Martin, "Emmanuel Bertrand-Bocandé (1812–1881): Un Nantais de Casamance (1818–1881)," *Bulletin de l'Institut Fondamental d'Afrique Noire, Série B: Sciences humaines* 31, no. 1 (1969): 292.

29. For more insights on the tributes Pakao's chiefs received from the French, see ARS, 13G 361: croquis sur le cours de la Casamance.

30. Bocandé, "Notes sur La Guinée Portugaise ou Sénégambie Méridionale."

31. See Schaffer, "A Study of Social Process among a Mandinko People of the Senegambia," 205–7. He mentions Bocandé's assessment of the ratio between Muslims and non-Muslims in the Middle Casamance by 1843.

32. Almamy Fossar Souané, interview, Sandiniéri, October 23, 2003; and Fina Malang Fenda Faty and Diéli Lamine Kouyaté who improvised a musical performance, Sédhiou, November 6, 2003.

33. Fenda Faty; and Konté, May 5, 2005.

34. ARS, 13 G 361: croquis sur le cours de La Casamance; Séju et dépendances; habitants et son commerce.

35. ARS, 13 G 361. Casamance, situation générale, 1845-1859; recensement de la population.

36. Bocandé, "Notes sur La Guinée Portugaise ou Sénégambie méridionale," 57–73.

37. El Hadji Kémo Demba, interview, Sédhiou, December 6, 2003, and Fina Malang Faty and Diéli Lamine Kouyaté, November 6, 2003.

38. Group interview, Sédhiou, November 17, 2003.

39. Almamy Fossar Souané, interview, Sandiniéri, October 24, 2004; and group interview, Karantaba, October 29, 2003. Souané said the marabout's visit occurred between 1846 and 1847 during which he encountered Alpha Molo and prayed for his family's success, in exchange for their hospitality; and Ndoura's appointment as the chief of Boudhié by the French may have been a direct consequence of the marabout's prayers. See also Roche, *Histoire de La Casamance*, 176.

40. Group interview, Karantaba, October 29, 2003.

41. The existing literature includes diverse epic performances dedicated to Muslim and non-Muslim leaders in the broader Mande world. See, for example, Niane's classical translation, *Sundiata; and* Sana Camara, *The Epic of Kelefaa Saane* (Bloomington: Indiana University Press, 2010).

42. Abdou Khadr Sylla, a schoolteacher and direct descendent of Syllaba, interview, Kounayan, November 4, 2003.

43. Leary, "Islam, Politics and Colonialism," 95–104.

44. Abdou Khadr Sylla, interview, Kounayan, November 4, 2003.

45. Abdou Khadr Sylla, interview, Kounayan, November 4, 2003.

46. Custom expects newly married couples to live with the grooms' families.

47. Balla Dramé interview, Sédhiou, November 16, 2003. When I asked him why Oudoukar and Darsilamé have both claimed "ownership" of Syllaba's father up to the present day, he responded by saying this is a reminder of the impressive skills he brought with him to the Middle Casamance.

48. Balla Dramé, interview. Because Syllaba's father died while Syllaba was too young, his descendants insisted, his maternal uncles took care of him until he became a grown man.

49. David Robinson, "Revolutions in the Western Sudan," in *The History of Islam in Africa*, ed. Nehemia Levtzion and Randall L. Pouwels (Athens: Ohio University Press, 2000), 131–52.

50. Sylla, interview, Kounayan, October 2, 2003; and Almamy Fossar Souané, interview, Sédhiou, October 29, 2003. Fouta Diallon and Fouta Touba were respected centers of Islamic education in Guinea. The latter was founded by the Diakahnké scholar Karamba Gassama (Diaby) (1730–1824).

51. Group interviews, Sédhiou, November 13 and 14, 2003.

52. Mori Kéba Lamine Cissé and Youssouf Corta, interview, Sédhiou, November 20, 2003.

53. Group interview, elders, Karantaba, December 6, 2003.

54. El Hadji Manding, interview, Karantaba, October 23, 2003; and Balla Dramé, interview, Darsilamé, November 20, 2003.

55. Group interview, Karantaba, November 7, 2003; and group interview led by Yoro Touré, Ndiama, September 12, 2001. In northern Senegambia as well, Qur'anic centers like Pire, Kokki, and Louga supported Muslims' propaganda for jihād. See Jean Boulégue, "La Participation possible des centres de Pir et de Ndogal à la révolution Islamique Sénégambienne de 1673," in *Contributions à l' histoire du Sénégal*, ed. Boulégue (Paris: Karthala, 1987), 119–25.

56. Robinson, "Revolutions in the Western Sudan," 132–52.

57. Syed's *Between Jihād and History.*

58. Schaffer, *Mandinko*, 74. Perhaps his informants exaggerated these numbers to underscore the Foula's massive military contribution to the jihād.

59. Abdou Khadr Sylla, interview, Kounayan, November 4, 2003.

60. ARS, 13G 459: correspondances du commandant Pelletier au commandant supérieur of Gorée entre Janvier et Décembre 1843.

61. Faty, interview, Sédhiou, October 17, 2003.

62. Mori Kéba Cissé and Youssouf Corta, Sédhiou, November 20, 2003.

63. Ibrahima Kékoye Konté , interview, Dioudoubou, May 5, 2005.

64. Imam Kémo Demba, interview, Sédhiou, December 3, 2003.

65. Imam Kémo Demba, interview, Sédhiou, December 3, 2003.

66. Balla Dramé, interview, Darsilamé, November 16, 2003; Cissé Mori Kéba Lamine, interview, Sédhiou, November 20, 2003; and Corta Youssouf, Katabina, November 20, 2003. One of Dabo's descendants, Lamine Dabo, is the maternal ancestor of El Hadji Sidiyya Dramé. Sidiyya was referred to as one the richest men in the Mandinka country by the time I began fieldwork. The Mandinka thought that his wealth derived from the prayers performed for the Dabo lineage by Pakao's holy men, as requested by his ancestor shortly before his death.

67. Schaffer, "A Study of a Social Process among a Mandinko People of the Senegambia," PhD diss., University of Oxford, 1976., 157.

68. Group interview, Kounayan, November 2, 2003; and group interviews, Karantaba, September 23, 2003, and Sédhiou, September 28, 2003.

69. Balla Dramé, interview, Darsilamé, November 16, 2003; and Chief Mamadou Mansaly, Bakoum, October 20, 2003.

70. Group interviews, Karantaba, Diatouma and Kounayan, October 23, 2003, November 2, 2003; and Almamy Fossar Souané, interview, Sandiniéri, October 24, 2003.

71. Fina Kéba Dakhaba, interview, Simbandi Birassou, January 10, 2004.

72. Oral narratives insist on the fact Mandouwarians' mystical practices were minimal because Niadoumassani was convinced that the Muslim camp lacked the courage to confront him.

73. Balla Dramé, interview, Darsilamé, November 16, 2003.

74. Mamadou Dramé, interview, Sédhiou, November 18, 2003.

75. Cissé Mori Kéba Lamine, interview, Sédhiou, November 20, 2003.

76. Dakhaba Yaya, interview, Simbandi Birassou, January 10, 2004; and Fina Malang Fenda Faty, interview, Sédhiou, November 6, 2003.

77. Group interview, Sédhiou, November 20, 2003.

78. Chief Mamadou Massaly, interview, Bakoum, October 20, 2003; and El Hadji Manding, interview, Karantaba, November 7, 2003.

79. I shielded the identity of this informant at his request.

80. Almamy Fossar Souané, interview, Sandiniéri, October 29, 2003.

81. Group interviews, Kounayan, November 6, 2003, and Sédhiou, October 29, 2003.

82. Abdou Khadr Sylla, interview, Kounayan, November 4, 2003.

83. Koubayo is an aquatic plant with large leaves resembling those of the pumpkin. This powerful source of vitamins generally grows in unsalted waters. Women wash, pound, and transform the grain into delicious couscous. See Dakhaba Yaya, interview, Simbandi Birassou, January 10, 2004; and Almamy Fossar Souané, Sandiniéri, October 24, 2003.

84. Almamy Fossar Souané, interview, Sandinieri, October 29, 2003.

85. Anonymous informant, interview, Sédhiou, December 22, 2003. At the beginning of the interview, he said: "I would not wish my children to have problems with their neighbors because of something I said in the past, and I hope you would respect that."

86. Anonymous source, Sédhiou, September 11, 2003. Some apparently well-informed individuals refused to recall this awful episode of their common past, arguing that they did not want to hurt their neighbors' feelings. Those who agreed to do so required that their identities be kept under seal.

87. Cissé Mori Kéba Lamine, interview, Sédhiou, November 20, 2003; Corta Youssouf, Katabina, November 20, 2003; Filidjié Mané, interview, Sédhiou, November 27, 2003; and Imam Demba of Sonkoudou, interview, Sédhiou, December 3, 2003.

88. Sylla, Kéba Dinding Cissé, and Boubacar Cissé, interview, Kounayan, November 3, 2003. All men are close relatives and belong to Kounayan's Cissé clerical lineage.

89. Malang Fenda Faty and Diéli Lamine Kouyaté, Sédhiou, November 6, 2003.

90. Group interview, Karantaba, October 23, 2003.

91. Like the Mandinka, the Diola used fire as a military weapon against the Bainounk of Takou and Bibira in the district of Yacine. The same is true for the French when they launched their deadly assaults against Fodé Kaba Doumbouya in Médina. See Roche, *Histoire de La Casamance*, 151.

92. ARS, 13 G 300: rapport du commandant de Gorée au gouverneur du Sénégal; chef du poste de Sédhiou confére avec le mansa (respect des traités de 1838); massacre des animistes par les musulmans, 9 avril 1843.

93. ARS, 1G 193: notice historique sur le Poste de Sédhiou de 1838 à 1883.

94. ARS, I G 193: notice historique sur le Poste de Sédhiou de 1838 à 1883.

95. ARS, 13 G 300: correspondance du commandant de Gorée au governeur du Sénégal.

96. African dealers denounced the unfair practices by the fort and the European trading houses. For instance, the Compagnie de Galam often cheated Africans, augmenting its profit margins with false measurement instruments. Written and oral sources agree that mutual trust, equity, and social justice were nonexistent in these exchanges, which only benefited Europeans. Group interview, Sédhiou, December 6, 2003. See also ANS, 4 B 8: les commandants particuliers de Gorée avec les gouverneurs, 1835-57).

97. ARS 1G 193: Notice historique sur le Poste de Sédhiou de 1838 à 1883.

98. ARS, B 432: lettre 55 du gouverneur du Sénégal au commandant du Poste de Séju, March 10, 1940.

99. Quinn, *The Mandingo Kingdoms of Senegambia*, 115. Serigne Maaba, who originated in Nioro in the Rip region of Senegal, was a revered representative of the Tidjaniyya. He developed close relationships with eminent Wolof scholars and rulers, including Mame Mor Anta Sally Mbacké, Cheikh Amadou Bamba's father, and Damel Lat Dior Diop of Kayor. Serigne Maba died in 1867 at the battle of Somb, which he fought alongside Lat Dior against Koumba Ndofféne Diouf, the ruler of Sine. See Glover, *Sufism and Jihad in Modern Senegal*, 65–69. According to David Skinner, the social movements that occurred in the Gambian River region in the second half of the nineteenth century should not be categorized as "jihãds," because territorial conquests and economic gains, not the propagation of Islam, were the primary motivations of those movements. See David Skinner, *States, Conflict and Islam: A Reconsideration of Jihãd in the Gambia River Region, 1850–1900*, Working Papers 2 (Evanston, IL: PAS/ISITA, 2017).

100. ARS, 13 G 300: correspondance du commandant de Gorée au gouverneur du Sénégal in 1859.

101. ARS, 4B 12: correspondances du commandant Dagorne au gouverneur du Sénégal, 9 avril et June 28 juin, 1843.

102. ARS, 4 B 12: correspondances de Dagorne: lettre 50 du 31 mars 1843.

103. ARS, 13G 459: correspondance du commandant Pelletier au gouverneur du Sénégal, 14 Juillet 1943; and Fina Kéba Dahaba, interview, Sédhiou, October 11, 2003.

104. ARS, 13 G 459: rapport du commandant de Séju au commandant particulier de Gorée, 2 mars 1943.

105. Group interview, Bakoum, December 2, 2003.

106. ARS, 4B 12: correspondances de Dagorne; commandant du fort de Séju au gouverneur du Sénégal, 9 avril et 28 juin, 1843.

107. Abdou Khadr Sylla, interview, November 4, 2003. If welcoming strangers was a widespread hallmark of hospitality across the Casamance for generations, he said, up until the recent past, Sylla clerics and other Muslim lineages who took part in this jihãd were denied "this right of hospitality" in some Bainounk communities.

108. ARS, B 434: lettres 59 et 62, 7 Septembre et 1 novembre 1, 1844; and 4 B 12: correspondance entre Dagorne et le gouverneur du Sénégal.

109. ARS, 13 G 300: rapport du commandant de Gorée au gouverneur du Sénégal.

110. ARS, 13 G 459: lettres adressées par le commandant de Séju au commandant particulier de Gorée, janvier-décembre 1843.

111. Group interviews, Darsilamé, October 17, 2003, and Karantaba, October 23 and November 11, 2003.

112. ARS, 4B13: lettre 72 de Dagorne au gouverneur du Sénégal, 6 novembre 1844.

113. ARS, 4 B 13: correspondances 35, 48, 57, 59 et 62 du commandant Dagorne du gouverneur au Sénégal, août 1844.

114. ARS, 3B 57: correspondances du commandant Thomas au gouverneur of Sénégal, 12 Octobre 1844.

115. ARS, 3 B 57.

116. ARS, 4B14: lettre 30, de Dagorne au gouverneur du Sénégal; lettre sur les pillages des magasins de la Maison Maurel & Prom, 9 mars 1845.

117. ARS, 4 B 16: lettre 55, du commandant Aumont au gouverneur du Sénégal, 15 juin, 1850.

118. ARS, 4 B 16: Lettre 60, 13 juillet 1850.

119. ARS, 1 G 193: Notice historique sur le Poste de Sédhiou de 1838 à 1883.

120. Quinn, *The Mandingo Kingdoms of Senegambia*,141–42.

121. ARS, 13 G 361: croquis sue le cours de la Casamance, 17 novembre 1858.

122. The French may have followed the lead of the Wolof, who have long referred to the Soninké as "*sarakholé*," and to the Mandinka as "*socé*."

123. Charles Bour, *Les Dépendances du Sénégal: Géographie, Population, Productions, Colonisation* (Paris: Librairie militaire de Baudouin et Cie, 1885), 21. For him, "these hardworking migrants" were present in the Casamance in 1825, but their number increased substantially by the 1860s.

124. François Manchuelle, *Willing Migrants: Soninke Labor Diasporas, 1848–1960* (Athens: Ohio University Press, 1977), 54–58.

125. Kenneth Swindell and Alieu Jeng, *Migrants, Credit and Climate: The Gambian Groundnut Trade, 1834–1934* (Boston: Brill, 2006), 40–67.

126. Swindell and Jeng, *Migrants, Credit and Climate.*

127. ARS, 13 G 361: recensement de la population placée sous la protection du fort de Séju.

128. ARS, 13 G 361: croquis sur le cours de la Casamance. Séju et dépendances, habitants et commerce.

129. ARS, 13G 361: Casamance, situation générale.

130. See Kenneth Swindell and Alieu Jeng (who cited Roche), *Migrants, Credit and Climate: The Gambian Groundnut Trade, 1834–1934* (Leiden, Brill, 2006), 48. These statistics resulted from a census sponsored by the fort in 1857 after the departure of the Bainounk. This shows that at this moment the Sarakholé were the second demographic group after the Mandinka, but other ethnic groups present in Sédhiou, including some Mandiago migrants from Guinea-Bissau. If the census was more inclusive by considering all the other population groups living in the wider Sédhiou land area at this time, these figures would probably be different.

131. Aristide Vallon, "La Casamance, Dépendance du Sénégal," *Revue maritime coloniale,* 6, Octobre-Décembre (Paris, 1862): 456–74.

132. Group interview, Sédhiou, December 13 and 17, 2003; and Roche, *Histoire de La Casamance,* 118.

133. The French policy to resettle the Sarakholé in Sédhiou was a generally short-lived one, but I found a few lineages of Sarakholé origin across town: Konaté, Sylla, Kanouté, Kanté, and Sidibé. Many retraced their ancestral origin back to "*tilibo,*" which means Mali or the towns of southeastern Senegal like Tamba, Bakel, and Kidira.

134. Ngaïdé, *L'esclave, le colon et le marabout,* 170–82.

135. Quinn, *The Mandinko Kingdoms of Senegambia,* 134.

136. ARS, 3 B 58: lettre 46, 20 Septembre, 1849: prétentions Portugaises en Casamance; and 2 B 30, Lettre 25, réclamations des négociants Anglais établis à Séju, 20 janvier, 1950.

137. ARS, 13 G 300: rapport du commandant de Gorée au gouverneur du Sénégal; and 13 G 361: croquis sur le cours de la Casamance.

138. Leary, "Islam, Politics and Colonialism," 77.

139. Group interview, Sédhiou, October 29, 2003.

140. ARS, 13 G 300: rapport du commandant de Gorée au gouverneur du Sénégal.

141. ARS, 13 G 4: traité signé avec Ndura, 25 mai, 1849. This apparent confusion was part of the French colonial psychology, regardless of the geographic and historical contexts. French officials' modus operandi included signing treaties with Africans in the name of the ideals of the French Republic (Liberty, Equality and Fraternity), only to reinterpret or modify these in conformity with their colonial agenda. In Southern Senegal, many such treaties ranged from "the right of commerce," "reconnaissance of sovereignty," and "the right to create establishments on riverbanks," to pacts of non-aggression," and "assurance of tranquility," to mention but a few. Because of space constraints, I do not provide here a detailed analysis of the letter and spirit of many such treaties between the French and Muslim leaders in this region. For more information see ANS: 13 G 461, which includes concrete examples concerning Souna, Pakao, Yacine and Boudhié.

142. Roche, *Histoire de la Casamance,* 90.

143. ARS, 13 G 4: traité de paix entre la République de France et la République de Boudhié, 4 février, 1850. Following Ndoura's dismissal as Boudhié's chief, other local authorities like "Alaisanou," Mour Dramé, Samba Aissata Diallo, and Ndoura's own son, Sounkari Yéri Kamara assumed the same function; their refusal bow to political pressure prevented them from having good, longlasting working relationships with the fort's authorities.

144. Malang Faty and Diéli Lamine Kouyaté, interview, Sédhiou, November 6, 2003; and Imam Demba, interview, Sédhiou, December 3, 2003.

145. Group interview, Sédhiou, November 30, 2003.

146. ARS, 1G 193: notice historique sur le Poste de Sédhiou de 1838 à 1883.

147. ARS, 13 G 4: traité de Paix conclu entre la République de France et la Répub-

lique du Bujé; ARS, 4 B 33: correspondance entre le commandant particulier de Gorée et le commandant de Séju..

148. ARS, 13 G 4: traités entre la France et les chefs de Kagnout, 25 mars, 1951.

149. ARS, 13 G 361: situation générale en Casamance de 1845 à 1859. Laprade succeeded Admiral Jean Bernard Jauréguibérry (1815–87) as governor of Senegal and spent twenty years in the colony before dying of cholera in Saint Louis. Governor Faidherbe helped lay the groundwork for the consolidation of the French colonial state in West Africa under the second French empire (1852–70).

150. I conducted group interviews on this issue in Sédhiou and Karantaba on November 17 and 24, 2003. It is hard to have a clear idea of these human casualties based on oral and written sources. But Almamy Fossar Souané persisted that these would have been much more devastating, if Mandinka clerics had not formulated sophisticated prayers designed to restrict the scope and magnitude of French military assaults.

151. ARS, 13 G 193: historique de Sédhiou.

152. Among the businesses that dominated the local economy in the Sédhiou land area were the Compagnie Française de l'Afrique de l'Ouest (CFAO), the Société Commerciale de l'Ouest Africain (SCOA), and the Compagnie Niger-France. See Catherine Boone, *Merchant Capital and the Roots of State Power in Senegal (1930–1985)* (Cambridge: Cambridge University Press, 1992); and Barrows Leland, "Faidherbe and Senegal: A Critical Discussion," *African Studies Review* 19, no. 1 (April 1976): 95–117.

153. Group interview, Sédhiou, November 13, 2003 and November 22, 2003; see also Schaffer, "A Study of Social Process Among a Mandinko People of the Senegambia," 210–12.

154. This legislation was authorized on August 9, 1861. See ANS, 3 B 83: correspondance entre le fort de Séju et Gorée.

155. ARS. Q 32: correspondance de Félix Cros, président de la chambre économique de Gorée au commandant particulier, Février 1882. Sounkari, one of cleric Maaba's disciples, was ambitious about extending his influence in the Middle Casamance; he died before achieving his objective when his compound was burned to the ground by the troops of Commandant Alfred Doods. See ARS 13 G.371: correspondance de Dodds au gouverneur du Sénégal. 9 mars, 1882.

156. ARS. 2D 5–4: traité entre la France et les chefs du Pakao, 19 janvier 1837.

157. Building mosques, opening Qur'anic schools, and forbidding the consumption of alcoholic beverages was theoretically part of the self-appointed mission of these new actors. Ibrahima Ndiaye particularly was a Wolof cleric and a businessman who teamed up with French traders. He mobilized his disciples and attacked some Diola groups who spared their lives by escaping to The Gambia in the 1890s. See ARS. 13 G. 370: correspondance entre commandant Grenouille et le commandant de Gorée, Janvier 1888; and Leary, "Islam, Politics and Colonialism," 102–115.

158. See, for example, Bour, *Les Dépendances du Sénégal*, 18.

159. Almamy Soly, interview, Karantaba, August 17, 2001, and El Hajj Manding,

interview, Karantaba, November 4, 2003. Soly was among the first Muslim clerics who illuminated my understanding of the key transitions in Karantaba's history.

160. Barry, *Senegambia and the Atlantic Slave Trade*, 243–49.

161. De Lamothe served as governor of Senegal from 1890 to 1895.

162. Schaffer, "A Study of Social Process Among a Mandinko People of the Senegambia,"210–12.

163. Mamadou Sarr and Khadiry Barro, Sédhiou, October 17, 2003. On this occasion, Barro did the same thing as Soly when he welcomed Sarr and me to his house in Sédhiou.

164. El Hadji Manding, interview, Karantaba, November 7, 2003; and Abdou Khadr Sylla, interview, Kounayan, November 4, 2003.

## CONCLUSION

1. Brooks, *Landlords and Strangers*, 38.

2. Martin Klein, *Islam and Imperialism in Senegal: Sine Saloum, 1847–1914* (Stanford: Stanford University Press, 1968).

3. For similar case studies, see Osborn, *Our New Husbands Are Here*. As previously mentioned, the institutions of *nabaya* and *fudunyolu* she discusses helped Maninka Mori propagate Islam in precolonial Guinea; and Semley, "Kétu Identities," 97–98 and 116–17. Semley contends that Haussa scholars originally resettled outside the walls of their Kétu host communities; that despite the foreigner-native distinction designed to identify people religiously, the populace benefitted from multiple forms of assistance provided by the Haussa; and that the outcome of these interactions was intermarriage between the two groups.

4. Jean Louis Triaud, "Islam in Africa under French Colonial Rule," in *The History of Islam in Africa*, ed. Nehemia Levtzion and Randall L. Pouwels (Athens: Ohio University Press, 2000), 169–88; David Robinson, *Paths of Accommodation*, and "France as a Muslim Power in West Africa," *Africa Today* 46, nos. 3–4 (Summer–Autumn 1999): 105–27.

5. Ruffié (1921–2004) was a French geneticist and biologist. President Senghor made this statement during an interview with Demba Dieng on Radio Senegal in the early 1980s; and in March 19, 1984, he said the same thing during his inauguration as the first African elected to the prestigious French Academy.

6. Many colleagues, students, or neighbors of mine categorized themselves ethnically as "half and half," implying their parents or grandparents belonged from two different ethnicities.

7. Some informants confirmed the importance of this dispersal for Bainounk groups who wanted to create a new identity for themselves.

8. Cobbinah, "The Casamance as an Area of Intense Language Contact,", 175–202. When Lüpke asked the Bainounk if they consider their ability to speak several languages

a gift, 96 percent of them agreed. When asked if they should renounce their mother tongue and only speak Mandingo or Diola, 96 percent or more said no. See Lüpke , "Language and Identity Flux," 159–68. While acknowledging the usefulness of linguistic plurality, Bainounk groups living between the Casamance and Guinea-Bissau now want to revive their heritage. I totally agree with Lüpke that "the linguistic diversity prevailing in the Casamance today and the legacy of colonial rule" have so far rendered this goal difficult to accomplish.

9. Group interviews, Sédhiou, October 31, and Simbandi Birassou, December 3, 2003.

10. Some informants openly talked about their "pride of being Bainounk" before vigorously denouncing others who lack the courage to do the same as "cowards." Amadou Fall spoke about this personal pride, saying, "both Robert Sagna and I descended from the Bainounk through our mothers." See Pape Cissokho, "Premier habitant de la Casamance." Fall is a bright scholar and historian whose public lectures have thrown light on many complicated dimensions of Bainounk history and culture. Sagna, an engineer, served as the mayor of Ziguinchor and a minister in Senegal (1980–2000).

11. El Hadji Khadiry Barro, interview, Sédhiou, November 13, 2003, and Almamy Fossar Souané, interview, Sédhiou, November 19, 2003.

12. Notwithstanding the propagation of Islamic knowledge across time and space, Karantaba has remained a fountainhead of Qur'anic education in southern Senegambia thanks to the dedication of old local schools such as Dar al-Qur'an and Dar al-qayri.

13. I attended the festival more than once during the month of May, meaning right before the rainy season, when the muddy terrain of the Middle Casamance causes serious transportation problems.

14. The enthusiasm exhibited by pilgrims captured my imagination particularly in 1994 and 1995, when I was hosted at the festival by the late Barrodi Bâ; he was the principal of the only elementary school existing in Karantaba at this moment.

15. In 2009, one of these pilgrims was Almamy Soussou Kamara, a Guinean trader who attended the festival many times.

16. Mbacké, *Sufism and Religious Brotherhoods in Senegal*, 15–22; Leary, "Islam, Politics and Colonialism,"214–16; and Paul Marty, "Cherif Younouss de Casamance," *Revue du Monde Musulman* (Paris, 1915): 431–69.

17. Unlike the other chérif, Younouss emigrated from Chad and sojourned in some countries before Malick Mané welcomed him to Bagnére, a small village located near Sédhiou, between the late nineteenth and early twentieth centuries. Paul Marty painted a vilifying picture of Chérif Younouss by caricaturing him as more a merchant than a scholar, given what he called "his lack of knowledge of Arabic." See Marty, "Cherif Younuss de Casamance," 431–69, and Paul Marty, *Etudes de l' Islam au Sénégal: Les Personnes*, book 1 (Paris: Ernest Leroux, 1917), 395–401. Informants rejected outright Marty's assertion, calling Chérif Younouss not solely a trader but also a dynamic Muslim

leader. Thanks to his popularity and Islamic knowledge, they insisted, he helped many individuals become Muslims and promote Qur'anic education in southern Senegambia.

18. Marty, "Cherif Younouss," 431–69.

19. Before settling among the Diola in the Lower Casamance, Chérif Makhfouss lived in Binako in the Middle Casamance, where French officials allocated him a large land concession. See ARS, 13 G. 513: objet de la correspondance de Paul Brocard; commandant de Sédhiou au gouverneur du Sénégal, 1908.

20. Around 1827, the marabout Khah immigrated to Niumi in The Gambia where he established the Qur'anic school of Medina Shaykh Maas; and the marabout Cherno founded Medina Bulofuto in the late 1890s. They devoted both their time and energy to the diffusion of Islamic values in The Gambia. Some scholars have retraced the road maps of these Foula scholars whose missionary activities are still relatively unknown, for the same reasons noted above. See Balla S. K. Saho, "Appropriation of Islam in a Gambian Village: Life and Times of Shaykh Maas Khah, 1827–1936,"*African Studies Quarterly* 12 (2010): 1–21, and Assan Sarr, "Islam, Spirits, and the History of a Toranka Cleric in The Gambia, c. 1890–1990," presented at the Annual Conference of the African Studies Association San Diego, November 2015.

21. Fina Fenda Faty, interview, Sédhiou, October 29, 2003; and Fodé Almamy Fossar Souané, interview, Sédhiou, October 31, 2003.

22. Group interviews, Sédhiou, November 19 and 22, 2003. A few individuals whose families have maintained close ties with the Bidan centers insisted that these rivalries never disappeared, despite the mediation of the French who wanted to profit from their close affinities with Chérif Younouss. See also Fatou Gassama, "Immigration Sénégalaise en France de 1914 á 1993: Etude de L' Implantation et du Rôle des Confréries Musulmanes," thése de doctorat d' histoire Université Charles De Gaulle (Lille), 2005, 36. One way Bidan clerics attempted to resolve their antagonistic relations was through matrimonial diplomacy. For example, during this reconciliation process Chérif Sidy proposed to marry his daughter, Fanta Aidara, to Chérif Makhfouss, who gladly accepted. This arrangement, which likely occurred in 1909, helped lessen tensions between the two groups. See Sagna, *La Casamance, l'Islam et La France*, 278 and 246–83. He explains well the itineraries and mystical prowess of these clerics, as well as their internal divisions tensions.

23. Diaby Gassama, interview, Sédhiou, November 29, 2003. Diaby and Gassama are interchangeable patronyms among the Diakhanké.

24. This statement came from Makhily Gassama, a former diplomat, poet, writer, and one of Mbaal Fodé Diaby's sons. He made this remark during an interview with Papa Moussa Samba entitled "Makhily Gassama: L'Africain," *Journal Xalima.com*, April 13, 2008. For recent insights on the roots of Diabi-Gassama clerics and their offshoots, see Sanneh, *Beyond Jihad*, 156–65.

25. Fodé Fossar Souané, interview, Sédhiou, January 5, 2004. Those who promoted the Diakhanké clerical dispersal helped establish many new communities in

West Africa. See Thomas Hunter, "The Jabi Ta'rikhs: Their Significance in West African Islam," *International Journal of African Historical Studies* 9, no. 3 (1976): 435–57; and Pierre Smith, "Les Diakhanké: Histoire d'une Dispersion," *Cahier du Centre de Recherche Anthropologique* 8, no. 3 (1965): 231–62.

26. This pious Tidjani scholar, who migrated from Thikité, a Foula community located in the Senegal River valley region, established Médina Gounass in the Upper Casamance. Until his death, he supported the creation of Muslim villages, the training of Qur'anic teachers, and the construction of mosques. See Cheikh Bâ, "Un Type de Conquête Pionniére en Haute Casamance (Senegal)," thése de doctorat de géographie, Sorbonne, Université de Paris, 1964; Abderrahmane Ngaïdé, "Les marabouts face à la modernité: Le dental de Madina Gounass á l'épreuve," in *Le Sénégal Contemporain*, ed. Momar Coumba Diop (Paris: Karthala, 2002), 617–52; and Yaya Wane, "Ceerno Muhamadu Sayed Baa: Le soufisme Integral de Medina Gunaas (Senegal)," *Cahiers d'études Africaines* 14, no. 56 (1974): 67–98.

27. Fina Malang Fata, interview, Sédhiou, November 6, 2003.

28. Fina Kéba Dakhaba, interview, Simbandi Birassou, January 10, 2004.

29. Mansaly Mamadou, interview, Bakoum, October 20, 2003.

30. Arreté 001941 of March 27, 2003 by the Ministry of Culture of Senegal. This same year, Karantaba also became the headquarters (*chef lieu*, French) of the Rural Community of Karantaba. During my last visit to the Casamance, I was convinced that this old landmark was on the verge of collapsing; and that Karantabans understood this growing existential threat. To satisfy the needs of the ever-increasing crowds of people who worship together at the mosque, in the early 2000s, local authorities "attached," as they liked to say, a bigger mosque to the original one, without modifying its original layout. The new mosque is equipped with fans, rugs, running water, clocks, electricity, and nicely painted but undecorated walls.

31. I agree with Mauro Nobili and Richard Reid that scholars must pay closer attention to the histories of Muslim clerical communities in the precolonial era, instead of just giving them "tangential attention." See Nobili (who cited Reid), "Reinterpreting the Role of Muslims in the West African Middle Ages."

## GLOSSARY OF FOREIGN TERMS

*Adansonia digitata*: scientific name of the baobab tree
*abai nounko* (Mandingo): those pushed away by the Mandinka
*abalanto* (Mandingo): those who refused cultural domination by the Mandinka
*afan gureng* (Diola): grandfathers of the forests in the Diola country
*ahadith* (sing. *hadith*, Arabic): Prophet Muhammad's sayings and deeds
*ajami* (Arabic): refers here to African languages written with the Arabic script
*al arbiyya* (Arabic): Wednesday
*al khulafa al-raashidoon* (Arabic): Prophet Muhammad's four caliphs
*alama* (Balante): chiefs
*al-baqara* (Arabic): Qur'anic chapter
*al-fatiyya* (Arabic): opening chapter of the Qur'an
*ali téli bé baa Kaa bili killing* (Mandingo): You are all members of the same family!
*al-jumuah* (Arabic): Friday congregational prayer
*alkaliyya* (Mandingo): alkaly's office
*alkaly* (Mandingo): village chief
*allah killing sotota* (Mandingo): God is one, unique; there is no God but God
*allahu akbar* (Arabic): God is great!
*allah long* (Mandingo): knowing God
*allouwwa* (Mandinka): wooden tablet used in Qur'anic school
*almamiyya* (Mandingo): imam's office
*almamy* (Mandingo): religious leader; corruption of al-imam (Arabic)
*almamy doko* (Mandingo): the stick carried by the almamy
*al-mulk* (Arabic): secular power
*al-qafirun* (Arabic): unbelievers
*arasa*: Balante group
*arfang* (Mandingo): Qur'anic schoolteacher
*asanthene* (Ashanti): king

*asi nine core* (Bainounk): no more place to go!
*associationisme* (French): means here the act of associating God with others, seen here as a big sin in Islam
*atenga bilenté* (Balante): leader of young male warriors
*ayatul kursiyyu* (Arabic): powerful Qur'anic verse in al-baqara
*ayya* (plural, *ayyat*, Arabic): Qur'anic verse, paragraph
*azan* (Arabic): call to prayer, happens before each of the five daily prayers
*ba* (Mandingo): great
*ba bilenté* (Balante): we the men
*ba, sin, mimara* (Arabic): letters of the Arabic alphabet
*baana saalo* (Mandingo): celebration of the Day of Sacrifice
*bainounko* (Mandingo): those pushed away by the Mandinka
*balafon* (Balante): sacred musical instrument, powerful symbol of Balante cultural heritage
*balantakounda* (Mandingo): Balante homeland in the Middle Casamance
*banko tiyyol* (Mandingo): landowners
*bantang* (Mandinka): type of tree
*bantang ba* (Mandingo): public square, palaver tree
*baraka* (Arabic): divine blessing
*baring* (Mandingo): uncle
*barkantang* (Mandingo): lazy
*barro mansiola* (Mandingo): Barro did not come to stay!
*batin* (Arabic): hidden knowledge
*bato* (Mandingo): mystical investigation
*baytil mahdis* (Arabic): Jerusalem
*bida* (Arabic): useless innovation, sin
*bilenté* (Balante): the men
*bideu kamil*: (Wolof): writing the entire Qur'an, exclusively through memorization
*bixirin* (Wolof): preacher, marabout, cleric
*boisé* (Balante): sacred groves
*bolong* (Mandingo): small river tributary, body of water
*boukout* (Diola): male circumcision
*boulsafé* (Mandingo): ritual marking beginning of Qur'anic schooling
*bounia* (Mandingo): hospitality
*bourba* (Wolof): royal title in Djolof
*bourouku chi or sikan* (Bainounk): red, deadly poison
*cadi* (Arabic): judge
*casa mansa* (Mandingo): title for king of Casa

*chegui choran* (Portuguese deformation): We arrive, they cry!
*cheikh* (shaykh, Wolof): prestigious title, venerated cleric
*chéfferies* (French): chiefdoms
*chef-lieu* (French): administrative center, capital, headquarter
*chérif* (Arabic deformation of Sharif, Wolof): descendant of Prophet Muhammad
*chinas* (Bainounk): supernatural spirits
*cola cordifolia:* scientific name of the taabo tree
*daara* (Arabic): Qur'anic school
*daka* (Foula): spiritual retreat
*dar al-Islam* (Arabic): Muslim land
*dar al-kafur* (Arabic): non-Muslim land
*dar al-qayri* (Arabic): Qur'anic school in Karantaba
*dar al-Qur'an* (Arabic): Qur'anic school in Karantaba
*diambadon* (Mandingo): "dance of leaves," public festival
*dekkou serigne* (Wolof): clerical homeland, where many Muslims live
*dénianké* (Foula): non-Muslim aristocracy in northern Senegal
*dentourao* (Foula): joking relationship
*dhu al-hijjah* (Arabic): last month of the Islamic lunar calendar
*dialan* (Mandingo): supernatural spirits, occult forces
*diallaloo* (Mandingo): plural of diéli
*dianatoul mouslimin* (Mandingo): Muslim paradise, name of Dianaba
*diatti yoo* (Mandingo): host, welcomer
*diéballou* (Wolof): submission, allegiance to a Muslim cleric
*diébé silla* (Bainounk): intermarriage, cross-cousin marriage
*diéli* (Mandingo): musician, storyteller, oral historian, bard
*diéliyya* (Mandingo): the diéli's profession
*dinoh* (Bainounk): supreme being
*dion* (Mandingo): slave
*dioula* (Mandingo): merchant
*djibé silla* (Bainounk): cross-cousin marriage
*dohorty guity* (Balante): elders' council
*dolo* (Mandingo): liquor, palm wine
*domorolaaba* (Mandingo): greedy person
*doua* (Mandingo): homemade ink
*doumassou* (Mandingo): lower village
*eid al-adha* (Arabic): celebration of the Day of Sacrifice
*eid al-fitr* (Arabic): end of Ramadan celebration
*eguregu* (Igbo, Nigeria): joking relationship

*emitai* (Diola): supreme being
*fanada* (Bainounk): male circumcision
*fanho* (Mandingo): sword
*farim* (Mandingo): governor in Kaabou
*farol* (Mandingo): rice fields
*fieryi yaab* (Balante): antiwitchcraft ceremony
*fildé alfa* (Foula): congratulations!
*fina* (Mandingo): storyteller, oral historian
*finayya* (Mandingo): the fina's profession
*finoloo* (Mandingo): plural of fina
*fiqh* (Arabic): Islamic jurisprudence
*fitna* (Arabic): ordeal, painful experience
*fodé* (Mandingo): distinguished scholar
*fodéyya* (Mandingo): highest institution in Mandinka Islam
*fondiké* (Mandingo): middle-aged man
*fromager* (French): silk cotton tree
*foutouwo* (Mandingo): marriage
*fudunyolu* (Malinké): "people with whom to marry"
*fuqara*: Muslim scholars, Nilotic Sudan
*gamou* (Wolof): Muslim festival
*gaya* (Wolof): sacred village, Tidjani site of memory in Senegal
*ginol* (Mandingo): supernatural spirits
*gniansou* (Mandingo): circumcised
*gningsaaté foulo bé ba killing né ti* (Mandingo): These two villages are indivisible!
*gning allah kalla diabita* (Mandingo): praised religious expert, specialist in the art of divination
*guelewar*: Sine's last ruling dynasty
*guignadou* (Balante): calabash
*gyara salla* (Haussa): fixing a prayer
*hafizatul Qur'an* (Arabic): female who has memorized the Qur'an
*hafizul Qur'an* (Arabic): male who has memorized the Qur'an
*hajj* (Arabic): annual pilgrimage to Mecca
*hansar* (Arabic): those who welcomed Prophet Muhammad and his followers to Yathrib (Medina)
*Harakat al-fallah* (Arabic): means here an Islamic reform group in Senegal
*hijira* (Arabic): Prophet Muhammad's immigration to Yathrib (Medina)
*homo kossi* (Bainounk): dead body
*horon* (Mandingo): highest social class
*ihsan* (Arabic): perfect worship, divine connection

*ihram* (Arabic): cloth worn by Muslim pilgrims
*ijtihad* (Arabic): independent reasoning, truthful explanation of Qur'anic teachings.
*ilia dos mosquitos* (Portuguese): Island of mosquitoes
*islam confrérique* (French): Sufi Islam
*istikhara* (Arabic): nocturnal prayers, meditations
*jabaal al-noor* (Arabic): mountain of light, birthplace of Islam
*jahiliyya* (Arabic): state of ignorance
*jibril* (Arabic): archangel Gabriel
*jihad al-akbar* (Arabic): bigger jihād
*jihad al-asghaar* (Arabic): smaller jihād
*jihad fi sabil allah* (Arabic): jihād in God's way
*Jam'atou ibadou rahmane* (Arabic): means here an Islamic reform group in Senegal
*jumuah* (Arabic): congregational prayer held on Friday
*kaaba* (Arabic): Muslim holy shrine in Mecca
*kaal, gamou* (Wolof): joking relationship
*kabanla banta* (Mandingo): forest in Yacine
*kabilas* (Mandingo): extended lineages, units
*kala nala* (Wolof): congratulations!
*kalla* (Mandingo): pen, deformation of *khlam*, Arabic
*kamathara* or *tabbith* (Mandingo): mystical practice
*kamathra* (Mandingo): untouchable
*kamil* (Wolof): integral, whole copy of the Qur'an
*kan minindang* (Mandingo): turban
*kanan toro* (Bambara): I am not tired!
*kankourang* (Mandingo): sophisticated spiritual mask
*kanta mansa* (Mandingo): prominent official in Kaabou
*karamo* (Mandingo): teacher
*karamols* (sing. *karamo*, Mandingo): teachers
*karan* (Mandingo): knowledge
*karanding* (Mandingo): knowledge seeker
*karanké, farba* (Mandingo): leatherworker
*karanta* (Mandingo): firewood
*karanta-dimba* (Mandingo): Qur'anic school at night
*kawalenak diak* (Diola Casa): hospitality
*kawando* (Mandingo): Qur'anic exegesis
*kéba kaffo* (Mandingo): council of male elders
*kéno* (Mandingo): type of wood

*khaala* (Balante): supreme being
*khabrou* (Arabic deformation, Wolof): burial ground; means here mausoleum
*khalwa* (Arabic): nightly meditation, prayer, more sophisticated than istikhara
*khassida* (Wolof): Cheikh Amadou Bamba's writings
*khatim* (Wolof): mystical, esoteric writing
*khlam* (Arabic): pen
*khutbah* (Arabic): sermon given during jumuah
*kibintay* (Balante): palaver tree
*kilemba* (Swahili): equivalent of the *fodéyya*
*killing* (Mandingo): one
*kintang* (Mandingo): circumcision camp supervisor
*kinwala adiadié* (Balante): hospitality
*khaya senegalensis*: type of tree, scientific name of the *cailcédrat*
*kolong thiossan* (Mandingo): old public well
*kookh* (Sérére Saféne): supreme being
*koringo* (Mandingo): key official in Kabou
*koubayo* (Mandingo): aquatic plant
*koumpo* (Mandingo): powerful spiritual mask
*kounda* (Mandingo): family, lineage unit
*koutouboulow* (Mandingo): type of tree
*kouyanding* (Mandingo): small circumcision
*kouyamba* (Mandingo): male circumcision
*bolon* (Mandingo): small tributary of a river, body of water
*ladiamo or ladiami* (Mandingo): deformation of *ajami*, Arabic
*la guerre des marabouts* (French): Muslim clerics' war against non-Muslims in Senegambia
*la guerre des races* (French): means here inter-ethnic wars
*lançado* (Portuguese): traders, born to Portuguese fathers and African mothers
*l'économie de traite* (French): French colonial system of economic exploitation of Africans
*"la verte Casamance"* (French): the green Casamance, alludes to the region's important rainfall and agro-economic asserts
*lenko* (Mandingo): old, famous tree in Karantaba, no longer exists
*lew* (Wolof): legal, portion of land
*lountang* (Mandingo): guest, stranger, visitor
*magal* (Wolof): biggest Mourid festival
*mahr* (Arabic): dowry
*mallam* (Haussa): clerics
*mancône* (Bainounk): type of tree

*mansa* (Mandingo): king, ruler
mansakounda (Mandingo): royal quarter, town, center of secular power
*mansa naffo* (Mandingo): royal hat, symbol of political power in Kaabou
*mansaba* (Mandingo): great king
*mansaring* (Mandingo): administrators in Kabou
*marifat* (Arabic): worship
*mary-bucks* (French deformation): marabouts
*maser* (Sérére): joking relationship
*masjid al-nabawi* (Arabic): Prophet Muhammad's mosque
*mawlud* (Arabic): celebration of Prophet Muhammad's birthday
*mbepp* (Wolof): sacred tree in Touba (the Mourids' capital), no longer exists
*mboumbourou* (Balante): ritual dance, musical instrument
*métis* (French): biracial people
*mihrab* (Arabic): semicircular niche inside the mosque
*minbar* (Arabic): pulpit inside the mosque
*misero* (Mandingo): prayer room, little mosque
*mongou* (Dogon): joking relationship
*mori* (Mandingo): teacher, scholar
*morikounda* (Mandingo): clerical town, village, center of religious power
*muhajirin* (Arabic): Prophet Muhammad's early followers in Mecca
*mukhadam* (Arabic): close religious associate, right hand man
*namoo* (Mandingo): kind of tax
*nabaya* (Malinké): Welcome here!
*nasso* (Mandingo): holy water
*naw mili* (Diakhanké): the equivalent of *fodéyya*
*nawet* (Wolof): rainy season
*nawetan* (Wolof): seasonal worker
*ndiokta* (Balante): dance of male warriors
*ndjiné* (Balante): mysterious, dark forest
*niamankalaw* (Mandingo): socio-professional groups
*ninki nanka* (Mandingo): dragon
*nke, nka* (Mandingo): suffix designating a specific lineage
*nooro* (Mandingo): divine light, rendition of noor, Arabic
*nor* (Wolof): dry season
*nounol* (Mandingo): blacksmiths
*nsinadié* (Mandingo): We will see!
*nter bilenté* (Balante): female leader
*nûn* (Bainounk): possible etymology of Bainounk
*nyancho* (Mandingo): honorable title for warrior

*oudiahére* (Bainounk): We, the hospitable people!
*ummah* (Arabic): the community of Muslims
*pangols* (Sérére): supernatural spirits
*penthie* (Wolof): public square
*puissance musulmane* (French): means here France ruling over African Muslim populations
*Pakao al-korano* or *Pakao al-qitabo* (Mandingo): Pakao's holy book
*qibla* (Arabic): Kaaba's direction during prayer
*rasul* (Arabic): God's messenger, prophet
*saabbah* (Arabic): caliph, successor of Prophet Muhammad
*salaf* (Arabic): ancestors, original generation of Muslims
*salat* (Arabic): prayer, one of the five Islamic pillars
*salylinko* (Mandingo): forest in Yacine
*sanakou* (Foula): banter
*sanankouyya* (Bambara): banter
*sanawwo, sanoyya* (Mandingo): joking relationship
*sano* (Mandingo): joking partner
*sanoma ké* (Mandingo): son of one's mother's brother, male cousin
*sanoma mousso* (Mandingo): daughter of one's father's sister, female cousin
*santassou* (Mandingo): upper village
*sapé* (Wolof): line formed by Muslims during prayer
*saté kourala* (Mandingo): village founders
*saté tiyyol* (Mandingo): village owners
*sawn* (Arabic): fasting, one of the five Islamic pillars
*serigne faakhtaal* (Wolof): clerical class
*serigne lamb* (Wolof): clerical class, Muslim scholar
*shahada* (Arabic): profession of faith
*sharia* (Arabic): Islamic law
*shirk* (Arabic): sin by associating God with others
*si dié* (Mandingo): Sit right there!
*signares* (Wolof, deformation of Portuguese): special class of women in Senegambia
*silsila* (Mandingo): chain of transmission of power
*sinkiro* (Mandingo): cooking fire, metaphorically means here household life
*siro* (Mandingo): pronunciation
*soss daa* (Wolof): harvesting ink
*soukouwo* (Mandingo): reading, recital of the Qur'an
*sounkar saalo* (Mandingo): celebration of the end of Ramadan
*sounkaro* (Mandingo): Ramadan; from soun (fasting) and karo (the moon)

*soutou* (Mandingo): dark, deep forest
*suf* (Arabic): woolen cloth
*sunna* (Arabic): prophetic tradition
*sura* (Arabic): Qur'anic chapter
*sura al-alaq* (Arabic): Qur'anic chapter
*sura al-jummah* (Arabic): Qur'anic chapter
*sura al-maidah* (Arabic): Qur'anic chapter
*taabo* (Mandingo): sacred tree, etymology of Karantaba, no longer exists
*tafsir* (Arabic): Qur'anic interpretation, explanation
*takhan matt* (Wolof): collecting firewood
*takkou deune* (Wolof): metaphorically means here compensation, punitive damage, part of joking relationship
*talibé* (deformation of *talib*, Arabic): student
*tang* (Mandingo): ten
*tarbiyyou* (Wolof): corruption from Arabic *tarbiyya*, dedication to a Muslim cleric
*tarikh* (Arabic): book
*tariqa* (Arabic): Sufi order
*tasavinyruivisro* (Ewe, Ghana): interward marriage
*tassawuf* (Arabic): Islam's mystical branch
*téranga* (Wolof): hospitality
*tiéddo* (Wolof): ruling class, unbeliever
*tiéddo kanama diobang* (Mandingo): Non-Muslim; unbeliever, do not finish my millet!
*tilibo* (Mandingo): east
*tilidji* (Mandingo): west
*tiombogne* (Wolof): hidden system of writing
*toubabo* (Mandingo): white man
*toubnan* (Arabic, Wolof): al-din's political movement
*tounka* (Soninké): king in pre-Almoravid Ghana
*tourouban kélo* (Mandingo): Kaabou–Fouta Diallon war
*wali* (Arabic): holy man
*waliollou* (Mandingo): holy men
*walla* (Mandingo, plural, *wallal*): Qur'anic wooden tablet, comes from *allouwwa*, Arabic
*wandane la* (Mandingo): muezzin, caller to prayer
*wasila* (Arabic): spiritual guide, religious leader
*wird* (Arabic): liturgical repetition of specific Qur'anic formula
*wotté* (Wolof): calling, Layénne festival

*wudu* (Arabic): ablutions before prayer
*yomal khiyama* (Arabic): Judgment Day
*yonou mourid* (Wolof): the Mourid way of practicing Islam
*zakaat* (Arabic): almsgiving, one of the five Islamic pillars
*ziara* (Arabic): pious visit to a sacred place or a religious figure
*zikr* (Arabic): praising God, repetition of God's multiple names

# BIBLIOGRAPHY

## SELECTED ORAL INTERVIEWS


Aidara Cheikh (Bagnére, October 22, 2003)
Barro Almamy (Karantaba, September 29, 2001)
Barro Khadiry El Hadji (Sédhiou, November 13, 2003)
Biaye Ansoumana (Sandiniéri, October 21, 2003)
Biaye Basso (Bambadion, January 9, 2009)
Biaye Khady (Kaour, October 18, 2008)
Bina Yara (Diatakounda, December 2, 2003)
Cissé Abdou Khadr (Kounayan, November 4, 2003)
Cissé Al Fouséyni (Binako, January 7, 2004)
Cissé Boubacar (Kounayan, November 2, 2003)
Cissé Dionsaba (Dianaba, September 3, 2009)
Cissé Karamo Dinding (Kounayan, October 13, 2003)
Cissé Khady (Sédhiou, August 13, 2003)
Cissé Mori Kéba Lamine (Sédhiou, November 20, 2003)
Cissé Omar (Karantaba, October 23, 2003)
Cissé Sitokoto (Dianaba, November 11, 2003)
Cissé Tida (Dianaba, October 24, 2003)
Cissé Tooribaly (Dioudoubou, August 19, 2009)
Cissé Toumbou (Dakar, September 25, 2003)
Cissé Y. Abdoulaye (Sédhiou, January 6, 2004)
Corta Youssouf (Katabina, November 20, 2003)
Dabo Boubacar (Bambadion, December 6, 2003)
Dabo Diané (Ndiama, August 3, 2009)
Dabo Fatoumata (Diatouma, August 13, 2003)
Dabo Nimbaly (Ndiama, August 13, 2009)
Dabo Younouss (Sédhiou, August 18, 2009)
Daffé El Hadji Nimbali (Sédhiou, January 4, 2004)
Dakhaba Kéba Fina (Simbandi Birassou, December 10, 2003)

Danfa Rocky (Bambadion, Dioudoubou, March 6, 2009)
Demba El Hadji Kémo (Sédhiou, December 3, 2003)
Dia Demba (Sédhiou, October 28, 2003)
Diafouné Nfally (Sédhiou, November 25, 2003.
Diallo Aminata (Sédhiou, December 3, 2003)
Diané Mariama (Kaour, October 17, 2008)
Diané Mariama (Sinkére-Bainounk, November 28, 2003)
Diassy Aida (Sédhiou, December 4, 2004)
Diatta Ibrahima (Sédhiou, October 17, 2003)
Diatta Ousmane Doua (Sédhiou, October 27, 2003)
Diatta Sanoussy (Sédhiou, November 10, 2003)
Diatta Séckou (Sédhiou, December 12, 2003)
Diba Kébouté (Karantaba, September 27, 2001)
Diba Sékouba (Karantaba, November 13, 2003)
Diédhiou Sokhna (Bignona, November 29, 2008)
Diémé Attab Cheikh (Bignona, November 29, 2008)
Diémé Tida (Bignona, November 29, 2009)
Diop Moustapha (Chicago, December 13, 2005)
Djitté Kéba (Sédhiou, December 12, 2003)
Djitté Sékou (Sédhiou, October 27, 2003)
Djitté Tamartha (Dioudoubou, March 5, 2009)
Dramé Ansoumana (Dioudoubou, August 19, 2009)
Dramé Bakari (Diatouma, November 23, 2003)
Dramé Balla (Darsilamé, November 16, 2003)
Dramé Doudou (Sédhiou, November 3, 2003)
Dramé El Hadji Manding (Karantaba, October 23, 2003)
Dramé Kissima (Karantaba, December 8, 2003)
Dramé Mansani (Diatouma, November 11, 2003)
Dramé Mourlaye (Dioudoubou, August 19, 2009)
Dramé Wandifa (Karantaba, August 12, 2009)
Dramé Yaya (Simbandi Birassou, January 10, 2004)
Faty Malang Fina Fenda (Sédhiou, November 6, 2003)
Gassama Diaby (Sédhiou, November 27, 2003)
Kamara Nato (Karantaba, October 19, 2003)
Kandé Amadou (Sédhiou, October 13, 2003)
Kéba Faty (Sédhiou, January 9, 2004)
Koma Malang Koussa (Dianaba, August 22, 2009)
Koma Nato (Dianaba, January 6, 2004)
Kombo Nano (Dioudoubou, December 17, 2009)
Konté Cissé Mariama (Ndiama, August 13, 2009)
Konté Ibrahima Kékoye (Dioudoubou, May 5, 2005)
Konté Kambo (Bambadion, March 5, 2009)

Konto Nato (Dianaba, October 24, 2003)
Kouyaté Lamine (Sédhiou, December 5, 2003)
Kouyaté Sirifo (Bounkiling, January 6, 2004)
Kouyaté Mori Kéba (Chicago, June 12, 2001)
Mané Bourama (Sédhiou August 18,2009
Mané Filidjié (Sédhiou, November 27, 2003)
Mané Ibrahima (Sédhiou, November 2, 2003)
Mané Ibrahima (Sédhiou, November 30, 2003)
Mané Walimata (Bambadion, March 5, 2009)
Manga Ansou (Sinkére-Bainounk, September 2, 2009)
Manga Maimouna (Sinkére-Bainounk, August 11, 2009)
Mansaly Mamadou (Bakoum, October 20, 2003)
Ndiaye Kane Fatou (Sédhiou, October 12, 2003)
Sadio Séckou (Brikama, November 20, 2003)
Sakho Kémo Soly (Karantaba, September 29, 2001)
Sarr Améth (Sédhiou, November 26, 2003)
Sarr Charlotte (Sédhiou, December 7, 2003)
Sarr Mamadou (Sédhiou, January 3, 2004)
Seydi Adja (Dianaba, November 11, 2003)
Seydi Fondalo El Hadji (Ndiama, August 13, 2009)
Seydi Mousa (Sédhiou, October 13, 2003)
Seydi Sana (Diatouma, November 12, 2003)
Seydi Sarba (Dianaba, January 6, 2004)
Soly Fakéba (Karantaba, November 7, 2003)
Soly Karamba El Hadji (Karantaba, September 29, 2001)
Soly Kémo (Karantaba, December 8, 2003)
Sonko Mousa (Sinkére-Bainounk, September 2, 2009)
Souané Almamy Fossar (Sandiniéri, October 24 and 29, 2003)
Souané Mamadou (Sandiniéri, October 21, 2003)
Souané Mousokéba (Dioudoubou, August 19,2009.
Sylla Abdou Khadr (Kounayan, November 2, 2003)
Touré Ibrahima (Karantaba, December 8, 2003)
Touré Yoro (Ndiama, September 12, 2003)

## ARCHIVES OF THE REPUBLIC OF SENEGAL (ARS)

1 G 23. Rapport de Bertrand Bocandé: voyage en 1850.
1 G 193: Notice historique sur le poste de Sédhiou de 1838 à 1883.
13 G 6. Les Français en Casamance en 1826.
13 G 4–9. Traité de fondation de Sédhiou: révolte des musulmans du Gabou; conventions conclues avec les chefs de Itou, 17 décembre 1839.

1 G 14. Mission Dagorne en Casamance; cession de terrains de Sédhiou; 1838, correspondance de Dagorne: Sandiniéri a brulé les cases de ses voisins.

13 G 13. Etat général du paiement des coutumes, 1783–1794.

13 G 300. Rapport du commandant de Gorée au gouverneur du Sénégal, 1859; chef du Poste de Sédhiou confére avec les mansa (respect du traité de 1838); massacre des animistes par les musulmans, 9 avril 1843.

13 G 361. Croquis sur le cours de la Casamance.

13 G 360. Casamance: politique générale du gouverneur, 1820–1842.

13 G 361. Casamance: situation générale; recensement de la population placée sous la protection du Fort de Sédhiou; musulmans contre non-musulmans, 1845–59

13 G 362. Sédhiou: Correspondance du commandant de Poste ; révoltes des Balant; relations Franco-Soninké; le début de la conquête, 1851

13 G 370. Correspondance du commandant de Gorée au gouverneur Grenouille, janvier 1888.

13 G 371. Correspondance du commandant Dodds au gouverneur du Sénégal, 9 mars 1882.

13 G 459. Correspondances de Sédhiou et Carabane au commandant particulier de Gorée, 1844–68.

13 G 461. Casamance: traités avec le souna, le Pakao, le Boudhié et le Yacine, 18 janvier 1873.

4 B 12. Arrestation par la virgie d'un négre Anglais; correspondances de Dagorne: lettre 50, du 31 mars 843.

13 G 365. Poste de Sédhiou et de Carabane: travaux et états des lieux,1858-1893

4 B 13. Lettres de Dagorne au gouverneur du Sénégal: hostilités à Sédhiou.

4 B 33. Nouveau Traité entre la France et Ndoura.

4 B 16. Lettres sur les pillages contre les mangasins de la Maison Maurel & Prom.

3 B 58. Correspondances du commandant Olivier, mars 1846.

4 B 14. Correspondances entre le chef de bataillon Caille et le gouverneur, lettre 44, du 18 Avril, 1845.

3 B 46. Correspondances entre le gouverneur et le commandant de Gorée, lettre 31, du 18 Juin 1839.

B 434. Signatures de traités avec les gens du Boudhié.

1 D 20. Affaires militaires: expéditions de Pinet-Laprade en moyenne Casamance

B 432. Correspondances des commandants de Poste Français en Casamance: Sédhiou.

2 D. Détails sur les guerres entre les mandingues, les Balantes et les Soninqués: conséquences désastreuses sur le commerce de la France.

2D 5/4. Traité signé entre la France et les chefs du Pakao, 19 janvier 1873.

1 G 193. Monographie sur Sédhiou par l'administrateur Adam

Q 32. Correspondance de Félix Cros au commandant particulier, Février 1882.

SECONDARY LITERATURE

*Alamjiri and Quranic Education*. Kaduna, Nigeria: Risbah Publishing, 2001.

Alidou, Ousseina. *Engaging Modernity: Muslim Women and the Politics of Agency in Postcolonial Niger.* Madison: University of Wisconsin Press, 2005.

Alidou, Ousseina. "Mwalim Bi Swafiya Muhashamy-Said: A Pioneer of the Integrated (Madrasa) Curriculum in Kenya and Beyond." In *Islamic Education in Africa: Writing Boards and Blackboards*, edited by Robert Launay, 195–210. Bloomington: Indiana University Press, 2016.

Ashforth, Adam. *Madumo: A Man Bewitched*. Chicago: University of Chicago Press, 2000.

Auberry, A. J. *Sufism*. London: Allen and Unwin, 1968.

Augis, Erin. "Jambaar or Jumbax-Out: How Sunnite Women Negotiate Power and Belief in Orthodox Islamic Femininity." In *New Perspectives on Islam in Senegal: Conversion, Migration, Wealth, Power and Femininity*, edited by Mamadou Diouf and Mara Leitchman, 211–33. New York: Palgrave Macmillan, 2009.

Austen, Ralph. A. *In Search of Sunjata*. Bloomington: Indiana University Press, 1999.

Ba, Alpha Oumarou. "Islam and Emancipation: Fuladu Fulani in the Kaabu Empire." In *Palgrave Handbook of Islam in Africa*, edited by Fallou Ngom, Mustapha H. Kurfi, and Toyin Folola, 117–31. London: Palgrave Macmillan, 2020.

Ba, Cheikh. "Un type de conquête pionniére en Haute Casamance (Sénégal)." Thése de doctorat de géographie, Sorbonne, 1964.

Ba, Oumar. "Le Royaume du Gabou." In "Actes du Colloque sur les Traditions Orales du Gabou," special issue, *Éthiopiques* (1980).

Babou, Cheikh A. M. "The Al-Azhar School Network: A Murid Experiment in Islamic Modernism." In *Islamic Education in Africa: Writing Boards and Blackboards*, edited by Robert Launay, 173–94. Bloomington: Indiana University Press, 2016.

Babou, Cheikh A. M. "Amadu Bamba and the Founding of the Muridiyya: The History of a Muslim Brotherhood in Senegal (1853–1913)." PhD diss., Michigan State University, 2002.

Babou, Cheikh A. M. "Educating the Murid: Theory and Practices of Education in Amadu Bamba's Thought." *Journal of Religion in Africa* 33, no. 3 (2003): 310–27.

Babou, Cheikh A. M. *Fighting the Greater Jihad: Amadou Bamba and the Founding of the Muridiyya of Senegal, 1853–1913*. Athens: Ohio University Press, 2007.

Barnes, Sandra. *Africa's Ogun*. Bloomington: Indiana University Press, 1997.

Barrows, Leland C. "Faidherbe and Senegal: A Critical Discussion." *African Studies Review* 19, no. 1 (1976): 95–117.

Barry, Boubacar. *Senegambia and the Atlantic Slave Trade*. Cambridge: Cambridge University Press, 1998.

Barth, Frederik, ed. *Ethnic Groups and Boundaries: The Social Organization of Cultural Difference*. Oslo: Bergen-Oslo Universitets, 1969.

Bathily, Abdoulaye. "The Land of Gold." *Journal of African History* 32, no. 3 (1991): 522–23.

Bathily, Abdoulaye. *Les Portes de L'or: Le Royaume du Galam (Sénégal) de L'ère Musulmane au Temps des Négriers (8th-18th).* Paris: L'Harmattan, 1989.

Batran, A. A. "The Kunta, Sidi al-Mukhtar al-Kunti, and the Office of Shaykh al-Tariqa'l Qadiriyya." In *The Cultivators of Islam*, vol. 1, edited by John Ralph Willis, 113–46. London: Frank Cass, 1979.

Battuta, Ibn. *Ibn Battuta and Black Africa.* Translated by Said Hamdun and Noël King. Princeton: Princeton University Press, 1994.

Baum, Robert M. "Crimes of the Dream World: French Trials of Diola Witches in Colonial Senegal." *International Journal of African Historical Studies* 37, no. 2 (2004): 201–28.

Baum, Robert M. *Shrines of the Slave Trade: Diola Religion and Society in Pre-colonial Senegambia.* Oxford: Oxford University Press, 1999.

Baum, Robert M. *West Africa's Women of God: Alinesitoué and the Diola Prophetic Tradition.* Bloomington: Indiana University Press, 2016.

Bendor-Samuel, John, and Rhonda L. Hartell, eds. *The Niger-Congo Languages.* Dallas: University Press of America, 1989.

Bérenger-Féraud, Laurent J. B. *Les Peuplades de La Sénégambie.* Paris: Ernest Leroux, 1879.

Berman, Bruce J. "African Ethnicity and the Politics of Knowledge." Paper presented at Mellon Sawyer Seminar, "Ethnicity in Africa: Historical, Comparative, and Contemporary Investigations," University of Michigan, Ann Arbor, December 2010.

Berry, Sara. *Chiefs Know Their Boundaries: Essay on Property, Power and the Past in Asante, 1896–1996.* Portsmouth, NH: Heinemann, 2001.

Bocandé, Bertrand E. "Notes sur La Guinée Portugaise ou Sénégambie méridionale." *Bulletin de la societé de Géographie*, serie 3, 11, (1849): 57–93.

Bocandé, Bertrand E. "Notes sur La Guinée Portugaise ou Sénégambie méridionale." *Bulletin de la societé de Géographie*, serie 3, 12 (1849): 265–350.

Bocandé, Bertrand J., Debrien Gabriel, and Y. J. Saint-Martin. "Emmanuel Bertrand Bocandé: Un Nantais en Casamance (1818–1881)." *Bulletin de l'Institut Fondamental d'Afrique Noire, Série B: Sciences humaines* 31, no. 1 (1969).

Bonate, Liazzat J. K. "Divergent Patterns of Islamic Education in Northern Mozambique: Qur'anic Schools of Angoche." In *Islamic Education in Africa: Writing Boards and Blackboards*, edited by Robert Launay, 95–118. Bloomington: Indiana University Press, 2016.

Bonner, Michael. *Jihad in Islamic History.* Princeton: Princeton University Press, 2008.

Boone, Catherine. *Merchant Capital and the Roots of State Power in Senegal (1935–1985).* Cambridge: Cambridge University Press, 1992.

Boulégue, Jean. "Aux Confins du Monde Malinké: Le Royaume du Kasa (Casamance)." Paper presented at the Congrés on Mande Studies, London School of Oriental and African Studies, July 1972.

Boulégue, Jean. *Contribution à l'histoire du Sénégal.* Paris: Afera, 1987.

Boulégue, Jean. "La Participation Possible des centres de Pir et Ndogal à la Révolution Islamique Sénégambienne de 1673." In *Contributions á l'histoire du Sénégal,* edited by Boulégue, 119–25. Paris: Karthala, 1987.

Boulégue, Jean. "La Sénégambie du Milieu du Quinziéme siécle au Début du dix septiéme siécle." Thése de doctorat, Université de Paris, 1968.

Boulégue, Jean. *Le Grand Jolof (XIII-XVI siecle).* Paris: Karthala, 1987.

Bour, Charles. *Les Dépendances du Sénégal: Géographie, Population, Commerce, Colonisation.* Paris: Librairie militaire de Baudouin et Cie, 1885.

Boyle, Helen. *Qur'anic Schools: Agents of Preservation and Change.* New York: Routledge, 2004.

Brawman, Bill. *Making Ethnic Ways: Communities and Their Transformations in Taita, Kenya, 1800–1950.* Portsmouth, NH: Heinemann, 1998.

Brenner, Louis. *Controlling Knowledge: Religion, Power, and Schooling in a West African Muslim Society.* Bloomington: Indiana University Press, 2001.

Brenner, Louis. *West African Sufi: The Religious Heritage and Spiritual Search of Cerno Bokar Salif Taal.* Berkeley: University of California Press, 1983.

Brooks, George. *Euro-Africans in West Africa: Commerce, Social Status, Gender, and Religious Observance from the Sixteenth to the Eighteenth Century.* Athens: Ohio University Press, 2003.

Brooks, George. *Landlords and Strangers: Ecology, Society, and Trade in West Africa, 1000–1630.* Boulder, CO: Westview Press, 1993.

Brooks, George. "A Provisional Historical Schema for Western Africa based on Seven Climate Periods (ca. 9000 B.C. to the 19th Century)." *Cahier d' études Africaines* 26, nos. 101–102 (1986): 43–62.

Brooks, George. "The Signares of Saint Louis and Gorée: Women Entrepreneurs in Eighteenth-Century Senegal." In *Women in Africa,* edited by Nancy J. Hafkin and Edna G. Bay, 19–44. Stanford: Stanford University Press, 1976.

Brooks, George. *Western Africa to C/1860 A.D.: A Provisional Historical Schema Based on Climatic Periods.* African Studies Program Working Papers Series 1, 97–126. Bloomington: Indiana University, 1995.

Bryant, Kelly M. D. *Education as Politics: Colonial Schooling and Political Debate in Senegal, 1850–1914.* Madison: University of Wisconsin Press, 2015.

Bühnen Stephan. "Place Names as an Historical Source: An Introduction with Examples from Southern Senegambia and Germany." *History in Africa* 19 (1992): 45–101.

Butler, Noah. "Collapsed Pluralities: Islamic Education, Learning, and Creativity in Niger." In *Islamic Education in Africa: Writing Boards and Blackboards,* edited by Robert Launay, 285–306. Bloomington: Indiana University Press, 2016.

Ca Da, Mosto. *Relation des Voyages sur la Côte Occidentale de L'Afrique, 1455–1457.* Translated by Charles Schefer. Paris: Leroux, 1895.

Camara, Sana. *The Epic of Kelefaa Saane.* Bloomington: Indiana University Press, 2010.

Cantone, Cleo. "The Shifting Space of Senegalese Mosques." In *New Perspectives on*

*Islam in Senegal: Conversion, Migration, Wealth, Power and Femininity*, edited by Mamadou Diouf and Mara Leichtman, 51–69. New York: Palgrave Macmillan, 2009.

Carmody, Brendan. *Religious Conversion: An African Perspective*. Edited by Carmody. Lusaka: Gadsden Publishers, 2015.

Carneiro, Robert L. "The Chiefdom: Precursor of the State." In *the Transition to Statehood in the World*, edited by G. D. Jones and R. R. Kantz. Cambridge: Cambridge University Press, 1981.

Carreira, Antonio, and A. M. de Meirles. "Quelques Notes sur les Mouvements Migratoires des Populations de la Province Portuguese de Guinée." *Bulletin de l'Institut Fondamental d'Afrique Noire, Série B: Sciences humaines* 3–4 (1960): 379–92.

Carrére, Frederic, and Paul Holle. *De la Sénégambia Française*. Paris: Librairie de Firmin, 1855.

Carvalho, George. "Contribution à L'histoire de la Casamance." *Afrique Documents* 91, no. 2 (1967): 131–45.

Chamberlain, John. "The Development of Islamic Education in Kano City, Nigeria with Emphasis on Legal Education in the Nineteenth and Twentieth Centuries." PhD diss., Columbia University, 1975.

Chamberlain, Michael. *Knowledge and Social Practice in Medieval Damascus, 1190–1350*. Cambridge: Cambridge University Press, 1994.

Chandra, Kanchan, ed. *Constructivist Theories of Ethnic Politics*. Oxford: Oxford University Press, 2012.

Chandra, Kanchan, ed. "How Ethnic Identity Changes." In *Constructivist Theories of Ethnic Politics*, edited by Kanchan Chandra, 132–78. Oxford: Oxford University Press, 2012.

Charpy, Jacques. "Casamance et Sénégal au Temps de La Colonisation Française." In *Pour Comprendre la Casamance*, 474–500. Dakar: Université Cheikh Anta Diop, 1994.

Cissé, Diango, and Monson Diabaté. *La Dispersion des Mandinka d'aprés un Récit du Généalogiste Kélé M. Diabaté*. Bamako: Editions Populaires du Mali, 1969.

Cissé, Nouha. "La Fin du Kaabu et les Débuts du Royaume du Fuladu." Mémoire de maîtrise (master's thesis), Université Cheikh Anta Diop, Dakar, 1978.

Cissoko, Sékéné M. "Introduction à L'histoire des Mandingues de L'Ouest." In "Colloque sur les Traditions Orales du Gabou," .special issue, *Éthiopiques* 81 (1980): 73–90.

Cissoko, Sékéné M. "La Royauté (Mansaya) chez les Mandingues Occidentaux d'aprés leurs Traditions Orales." *Bulletin de l'Institut Fondamental d'Afrique Noire, Série B: Sciences humaines* 31, no. 2 (1969): 325–38.

Cissoko, Sékéné M. "Prophéties du Roi Mandingue, Mansa Dali." *Notes Africaines* 120 (1968): 123–24.

Cissokho, Pape. "Premier Habitant de Casamance au Sénégal: Le Bainounk, le 'bienvéillant' envers l'étranger." *Journal Societé*, September 13, 2015.

Cleveland, Timothy. "Islam and the Construction of Social Identity in the Nineteenth-Century Sahara." *Journal of African History* 39, no. 3 (1988): 365–66.

Cobbinah, Alexander. "The Casamance as an Area of Intense Language Contact: The Case of the Bainounk of Gubaher." In "Multilingualism and Language Contact in West Africa," special issue, *Journal of Language Contact and Discourse* 3 (2010): 175–202.

Colvin, Lucie G. "The Shaykh's Men: Religion and Power in Senegambian Islam." In *Rural and Urban in West Africa*, edited by Nehemia Levtzion and Humphrey J. Fisher, 55–65. Boulder, CO: Lynne Rienner, 1987.

Conrad, David. *Sunjata, a West African Epic of the Mande Peoples*. Narrated by Djanka Tassey Condé and translated by Conrad. Indianapolis: Hackett, 2004.

Coquery-Vidrovitch, Cathérine. *The History of African Cities South of the Sahara: From the Origins to Colonization*. Translated by Mary Baker. Princeton, NJ: Markus Wiener Publishers, 2005.

Corréa Ndiaye, Génévíeve. "Etude F.C.A. ou Balante: Dialecte Ganja." *Annales de la faculté des Lettres et des Sciences Humaines* 3 (Dakar: Université Cheikh Anta Diop, 1973).

Coulon, Christian, and Odile Reveyrand. *L'Islam au Féminin: Sokhna Magat Diop, Cheikh de la Confrérie Mouride du Sénégal*. Bordeaux: Institut d' études Politiques, 1990.

Courlander, Harold. *A Treasury of African Folklore*. New York: Marlowe and Company, 1996.

Creissels, Denis, and Sékou Biaye. *Le Balante Ganja: Phonologie, Morphosyntaxe et Liste Lexicale*. Dakar: I.F.A.N., 2016.

Cronk, Lee. *From Mukogodo to Maasai: Ethnicity and Cultural Change in Kenya*. Boulder, CO: Westview, 2004.

Cultru, Proper. "Le Faux d'un Historien du Sénégal." *La Quinzaine Coloniale* (1910): 399–402.

Cultru, Proper. *Premier Voyage du Sieur la Courbe in 1685*. Paris: Libraries de la Société des Colonies Françaises, 1913.

Curtin, Philip. *Economic Change in Precolonial Africa: Senegambia in the Era of the Slave Trade*. Madison: University of Wisconsin Press, 1975.

Curtin, Philip D. "Jihad in West Africa: Early Phases and Inter-relations in Mauritania and Senegal," *Journal of African History* 12, no. 1 (1971): 11–24.

Dalby, David. "Distribution and Nomenclature of the Manding People and Their Language." In *Papers on the Manding*, edited by Carleton T. Hodge, 1–3. Bloomington: Indiana University Press, 1971.

Da Mosta, Teixeira. "Les Relations de l'Ancien Cabou avec quelques Etats voisins." Paper presented at the Colloque sur les Traditions Orales du Gabou, Dakar, May 1980.

D'Aoust, Sophie. "Ecoles Franco-arabes Publiques et Daaras Modernes au Sénégal: Hybridation des Ordres Normatifs concernant l'éducation." *Cahiers de la Recherche sur l Education et les Savoirs* (2013): 313–38.

De Benoit, Joseph Roger. *Histoire de L'église Catholique: Du Milieu du Quinziéme Siècle à l'Aube du Troisiéme Millénaire*. Paris: Karthala, 2008.

Debrien, Gabriel. "Bertrand Bocandé (1821–810): Un Nantais de Casamance." *Bulletin de l'Institut Fondamental d'Afrique Noire, Série B: Sciences humaines* 34 (1970): 440–98.

Decressac-Villagrand, Marcel. *Souvenirs du Sénégal: Lettre sur la Gambie et la Casamance.* Guéret: Imprimerie P. Amiault, 1890.

De Jong, Ferdinand. "A Joking Nation: Conflict Resolution in Senegal (Casamance)." *Canadian Journal of African Studies* 39, no. 2 (2005): 389–413.

De Jong, Ferdinand. *Masquerades of Modernity: Power and Secrecy in Casamance, Senegal.* Bloomington: Indiana University Press, 2007.

De Lespinay, Charles. "Action sur le Territoire, Marqueurs Toponymiques et Enjeux Socio-Juridiques en Casamance (Senegal)." In *Noms et Renoms*, edited by Salih Akin, 165–81. Rouen: Publications de L'Université de Rouen, 1999

Delong-Bass, Natana J. *Wahhabi Islam: From Revival and Reform to Global Jihad.* Oxford: Oxford University Press, 2004.

Diagne, Amadou Mapathé. "Contributions à L'étude des Coutumes des Balantes de Sédhiou." *Bulletin de l'Enseignement de l A.O.F.* 83 ( April–May 1933): 137–49.

Diallo, El Hadji Samba. *La Tijãniyya sénégalaise: Les métamorphoses des modéles de succession.* Paris: Publisud, 2010.

Diallo, Ibrahima. "Every Little Tree Has Its Own Bit of Shade: Qur'an-Based Literacy of the Peul Fuuta Community." *International Journal of Pedagogies and Learning* 7, no. 3 (2012): 227–38.

Diallo, Thierno. *Les Institutions Politiques du Fouta-Djallon au XIXè siécle.* Dakar: Université Cheikh Anta Diop, 1972.

Diallo, Youssouf. "Identités et Relations de Plaisanteries chez les Peuls de l' ouest du Burkina Faso." *Cahier d'études Africaines* 184 (2008): 779–94.

Diatta, Oumar. *Essai sur le Destin Tumultueux d'une Région.* Paris: Karthala, 2006.

Diédhiou, Paul. *L'Identité Joola en Question (Casamance).* Paris: Karthala, 2011.

Diop, Abdoulaye B. *La Societé Wolof: Tradition et Changement: Les Systémes d' inéqualités et de Domination.* Paris: Karthala, 1981.

Diouf, Makhtar. *Sénégal: Les Ethnies et la Nation.* Paris: L'Harmattan, 1994.

Diouf, Mamadou. *Histoire du Sénégal: Le Modéle Islamo-Wolof et ses Périphéries.* Paris: Maisonnneuve & Larose, 2001.

Diouf, Mamadou. *Le Kajoor au Dix-neuviéme siécle: Pouvoir Ceddo et Conquête Coloniale.* Paris: Karthala, 1990.

Diouf, Mamadou, and Mara Leichtman, eds. *New Perspectives on Islam in Senegal: Conversion, Migration, Wealth, Power and Femininity.* New York: Palgrave Macmillan, 2009.

Diouf, Sylviane. *Servants of Allah: African Muslims Enslaved in the Americas.* New York: New York University Press, 1992.

Donelha, André. *Description de la Sierra Leone et des Rives de la Guinée et du Cap Vert (1625).* Lisbon: Junta de Investigações Científicas do Ultramar, 1977.

Dramé, Aly. "Life-cycle Celebrations in Senegal: The Balafon's Role in Early Balante Culture." *International journal of African Historical Studies* (forthcoming, 2025).

Dramé, Aly. Review of *Islam, Power and Dependency in the Gambia River Basin: Politics of Land Control, 1790–1940*, by Assan Sarr." *International Journal of African Historical Studies* 50, no. 1 (2016): 12–13.

Dramé, Aly. "From Bulsafay to Fodeyya: Qur'anic Education among Mandinka Muslims in Senegal." *Journal of Mande Studies* 13 (2014): 91–123.

Dramé, Aly. "Migration, Marriage and Ethnicity: The Early Development of Islam in Precolonial Middle Casamance." In *New Perspectives of Islam in Senegal: Conversion, Migration, Wealth, Power and Femininity*, edited by Mamadou Diouf and Mara Leichtman, 169–88. New York: Palgrave Macmillan, 2009

Dramé, Aly. "Planting the Seeds of Islam: Karantaba, a Mandinka Muslim Center in Casamance, Senegal." PhD diss., University of Illinois at Chicago, 2006.

Dramé, Djim. *L'enseignement Arabo-islamique au Sénégal: Le daara de Koki*. Paris: L'Harmattan, 2015.

Dramé, Kandioura. *Epopée de Naling Sonko.* Dakar: I.F.A.N., 1970.

Dubois, E. *Relation Historique de la Campagne du Senegal (1861): Extrait du Journal d'un Capitaine de Tirailleurs Algériens.* Blidah: Imprimerie Arnavon, 1863.

Duran, Jean B. *Voyage au Sénégal ou Mémoires Historiques, Philosophiques et Politiques sur les Découvertes, les Etablissements et le Commerce des Européans dans les Mers de L'Océan Atlantique*. Paris: Henri Agasse, 1802.

Eickelman, Dale. *Knowledge and Power in Morocco: The Education of a Twentieth-Century Notable*. Princeton: Princeton University Press, 2009.

Foulquier, Jacques. *Les Français en Casamance de 1826 à 1854: Mémoire de Diplôme d' études Supérieures*. Dakar: Université de Dakar, 1966.

Fernandes, Valentin. *Description de la Côte Occidentale d' Afrique, du Sénégal au Cap de Monte Archipels, 1500–1510*. Translated by Theodore Monod. Bissau: Centro de Estudos da Guine Portuguesa, 1951.

Ferraro, Gary. *Cultural Anthropology: An Applied Perspective*. 7th ed. Belmont, CA: Tomson Learning, 2008.

Fisher, Humphrey. "Conversion Reconsidered: Some Historical Aspects of Religious Conversion in Black Africa." *Africa* 43, no. 1 (1973).

Fisher, Humphrey. "Dreams and Conversion in Black Africa." In *Conversion to Islam*, edited by Nehemia Levtzion, 217–35. New York: Holmes and Meier, 1979.

Fisher, Humphrey. "The Horse in the Central Sudan II." *Journal of African History* 14 (1972): 355–79.

Fisher, Humphrey. "The Juggernaut's Apology: Conversion to Islam in Black Africa." *Africa* 55, no. 2 (1985): 153–73.

Fortier, Corinne. "Orality and the Transmission of Islamic Knowledge in Mauritania." In *Islamic Education in Africa*, edited by Robert Launay, 61–78. Bloomington: Indiana University Press, 2016.

Foster, Elizabeth. *Faith in Empire: Religion, Politics, and Colonial Rule in French Senegal, 1880–1940*. Stanford: Stanford University Press, 2013.

Founou-Tchuigoua, Bernard. *Fondements de L'économie de Traite au Sénégal: La Surexploitation d'une Colonie de 1880 à 1960*. Paris: Silex Editions, 1981.

Frede, Britta. "Female Muslim Scholars in Africa." In *The Palgrave Handbook of Islam in Africa*, edited by Fallou Ngom, Mustapha H. Kurfi, and Toyin Falola, 221–32. London: Palgrave Macmillan, 2020.

Fuglestad, Finn. "A Reconsideration of Haussa History before the Jihad." *Journal of African History* 19 (1978): 319–63.

Fyfe, Christopher, and V. R. Dorjahn. "Landlord and Stranger: Change in Tenancy Relations in Sierra Leone." *Journal of African History* 33, no. 3 (1962): 391–97.

Gaillard, Gerard. "Introduction." *Colloquium on the Lower Guinean Coasts*. December. Lille: University of Lille, 1997..

Gardner, Gerald B. *Witchcraft Today*. New York: Kensington Publishing, 2004.

Gassama, Fatou. "Immigration Sénégalaise en France de 1914 á 1993: Etude de L'Implantation et du Rôle des Confréries musulmanes." Thése de doctorat, Université Charles De Gaulle, 2004.

Gaucher, Joseph. *Les Débuts de l'enseignement Francophone en Afrique: Jean Dard et l école Mutuelle de Saint Louis au Sénégal*. Paris: le Livre Africain, 1968.

Geertz, Clifford, ed. *The Interpretation of Culture: Selected Essays*. New York: Basic Books, 1973.

Giesing, Cornelia, and Denis Creissels. *Les Memoires de Mala Galisa sur le Royaume Confédéré du Kaabu*. Leiden: Brill, 2017.

Giesing, Cornelia, and Valentin Vydrine. *Ta:rikh Mandinka de Bijini (Guinee-Bissau)*. Leiden: Brill, 2007.

Girard, Jean. *Genése du Pouvoir Charismatique en Basse Casamance*. Dakar: I.F.A.N., 1969.

Glover, John. "The Hope in This World and the Next: Maam Cerno and the Settlement of Darou Mousty, 1912–47." PhD diss., University of Illinois at Chicago, 2000.

Glover, John. "The Prophet Muhammad Reincarnated and His Son, Jesus: Re-centering Islam among the Layenne of Senegal." *Journal of Historical Geography* 42 (2013): 24–35.

Glover, John. *Sufism and Jihad in Modern Senegal: The Murid Order*. Rochester: University of Rochester Press, 2007.

Golbéry, Sylvian. *Fragments d'un Voyage en Afrique: fait dans les annees 1785, 86 et 87 dans les Contrees de ce continent*Book 2, 396–98. Paris: Libraires de la Nouvelle Societé des Colonies Françaises, 1802.

Gomez, Michael. *Pragmatism in the Age of the Jihad: The Precolonial State of Bundu*. Cambridge: Cambridge University Press, 1992.

Gomez-Perez, Muriel. "Un Mouvement Culturel vers l'indépendance: Le Réformisme Musulman au Senegal (1956–1960)." In *Le Temps des Marabouts,* edited by David Robinson and Jean Louis Triaud. Paris: Karthala, 1997.

Goody, Esther. *Contexts of Kinship: An Essay in the Family Sociology of the Gonja of Northern Ghana*. Cambridge: Cambridge University Press, 1973.

Goody, Jack. "The Impact of Islamic Writing on the Oral Cultures of West Africa." *Cahier d' études Africaines* 11, no. 43 (1971): 455–66.

Goody, Jack. "Restricted Literacy in Northern Ghana." In *Literacy in Traditional Societies*, edited by Goody, 198–246. Cambridge: Cambridge University Press, 1975.

Goody, Jack. *The Social Organization of the Lo Wiili*. Oxford: Oxford University Press, 1967.

Goody, Jack. *Technology, Tradition and the State in West Africa*. Oxford: Oxford University Press, 1971.

Gravrand, P. R. "Le Gabou dans les traditions rales Sereer et Guelwar."In *Colloque sur les traditions orales du Gabou, special issue. Ethiopiques* (1980): 40–59.

Gray, J. M. *A History of The Gambia*. Cambridge: Cambridge University Press, 1940.

Gray, William. *Travels in West Africa in the Years, 1818, 19, 20, 21*. London: John Murray, 1825.

Green, Sandra. *Gender, Ethnicity and Social Change on the Upper Slave Coast*. Portsmouth, NH: Heinemann, 2009.

Griaule, Marcel. "L'alliance cathartique." *Africa* 18, no. 4 (1948): 242–58.

Griffeth, Robert. "The Dyula Impact on the Peoples of the West Volta Region." In *Papers on the Manding*, edited by Carleton T. Hodge, 166–81. Bloomington: Indiana University Press, 1971.

Guéye, Mbaye. "Les Guélowares et le Sine." *Éthiopiques* 28 (1981).

Haar, Gerrie Ter. *Imagining Evil: Witchcraft Beliefs and Accusations in Contemporary Africa*. Trenton, NJ: Africa World Press, 2007.

Halevi, Leor. *Muhammad's Grave: Death Rites and the Making of Islamic Society*. New York: Columbia University Press, 2007.

Hanka, Mulongo. "Oral Traditions in Historical Writings." In *Oral Traditions in Southern Africa*, . Lusaka, Zambia: Institute for African Studies, 1986.

Hanson, John. *Migration, Jihad, and Muslim Authority in West Africa: The Futanke Colonies of Kaarta*. Bloomington: Indiana University Press, 1996.

Hartell, Rhonda L., and John Bendor-Samuel. *The Niger-Congo Languages*. Dallas, TX: University Press of America, 1989.

Hassane, Moulaye. "Ajami in Africa: The Use of Arabic Script in the Transcription of African Languages." In *The Meanings of Timbuktu*, edited by Souleymane B. Diagne and Shanil Jeppie, 109–22. Dakar: CODESRIA/HSRC, 2008.

Hawthorne, Walter. *From Africa to Brazil: Culture, Identity and an Atlantic Slave Trade (1600–1830)*. Cambridge: Cambridge University Press, 2010.

Hawthorne, Walter. "Nourishing a Stateless Society during the Slave Trade: The Rise of Balanta Paddy Rice Production in Guinea-Bissau." *Journal of African History* 42, no. 1 (2000): 1–24.

Hawthorne, Walter. *Planting Rice and Harvesting Slaves: Transformations along the Guinea-Bissau Coast, 1400–1900*. Portsmouth, NH: Heinemann, 2003.

Hecquard, Hyacinthe. "Rapport sur un Voyage dans La Casamance." *Revue Coloniale* 6 (Paris, 1852).

Hecquard, Hyacinthe. *Voyage sur la Côte et dans L'Interieur de L'Afrique Occidentale.* Paris: Benard et compagnie, 1855.

Hegel, Frederik. *The Philosophy of History*. New York: Dover, 1985.

Herbst, Jeffrey. *States and Power in Africa: Contemporary Lessons in Authority and Control.* Princeton: Princeton University Press, 2000.

Hill, Joseph. *Wrapping Authority: Women Islamic Leaders in a Sufi Movement in Dakar, Senegal.* Toronto: University of Toronto Press, 2018.

Hiskett, Mervyn. *The Sword of Truth: Life and Times of the Sheku Usman Dan Fodio.* Evanston, IL: Northwestern University Press, 1994.

Hobsbawm, Eric, and Terence Ranger, eds. *The Invention of Tradition.* Cambridge: Cambridge University Press, 1983.

Hoffman, Barbara. *Griots at War: Conflict, Conciliation, and Caste in Mande.* Bloomington: Indiana University Press, 2000.

Holy Qur'an.

Hoppe, Kirk A. *Lords of the Fly: Sleeping Sickness Control in British East Africa (1900–1960).* Westport, CT: Praeger, 2003.

Horton, Robert. "On the Rationality of Conversion, Part One." *Africa* 45, no. 3 (1975): 219–35.

Horton, Robert. "Stateless Societies in the History of West Africa." In *History of West Africa*, edited by J. F. Adeajayi and Michael Crowder. New York: Longman, 1985.

Howard, Allen M., and Richard M. Shain. *The Spatial Factor in African History.* Leiden: Brill Academic Publishers, 2005.

Human Rights Watch. *Off the Backs of the Children: Forced Begging and Other Abuses against Talibés in Senegal.* April 15. New York: Human Rights Watch, 2010.

Hunter, Thomas C. "The Development of an Islamic Tradition of Learning among the Jakhanke of West Africa." PhD diss., University of Chicago, 1977.

Hunwick, John. "A Historical Whodunit: The So-Called 'Kano Chronicle' and Its Place in the Historiography of Kano." *History in Africa* 21 (1994): 127–46.

Hunwick, John. *Literacy and Scholarship in Muslim West Africa in the Pre-colonial Period.* Nsukka, Nigeria: Institution of African Studies, 1972.

Hunwick, John. *Timbuktu and the Songhay Empire: Al-Sadis'Tar'rikh al-sudan down to 1613 and Contemporary Documents.* Leiden: Brill, 2003.

Innes, Gordon. *Sunjata: The Three Mandinka Versions.* London: Routledge, 2001.

Isaacs, Harold. *The Idols of the Tribe: Group Identity and Political Change.* Cambridge: Harvard University Press, 1975.

Jansen, Jan. *Epopée, Histoire et Societé.* Paris: Karthala, 1987.

Janson, Marloes. *Islam, Youth and Modernity in the Gambia: The Tablighi Jama'at.* Cambridge: Cambridge University Press, 2013

Janson, Marloes. "Searching for God: Young Gambian Conversion to the Tabligh Jama'at." In *New Perspectives on Islam in Senegal: Conversion, Migration, Wealth, Power and Femininity*, edited by Mamadou Diouf and Mara Leitchman, 138–66. New York: Palgrave Macmillan, 2008.

Janson, Marloes. "We Are the Sauce on Top of the Rice." *Journal of Mande Studies* 8 (2006): 183–205.

Jeng, Alieu and Swindell, Kenneth. *Migrants, Credit and Climate: The Gambian Groundnut Trade, 1834–1934*. Leiden: Brill, 2006.

Jimoh, Lak. *Llorin: The Journey So Far*. Llorin, Nigeria, 1994.

Jobson, Richard. *The Golden Trade*. London: Dawsons of Pall Mall, 1623.

Johnson, Michele. "On the Road to Alijana: Reconfiguring Islam and 'Mandiga-ness' in the New African Diaspora." Paper Presented at the Annual Conference of the African Studies Association, Houston, 2001.

Johnson, William. *The Epic of Son-Jara*. Bloomington: Indiana University Press, 2003.

Jones, Rachel . "You Eat Beans! Kin-Based Joking Relationships, Obligations, and Identity in Urban Mali." Anthropology honor project, Macalester College (Saint Paul, MN), 2007.

Kaba, Lansiné. "The Pen, the Sword and the Crown: Islam and Revolution in Songhay Reconsidered, 1464–1493." *Journal of African History* 25, no. 3 (1984): 241–56.

Kaba, Lansiné. *The Wahhabiyya: Islamic Reform and Politics in French West Africa*. Evanston, IL: Northwestern University, 1973.

Kamara, Doudou. "La Societé Traditionnelle Mandinka et la Dynamique Intégrationniste." Paper presented at the Colloque International sur la Culture Mandingue comme Facteur d' intégration Ouest Africaine, Sédhiou, November 30-October 2, 1991.

Kane, Cheikh Amidou. *L'Aventure Ambigue*. Translated by Katherine Wood, London: Heinemann, 1972.

Kane, Omar. "Essai de Chronologie des Satigis au dix-huitiéme siècle." *Bulletin de l'Institut Fondamental d'Afrique Noire, Série B: Sciences humaines* 32, no. 3(1970): 755–65.

Kane, Ousmane Oumar. *Beyond Timbuktu: An Intellectual History of Muslims in West Africa*. Cambridge: Harvard University Press, 2016.

Kea, Pamela J. *Land, Labour and Entrustment: West African Female Farmers and the Politics of Difference*. Leiden: Brill, 2010.

Kesteloot, Lilyan. "Les Mandingues de Casamance: Kankurang, Castes et Kora." In *Pour Comprendre la Casamance: Chronique d'une Intégration Contrastée*, edited by Francois-George Barbier-Wiesser, 97–117. Paris: Karthala, 1994.

Khaldun, Ibn. *Muhaddimah*. Translated by N. J. Dawood. Princeton: Princeton University Press, 2015.

Ki Zerbo, Joseph. *Histoire Générale de l'Afrique*. Paris: Hatier, 1977.

Klein, Martin. *Islam and Imperialism in Senegal: Sine Saloum, 1847–1914*. Stanford: Stanford University Press, 1968.

Klein, Martin. "Social and Economic Factors in the Muslim Revolution in Senegambia." *Journal of African History* 13 (1972): 419–41.

Kopytoff, Igor. *The African Frontier: The Reproduction of Traditional African Societies*. Bloomington: Indiana University Press, 1987.

Korn, Francis. *Elementary Structures Reconsidered: Levi-Strauss on Kinship*. Berkeley: University of California Press, 1973.

Labat, Jean Baptiste. *Nouvelle Relation de l'Afrique Occidentale*. Paris: Pierre François Giffart, 1728.

Labouret, Henri. *Les Manding et Leur Langue*. Paris: Larose, 1934.

Lasnet, Alexandre. *Une Mission au Sénégal: Les Races du Sénégal, Sénégambie et Casamance*. Paris: Challamel, 1900.

Launay, Robert. *Beyond the Stream: Islam and Society in a West African Town*. Berkeley: University of California Press, 1992.

Launay, Robert, ed. *Islamic Education in Africa: Writing Boards and Blackboards*. Bloomington: Indiana University Press, 2016.

Launay, Robert. "Practical Joking." *Cahiers d'études africaines* 184 (2006).

Launay, Robert. *Traders without Trade: Responses to Changes in Two Dyula Communities*. Cambridge: Cambridge University Press, 1982.

Law, Robin. The *Horse in West Africa History*. Oxford: Oxford University Press, 1980.

Leary, Ann Frances. "Islam, Politics, and Colonialism: A Political History of Islam in the Casamance Region of Senegal, 1850–1914." PhD diss., Northwestern University, 1974.

Leary, Anne Frances. "The Role of the Mandinka in the Islamization of the Casamance, 1840–1901." In *Papers on the Manding*, edited by Carleton T. Hodge, 227–48. Bloomington: Indiana University Press, 1971.

Lee, Cronk. *From Mukogodo to Maasa: Ethnicity and Cultural Change in Kenya*. Boulder, CO: Westview, 2004.

Leichtman, Mara A. "The Authentication of a Discursive Islam." In *New Perspectives on Islam in Senegal: Conversion, Migration, Wealth, Power and Femininity*, edited by Mamadou Diouf and Mara Leichtman, 111–38. New York: Palgrave Macmillan, 2009.

Leichtman, Mara A. *Shi'i Cosmopolitanisms in Africa: Lebanese Migration and Religious Conversion in Senegal*. Bloomington: Indiana University Press, 2015.

Leinweber, Asley E. "The New Muslim Public School in the Democratic Republic of Congo." In *Islamic Education in Africa*, edited by Robert Launay, 149–69. Bloomington: Indiana University Press, 2016.

Lemos Coelho, Francisco de. *Description of the Coast of Guinea (1684)*. Translated by P. E. Hair. Unpublished document. Liverpool: University of Liverpool.

Lentz, Carola. *Ethnicity and the Making of History in Northwestern Ghana*. Edinburgh: Edinburgh University Press, 2006.

Lentz, Carola. *Land, Mobility, and Belonging in West Africa*. Bloomington: Indiana University Press, 2013.

Le Prince, Jules. "Notes sur deux Tribus de la Casamance." *Revue Coloniale, 33* (Paris: Librairie Maritime Coloniale, 1905), 513–27 and 581–605.

Levi-Strauss, Claude. *Les Structures Elementaires de la Parentée* [Elementary structures of kinship]. Paris: Presses Universitaires de France, 1949.

Levtzion, Nehemia. "Islam in the Bilad al-Sudan to 1800." In *History of Islam in Africa*, edited by Nehemia Levtzion and Randall L. Pouwels, 61–91. Athens: Ohio University Press, 2000.

Levtzion, Nehemia. "Merchants vs. Scholars and Clerics in West Africa: Differential and Complementary Roles." In *Rural and Urban Islam in West Africa*, edited by Nehemia Levtzion and Humphrey Fisher, 21–37. London: Lynne Rienner, 1987.

Levtzion, Nehemia, and Humphrey Fisher, eds. *Rural and Urban Islam in West* Africa. Boulder, CO: Lynne Rienner, 1987.

Levtzion, Nehemia, and Jay Spaulding. *Medieval West Africa*. Princeton, NJ: Markus Wiener Publishers, 2007.

Levtzion, Nehemia, Ivor Wilks, and Bruce Haight. *Chronicles from Gonja: A Tradition of West African Muslim Historiography*. Cambridge: Cambridge University Press, 1987.

Lévy-Bruhl, Lucien. *How Natives Think*. Princeton: Princeton University Press, 2008.

Linares, Olga. *Power, Prayer and Production: The Jola of Casamance, Senegal*. Cambridge: Cambridge University Press, 1992.

Llife, John. *A Modern History of Tanganyika*. Cambridge: Cambridge University Press, 1979.

Loimeier, Roman. "L'islam ne se vend pas: The Islamic Reform Groups and the State in Senegal." *Journal of Religion in Africa* 30, no. 2 (2000): 168–90.

Loimeier, Roman. "Muslim Scholars, Organic Intellectuals, and the Development of Islamic Education in Zanzibar in the Twentieth Century." In *Islamic Education in Africa: Writing Boards and Blackboards*, edited by Robert Launay, 137–48. Bloomington: Indiana University Press, 2016.

Lopes, Carlos. "Kabou and Its Neighbors: A Historical and Territorial Interpretation of Conflicts." *Journal of Mande Studies* 5 (2003): 113–26.

Lovejoy, Paul. *Jihad in West Africa during the Age of Revolution*. Athens: Ohio University Press, 2016.

Lovejoy, Paul. *Transformations of Slavery: A History of Slavery in Africa*. Cambridge: Cambridge University Press, 2000.

Lüpke Friederike. "Language and Identity Flux: In Search of Baïnounk." *Journal of Language Contact* 3, no. 1 (2010): 155–74.

Ly-Tall, Madina. "The Decline of the Mali Empire." In *General History of Africa 4: Africa from the Twelfth to the Sixteenth Century*, 172–86. Paris: International Scientific Committee for the Drafting of a General History of Africa, UNESCO, 1984.

Ly-Tall, Madina. *L'histoire du Mandé d'aprés le Jeli Kanku Madi Diabaté de Kela*. Bamako, Mali: Association SCOA pour la recherche scientifique en Afrique noire, 1987.

Ly-Tall, Madina. "Quelques Précisions sur les Relations entre l'empire du Mali et le Gabou." In "Colloque sur les Traditions Orales du Gabou," special issue, *Éthiopiques* (1980): 124–27.

Mack, Beverly B., and Jean Boyd. *One Woman's Jihad: Nana Asmau, Scholar and Scribe*. Bloomington: Indiana University Press, 2000.

Maclean, Lauren M. "The Everyday, Local, and Informal Sources of Ethnic Identity

Construction in African Politics." Paper presented at the Mellon Sawyer Seminar, "Ethnicity in Africa: Historical, Comparative, and Contemporary Investigations," University of Michigan, Ann Arbor, December 2010.

Magassouba, Moriba. *L'islam au Senegal: Demain les Mollah*. Paris: Karthala, 1985.

Manchuelle, François. *Willing Migrants: Soninke Labor Diasporas, 1848–1960*. Athens: Ohio University Press, 1977.

Mané, Idrissa. "Les 'Ibadou' du Senegal: Logiques Religieuses, Logiques Identitaires." Thése de doctorat en éthnologie, Université de Pau, 2018. http://www.theses.fr/2018PAUU1049/document

Mark, Peter. *A Cultural, Economic, and Religious History of the Basse Casamance since 1500*. Stuttgart: Franz Steiner, 1985.

Mark, Peter. *"Portuguese" Style and Luso-African Identity: Precolonial Senegambia, Sixteenth-Nineteenth Centuries*. Bloomington: Indiana University Press, 2002.

Mark, Peter. "The Rubber and Palm Produce Trade and the Islamization of the Joola Boulouf, 1800–1940." *Bulletin de l'Institut Fondamental d'Afrique Noire, Série B: Sciences humaines* 39 (1977): 34–61.

Mark, Peter. "The Senegambian Horned Mask: History and Provenance." *Art Bulletin* 69, no. 4 (1987): 626–40,

Mark, Peter. *The Wild Bull and the Sacred Forest: Forms, Meaning and Change in Senegambian Initiation Masks*. Cambridge: Cambridge University Press, 1992.

Martin, Susan M. *Palm Oil and Protest: An Economic History of the Ngawa Region, Southeast Nigeria, 1800–1980*. Cambridge: Cambridge University Press, 1988.

Marty, Paul. "Les Mandingues, Element Islamisé de la Casamance." *Revue du Monde Musulman* 31 (Paris, 1915): 443–68.

Marty, Paul. *Etudes sur L'Islam au Sénégal: Les Personnes*. Book 1. Paris: Ernest Leroux, 1917.

Marty, Paul. *Etudes sur L'Islam au Sénégal: Les Doctrines et les Institutions*. Book 2. Paris: Ernest Leroux, 1917.

Marty, Paul. "Cherif Younuss de Casamance." *Revue du Monde Musulman* (Paris, 1915): 431–69.

Marty, Paul. *Islam en Guinée: Fuuta Diallon*. Paris: Ernest Leroux, 1921.

Marut, Jean. C. *Le Conflit de Casamance: Ce que Disent les Armes*. Paris: Karthala, 2010.

Mbacké, Khadim. *Etudes Islamiques: Daaras et Droit de L Enfant*. Dakar: Publifan, 1994.

Mbacké, Khadim. "Le rôle du Mouvement réformiste dans le developpement du Senegal au vingtiéme siécle." *Africa* 57, no. 1 (2002): 87–101.

Mbacké, Khadim. *Sufism and Religious Brotherhoods in Senegal*. Edited by John Hunwick and translated by Eric Ross. Princeton, NJ: Markus Wiener Publishers, 2005.

Mbaye, Rawane. "L'Islam au Sénégal." Thése de doctorat troisiéme cycle, Department d'Arabe, Université de Dakar, 1975.

Mbiti, John. *African Religions and Philosophy, Second Edition*. Portsmouth, NH: Heinemann, 1990.

Mbow, Penda. "L'islam et la Femme Sénégalaise." *Éthiopiques* 66–67, no. 2 (2001).

Mbow, Penda. "Secularism, Religious Education, and Human Rights in Senegal." *Institute for the Study of Islamic Thought in Africa Working Paper No. 09-007*. Evanston, IL: Northwestern University, 2009.

McCann, James C. "Climate and Causation in African History." *International Journal of African Historical Studies* 32, no. 3 (1999): 261–70.

McIntosh, Susan K. *Beyond Chiefdoms: Pathways to Complexity in Africa*. Cambridge: Cambridge University Press, 2005.

Mollien, Gaspard. *Travels in the Interior of Africa to the Sources of the Senegal and Gambia*. London: E. Bowdich, 1820.

Mommersteeg, Geert. "Learning the Word of God: The Primitive City of Timbuktu." *Saudi Aramco World Magazine* 42 (1991): 2–11.

Monteil, Charles. *Les Kassonké: Monographie d'une Peuplade du Soudan Français*. Paris: Ernest Leroux, 1915.

Moodie, Dumbar. *Going for Gold: Men, Mining, and Migrations*. Berkeley: University of California, 1994.

Moore, Francis. *Travels into the Inland Parts of Africa*. London: E. Cave, 1738.

Mouser, Bruce L. "Landlords and Strangers: A Process of Accommodation." *International Journal of African Historical Studies* 8, no. 3 (1975): 425–40.

Murphy, William, and Caroline H. Bledsoe. "The Importance of Being First: Kingship and Territory in the History of a Kpelle Chiefdom (Liberia)." In *The African Frontier: The Reproduction of Traditional African Societies*, edited by Igor Kopytoff, 123–48. Bloomington: Indiana University Press, 1987.

Ndiaye, Gana. "Private Islamic Education in Africa." In *The Palgrave Handbook of Islam in Africa*, edited by Fallou Ngom, Mustapha H. Kurfy, and Toyin Falola, 577–98. London: Palgrave Macmillan, 2020.

Neuwinger, Hans D. *African Ethnobotany*. London: Chapman and Hall, 1966.

Ngaïdé, Abderrahmane. "Domination politique et Influences socioculturelles des mandingues sur les Peuls du Fuladu (Kold-Senegal)." In *Peuls et Mandingues: Dialectique des constructions identitaires*, edited by Mirjam Bruijn and Han van Dijk, 147–64. Paris: Karthala, 1997.

Ngaïdé, Abderrahmane. *L'esclave, le colon et le marabout: Le Royaume Peul du Fuladu de 1867 á 1936*. Paris: L'Harmattan, 2012.

Ngaïdé, Abderrahmane. "Les Marabouts face à La Modernité: Le Dental de Madina Gounass á l'épreuve." In *Le Sénégal Contemporain*, edited by Momar Coumba Diop, 617–52. Paris: Karthala, 2002.

Ngom, Birame. *La Question Guélwar et l'Histoire du Siin: Mémoire de Diplôme d'études Appronfondies*. Dakar: Université Cheikh Anta Diop, 1987.

Ngom, Fallou. *Muslims beyond the Arab World: The Odyssey of Ajami and the Muridiyya*. Oxford: Oxford University Press, 2016.

Niane, Djibril T. *Histoire des Mandingues de l'Ouest*. Paris: Karthala, 1989.

Niane, Djibril T. *Soundiata ou l'Epopée Mandingue*. Paris: Karthala, 1960.

Nicholson, Sharon E. "Climatic Variations in the Sahel and Other Regions during the Past Five Centuries." *Journal of Arid Environments* 1, no. 1 (1978): 3–24.

Nigro, Jenna. "Colonial Logics: Agriculture, Commercial, and Moral Experiments in the Making of French Senegal, 1763–1870." PhD diss., University of Illinois at Chicago, 2013.

Nnoruga, James N. "Fisher's Historical Approach to the Religious Change in Igboland." *African Journal of Multidisciplinary Research* 15, no. 1 (2020): 72–85.

Nobili, Mauro. "Reinterpreting the Role of Muslims in the West African Middle Ages." *Journal of African History* 61, no. 3 (2021): 1–60.

O'Fahey, R. S. "Islam, State, and Society in Dar Fur." In *Conversion to Islam*, edited by Nehemia Levtzion, 189–206. New York: Holmes and Meier, 1979.

Osborn, Emily L. *Our New Husbands Are Here: Households, Gender, and Politics in a West African State from the Slave Trade to Colonial Rule*. Athens: Ohio University Press, 2011.

Owohaene-Acheampong, Stephen, and Charles Prempeh. "Contemporary Zongo Communities in Accra Interfaith Marriages: The Case of Muslims and Christians in Accra." *African Studies Quarterly* 19, no. 1 (2020): 23–40.

*Pakao-al -Kitabo*. [The holy book of Pakao]. Manuscript (no specific authors).

Park, Mungo. *Les Trois Voyages de Mungo Park au Maroc et dans L'Interieur de L'Afrique, 1787–1804*. Paris: M. Dreyfous, 1882.

Park, Mungo. *Travels to the Interior Districts of Africa*. Durham: Duke University Press, 2000.

Patton, Adell. "An Islamic Frontier Polity: The Niger Mountains of Northern Nigeria, 1846–1902." In *The African Frontier: The Reproduction of Traditional African Societies*, edited by Igor Kopytoff, 195–213. Bloomington: Indiana University Press, 1987.

Pawlikova-Vilhanova, Viera. "Islam and Christianity in Africa." In *Palgrave Handbook of Islam in Africa*, edited by Fallou Ngom, Mustapha H. Kurfy, and Toyin Falola, 233–51. Cham, Switzerland: Palgrave Macmillan, 2020.

Peel, J. D. Y. *Christianity, Islam, and Orisa-Religion: Three Traditions in Comparison and Interaction*. Oakland: University of California Press, 2015.

Pélissier, Paul. "Les Paysans du Sénégal." Thése de doctorat de geographie, Sorbonne, 1966.

Pélissier, Paul. *Les Paysans du Sénégal: Les civilisations agraires du Cayor à La Casamance*. Saint Yrieix: Imprimerie Faberge, 1966.

Pereira, Duarte Pacheco. *Esmeraldo De Situ Orbis*. Translated and edited by G. H. T. Kimble. London: Hakluyt Society, 1937.

Person, Yves. "The Coastal Peoples: From Casamance to the Ivory Coast Lagoons." *General History of Africa* 4 (1982): 301–23.

Person, Yves. "Les Problémes de l'histoire du Gabou." In "Actes du Colloque sur les Traditions Orales du Gabou," special issue, *Éthiopiques* (1980): 60–71.*

Peters, Rudolph. *Jihad in Classical and Modern Islam*. Princeton, NJ: Markus Wiener Publishers, 1995.

Pope John Paul II. *On Human Work*. Rome: Liberia Editrice Vaticano, 1981.

Post, Arjan. "A Glimpse of Surface in the Circle of Ibn Taymiyya." *Journal of Sufi Studies* (2016): 156–87.

Quinn, Charlotte. *The Mandingo Kingdoms of Senegambia: Traditionalism, Islam and European Expansion*. Evanston, IL: Northwestern University Press, 1972.

Quinn, Charlotte. *Pride, Faith and Fear*. Oxford: Oxford University Press, 2003.

Radcliffe, A. R. "On Joking Relationships." *Africa: Journal of International African Institute* 13, no. 3 (1940): 195–210.

Raffenel, Anne. *Voyage dans l'Afrique Occidentale, 1843–44*. Paris: Arthus Bertrand, 1846.

Ranger, Terrence. "The Invention of Tradition in Colonial Africa." In *The Invention of Tradition*, edited by Eric Hobsbawm and Terence Ranger, 211–62. Cambridge: Cambridge University Press, 1983.

Ray, Benjamin. *African Religions: Symbol, Ritual, and Community*. New Jersey: Prentice-Hall, 2000.

Reichmuth, Stephan. "Islamic Learning and its Interaction: Western Education in Ilorin, Nigeria." In *Muslim Identity and Social Change in Sub-Saharan Africa*, edited by Louis Brenner, 127–50. Bloomington: Indiana University Press, 1993.

Reid, Richard. "Past and Presentism: The 'Precolonial' and the Foreshortening of African History." *Journal of African History* 2, no. 2 (2011): 135–55.

Roberts, Richard. *Warriors, Merchants, and Slaves: The State and the Economy of the Middle Niger Valley, 1770–1914*. Stanford: Stanford University Press, 1987.

Robinson, David. *Chiefs and Clerics: Abdul Bokar Kan and Futa Toro, 1853–1891*. Oxford: Oxford University Press, 1975.

Robinson, David. "France as a Muslim Power in West Africa." *Africa Today* 46, nos. 3–4 (Summer/Autumn 1999): 105–27.

Robinson, David. *The Holy War of Umar Tal: The Western Sudan in the Mid-Nineteenth Century*. Oxford: Oxford University Press, 1985.

Robinson, David. *Muslim Societies in African History*. Cambridge: Cambridge University, 2004.

Robinson, David. *Paths of Accommodation: Muslim Societies and French Colonial Authorities in Senegal and Mauritania, 1880–1920*. Athens: Ohio University Press, 2000.

Robinson, David. "Revolutions in the Western Sudan." In *The History of Islam in Africa*, by Nehemia Levtzion and Randall L. Pouwels, 130–52. Athens: Ohio University Press, 2000.

Roche, Christian. *Histoire de la Casamance: Conquête et Résistance, 1850–1920*. Paris: Karthala, 1985.

Roche, Christian. *La Casamance Face à son Destin*. Paris: L'Harmattan, 2015.

Roche, Christian. "Portraits des Chefs Casamançais du dix-neuviéme siécle." *Revue Française d' histoire d' outré-mer* (1970): 451–67.

Rodney, Walter. *A History of the Upper Guinea Coast (1545–1800)*. New York: Monthly Review Press, 1970.

Ross, Eric. *Sufi City: Urban Designs and Archetypes in Tuba*. Rochester: University of Rochester Press, 2006.

Sadio, Balla M. "Les Balante de Gan-JAA (BIJAA-N'GAnJAA): Répartition spatiale, Organisation sociale et administrative, Evolution socio-culturelle et Politique: De l'éviction des Bainounk á la mise en place de l' Administration Coloniale, 1830–1899." Mémoire de maîtrise (master's thesis), Université Cheikh Anta Diop, Dakar, 2002.

Sadio, Sény. "Le Peuple de Beeja ou Balante: Du Périple á la Sédentarisation." Mémoire de maîtrise (master's thesis), Université Cheikh Anta Diop, Dakar, 2006

Sagna, S. Séga. *La Casamance, l'Islam et la France*. Paris: L'Harmattan, 2017.

Sagna, S. Séga. "La Longue Marche de l'islam en Casamance." *Lettres d'Ivoire* 3 (2007): 147–64.

Saho, Balla S. K. "The Appropriation of Islam in a Gambian Village: Life and Times of Shaykh Maas Khah, 1827–1936." *African Studies Quarterly* 12 (2010): 1–21.

Samb, Amar. "L'islam et le Ngabou." In "Colloque International sur les Traditions Orales du Gabu," special issue, *Éthiopiques* 28 (1980): 116–23.*

Samba, Moussa P. "Makhili Gassama: L'African." *Journal Xalima.com*, April 13, 2008.

Sambou, Kaussou. *Recueil des Traditions Orales des Mandingues de Gambie et de Casamance*. Bloomington: Indiana University Press, 2009.

Sambou, Saliou. *La Légende d' Aguéne et de Diambone*. Dakar: Niamagne Editions, 2005.

Sanneh, Lamin. *Beyond Jihad: The Pacifist Tradition of West African Islam*. Athens: Ohio University Press, 2016.

Sanneh, Lamin. *The Crown and the Turban: Muslims and West African Pluralism*. London: Routledge, 1996.

Sanneh, Lamin. *The Jahanke Muslim Clerics: A Religious and Historical Study of Islam in Senegambia*. New York: University Press of America, 1989.

Santerre, Roger. *Pédagogie Musulmane d' Afrique Noire: L'école Coranique Peule du Cameroun*. Montreal: Presse de l'Université de Montréal, 1973.

Sapir, David. *A Grammar of Diola-Fogny: A Language Spoken in the Basse Casamance Region of Senegal*. Cambridge: Cambridge University Press, 1965.

Sarr, Assan. "Islamic Philosophy in Africa." In *Palgrave Handbook of Islam in Africa*, edited by Fallou Ngom, Mustapha H. Kurfi, and Toyin Falola. Cham, Switzerland: Palgrave Macmillan, 2020.

Sarr, Assan. *Islam, Power, and Dependency in the Gambia River Basin: The Politics of Land Control, 1790–1940*. Rochester: University of Rochester Press, 2016.

Sarr, Assan. "Islam, Spirits, and the History of a Toranka Cleric in The Gambia c. 1890–1990." Paper presented at the Annual Conference of the African Studies AssociationSan Diego, November 2015.

Saul, Mahir. "Stratification and Leveling in the Farming Economy of a Voltaic Village." PhD diss., Indiana University, 1982.

Schaffer, Matt. "Bound to Africa." *History of Africa* 32 (2005): 321–69.

Schaffer, Matt. *Djinns, Stars and Warriors: Mandinka Legends from Pakao, Senegal.* Leiden: Brill, 2003.

Schaffer, Matt. *Mandinko: The Ethnography of a West African Holy Land.* Waveland, IL: Prospect Heights Press, 1980.

Schaffer, Matt. "'Pakao Book': An Introduction to Pakao Expansion and Social Structure by Virtue of an Indigenous Manuscript." *African Languages* (1975): 96–123.

Schaffer, Matt. "A Study of a Social Process among a Mandinko People of the Senegambia." PhD diss., University of Oxford, 1976.

Schapera, Isaac. "Marriage of Near Kin among the Twana." *Africa* 27, no. 2 (1957): 139–59.

Searing, James. "The Greater Jihad and Conversion: Sereer Interpretations of Sufi Islam in Senegal" In *New Perspectives on Islam in Senegal: Conversion, Migration, Wealth, Power and Femininity*, edited by Mamadou Diouf and Mara Leichtman, 91-110. New York: Palgrave Macmillan, 2009.

Searing, James. "Conversion to Islam: Military Recruitment and Generational Conflict in a Sereer-Safen Village (Bandia), 1920–38." *Journal of African History* 44 (2003): 73–94. .

Searing, James. *"God Alone Is King": Islam and Emancipation in Senegal; The Wolof Kingdoms of Kajoor and Bawol, 1859–1914.* Portsmouth, NH: Heinemann, 2002.

Searing, James. "No Kings, No Lords, No Slaves: Ethnicity and Religion among the Sereer-Safen of Western Bawol, 1700–1914." *Journal of African History* 43 (2002): 407–29.

Searing, James. "Time of Conversion: Christians and Muslims among the Sereer-Safen of Senegal, 1914–1950s." In *Muslim-Christian Encounters*, edited by Bejamin F. Soares, 115–91. Leiden: Brill, 2006.

Searing, James. *West African Slavery and Atlantic Commerce: The Senegal River Valley, 1700–1860.* Cambridge: Cambridge University Press, 1993.

Seck, Assane. "La Moyenne Casamance: Etude de Géographie Physique." *Revue de Géographie Alpine* 43–44 (1955): 707–55.

Seck, Assane. *Sénégal, Emergence d' une Démocratie Moderne.* Paris: Karthala, 2005.

Seck, Ibrahima. "The Relationships between Saint Louis, Its Hinterlands, and Colonial Louisiana." Translated by Joanna E. Burnett. In *French Colonial Louisiana and the Atlantic World*, edited by Bradley G. Bond, 265–90. Baton Rouge: Louisiana State University Press, 2005.

Seck, Mamarame. *Narratives as Muslim Practice in Senegal.* New York: Peter Lang, 2013.

Seesemann, Rüdiger. "Changes in Islamic Knowledge Practices in Twentieth Century Kenya." In *Islamic Education in Africa: Writing Boards and Blackboards*, edited by Robert Launay, 212–33. Bloomington: Indiana University Press, 2016.

Seesemann, Rüdiger. "Sufism in West Africa." *Religion Compass* 4, no. 10 (2010): 606–14.

Semley, Denise. "Kétu Identities: Islam, Gender, and French Colonialism in West Africa, 1850s-1860s." PhD diss., Northwestern University, 2002.

Shaw, Thurstan, et al. *The Archaeology of Africa.* London: Routledge, 1995.

Skinner, David E. *States, Conflict, and Islam: A Reconsideration of Jihād in the Gambia River Region, 1850–1900*. Evanston, IL: PAS/ISITA Working Papers 2, 2017.

Smith, Etienne. "La Nation par le côté: Politique des Cousinages au Senegal." *Cahier d'études Africaines* 184 (2006): 907–65.

Smith, Etienne, and Cécile Canut. "Pactes, Alliances et Plaisanteries." *Cahier d'études Africaines* 46, no. 184 ( 2006): 687–754.

Smith, Mary F. *Baba of Kano: A Woman of the Muslim Hausa*. New Haven: Yale University Press, 1954.

Smith, Pierre. "Les Jahanke, Histoire d'une Dispersion." *Bulletins et Mémoires de la Société d' Anthropologie* (1965).

Soares, Benjamin F. *Islam and the Prayer Economy: History and Authority in a Malian Town*. Ann Arbor: University of Michigan Press, 2005.

Soares, Benjamin F. "Muslim Saints in the Age of Neoliberalism in Producing African Futures." In *Ritual and Reproduction in a Neoliberal Age*, edited by Brad Weiss, 79–105. Leiden: Brill, 2004.

Soares, Benjamin F. "New Muslim Public Figures in West Africa." In *Islamic Education in Africa: Writing Boards and Blackboards*, edited by Robert Launay, 268–84. Bloomington: Indiana University Press, 2016.

Souané, Fossar. "Les Mandingues de la Moyenne Casamance: Evolution Economique, Politique et Sociale, 1837–1900." Mémoire de maîtrise (master's thesis). Université Cheikh Anta Diop, Dakar, 1990.

Sounaye, Abdoulaye. "Walking to the Makaranta: Production, Circulation, and the Transmission of Islamic Learning in Urban Niger." In *Islamic Education in Africa: Writing Boards and Blackboards*, edited by Robert Launay, 234–52. Bloomington: Indiana University Press, 2016.

Spaulding, Jay. *Medieval West Africa*. Princeton, NJ: Markus Wiener Publishers, 2007.

Spaulding, Jay. "Precolonial Islam in the Eastern Sudan." In *History of Islam in Africa*, edited by Nehemia Levtzion and Randall L. Pouwels, 115–29. Athens: Ohio University Press, 2000.

Spear, Thomas. "Neo-traditionalism and the Limits of Invention in British Colonial Africa." *Journal of African History* 44 (2003): 3–27.

Stewart, Charles. *Islam and Social Order in Mauritania: A Case Study from the Nineteenth Century*. Oxford: Clarendon Press, 1973.

Sweet, James. *Culture, Kingship, and Religion in the African-Portuguese World (1441–1770): Recreating Africa*. Chapel Hill: University of North Carolina Press, 2003.

Swindell, Kenneth, and Alieu Deng. *Migrants, Credits and Climate*. Boston: Brill, 2006.

Syed, Amir. "*Between Jihād and History: Reconceptualizing the Islamic Revolutions of West Africa." In Palgrave Handbook of Islam in Africa*, edited by Fallou Ngom, Mustapha H. Kurfy, and Toyin Falola, 93116. Cham, Switzerland: Palgrave Macmillan, 2020.

Syed, Amir. "Al-Hajji Umar Tal and the Realm of the Written: Mastery, Mobility, and

Islamic Authority in Nineteenth-Century West Africa." PhD diss., University of Michigan, 2017.

Tamari, Tal. "The Development of Caste Systems in West Africa." *Journal of African History* 32 (1991): 221–50.

Tamari, Tal. "Styles of Islamic Education: Perspectives from Mali, Guinea, and The Gambia." In *Islamic Education in Africa: Writing Boards and Blackboards*, edited by Robert Launay, 29–60. Bloomington: Indiana University Press, 2016.

Tandjigora, Abdou K. *Colonisation et Inégalités au Sénégal: Le Boundou et le Gadiaga, 1885–1985*. Paris: L'Harmattan, 2015.

Tayob, Abdulkader. *Islam in South Africa: Mosques, Imams, and Sermons*. Gainesville: University of Florida Press, 1999.

Temudo, Marina Padrao. "From the Margins of the State to the Presidential Palace: The Balanta Case in Guinea-Bissau." *African Studies Review* 52, no. 2 (2009): 47–67.

Tendeng, Antoine. *Les Sources de l'Histoire de La Casamance aux Archives du Sénégal, 1816–1920*. Dakar: Archives du Senegal, 1974.

Thiam, Iba D. "Les Daaras au Sénégal: Rétrospective Historique." *Alfiyahi.org*, March 2013.

Thomas, Louis V. *La Mort Africaine*. Paris: Payot, 1982.

Thomson, Steven. "Revisiting 'Mandingization' in Coastal Gambia and Casamance ( Senegal): Four Approaches to Ethnic Change." *African Studies Review* 54, no. 2 (2011): 95–121.

Thornell, Christina. *La Vitalité de la Langue Balant-ganja au Senegal*. Dallas, TX: SIL International, 2019.

Thornton, John. "Ethnicity in Pre-colonial Africa." Paper presented at the Mellon Sawyer Seminar on "Ethnicity in Africa: Historical, Comparative, and Contemporary Investigations," University of Michigan, Ann Arbor, December, 2010.

Thurston, Alexander. "Colonial Control, Nigerian Agency, Arab Outreach, and Islamic Education in Northern Nigeria." In *Islamic Education in Africa: Writing Boards and Blackboards*, edited by Robert Launay, 119–36. Bloomington: Indiana University Press, 2016.

Thurston, Alexander. *Salafism in Nigeria*. Cambridge: Cambridge University Press, 2016.

Touré, Lamine. "Etudes des Valeurs chez les Manding de Casamance (au sud du Sénégal): Enquête Réalisée á partir des Chants." Thése de doctorat, Université Assane Seck (Ziguinchor), 2022.

Traoré, Makhroufi Ousmane. *Assassinations, Affections, and Negotiations: The Soninke People of Senegambia in the Atlantic Slave Trade, 1732–1848* (forthcoming).

Traoré, Makhroufi Ousmane. *Slavery, Resistance and Identity in Early Modern West Africa: The Ethnic-State of Gajaaga*. Cambridge: Cambridge University Press, 2023.

Triaud, Jean L. "Islam in Africa under French Colonial Rule." In *The History of Islam in Africa*, edited by Nehemia Levtzion and Randall L. Pouwels, 169–88. Athens: Ohio University Press, 2000.

Triaud, Jean L. "Quelques remarques sur l'islamisation du Mali des origines à 1300." *Bulletin de l'Institut Fondamental d'Afrique Noire, Série B: Sciences humaines* 30, no. 4 (1968): 13–35.

Triaud, Jean L., and David Robinson, eds. *Le Temps des Marabouts: Itinéraires et Stratégies Islamiques en Afrique Occidentale Française, 1880–1960*. Paris: Karthala, 1997.

Trimingham, J. Spencer. *Islam in West Africa*. Oxford: Oxford University Press, 1959.

Umar, Muhammad S. "Islamic Education and the Intellectual Pedigree of Al-Hajji Umar Falke." In *Islamic Education in Africa: Writing Boards and Blackboards*, edited by Robert Launay, 79–91. Bloomington: Indiana University Press, 2016.

Umar, Muhammad S. "Mass Islamic Education and the Emergence of Female Ulema in Northern Nigeria: Background, Trends and Consequences." In *Transmission of Learning in Islamic Africa*, edited by Reese Scott, 99–120. Leiden: Brill, 2009.

Vallon, Aristide. "La Casamance, Dépendence du Sénégal." *Revue Maritime Coloniale* Tome 6, October–December. (Paris, 1862): 456–74.

Villard, André. *Histoire du Sénégal*. Dakar: Maurice Vial, 1943.

Waller, Richard, and Thomas Spear. *Being Maasai*. Athens: Ohio University Press, 1993.

Wane, Yaya. "Ceerno Muhamadu Sayed Baa: Le Soufisme Intégral de Médina Gunass (Sénégal)." *Cahiers d' Etudes Africaines* 14, no. 56 (1974): 67–98.

Wane, Yaya. *Les Toucouleur du Fouta Tooro: Stratéfication Sociale et Structure Familiale*. Dakar: I.F.A.N., 1966.

Ware, Rudolph T., III. "Knowledge, Faith, and Power: A History of Quranic Schooling in Twentieth-Century Senegal." PhD diss., University of Pennsylvania, 2004.

Ware, Rudolph T., III. "Njangaan: The Daily Regime of Qur'anic Students in Twentieth-Century Senegal." *International Journal of African Historical Study* 37, no. 3 (2014): 515–38.

Ware, Rudolph T., III. *The Walking Qur'an: Islamic Education, Embodied Knowledge, and History in West Africa*. Chapel Hill: University of North Carolina Press, 2014.

Ware, Rudolph T., III, and Robert Launay, eds. "How (Not) to Read the Qur'an? Logics of Islamic Education in Senegal and Côte d'Ivoire." Translated by Robert Launay. In *Islamic Education in Africa: Writing Boards and Blackboards*, edited by Robert Launay, 255–68. Bloomington: Indiana University Press, 2016.

Ware, Rudolph T., III, Zachary Wright, and Amir Syed. *Jihad of the Pen: The Sufi Literature of West Africa*. Cairo: American University in Cairo Press, 2018.

Wariboko, Nimi. "Robin W. G. Horton (1932–2019): His Life and Work." *Journal of the International African Institute* 90, no. 4 (2020): 822–30.

Weil, Paul. "The Mask Figure and Social Control: The Mandinka Case." *Africa* 41, no. 4 (1971): 279–93.

Wiley, Katherine Ann. "Joking Market Women: Critiquing and Negotiating Gender and Social Hierarchy in Kankossa, Mauritania." *Africa* 84, no. 1 (2014): 101–18.

Wilks, Ivor. "The Juula and the Expansion of Islam into the Forest." In *The History of Islam in Africa*, edited by Nehemia Levtzion and Randall L. Pouwels, 93–108. Athens: Ohio University Press, 2000.

Wilks, Ivor. "The Transmission of Islamic Learning in the Western Sudan." In *Literacy in Traditional Societies*, edited by Jack Goody, 162–97. Cambridge: Cambridge University Press, 1975.

Wilks, Ivor, Nehemia Levtzion, and Bruce Haight. *Chronicles from Gonja: A Tradition of West Africa Muslim Historiography*. Cambridge: Cambridge University Press, 1987.

Willis, John R. "Introduction: Diffusion of Islam." In *Studies in West African Islamic History*, vol. 1, *The Cultivators of Islam*, edited by Willis, 1–39. London: Frank Cass, 1979.

Willis, John R. "Reflections on the Diffusion of Islam in West Africa." In *Studies in West African Islamic History*, vol. 1, *The Cultivators of Islam*, edited by Willis, 1–39. London: Frank Cass, 1979.

Willis, John R. *Studies in West African Islamic History*. Vol. 1, *The Cultivators of Islam*, edited by Willis. London: Frank Cass, 1979.

Wise, Christopher. *Ta' rikh al-Fattash: Timbuktu Chronicles 1493–1599*. Translated by Al Hajj Mahmud Kati, edited by Wise. Trenton, NJ: Africa World Press, 2011.

Wright, Donald. *The World and a Very Small Place in Africa: A History of Globalization in Niumi, The Gambia*. New York: M. E. Sharpe, 2000.

Wright, Zachary Valentine. *Living Knowledge in West African Islam: The Sufi Community of Ibrahim Niasse*. Leiden: Brill, 2015.

Wright, Zachary. "The Sufi Scholarship of Islamic West Africa." In *Jihad of the Pen: The Sufi Literature of West Africa*, edited by Rudolph Ware, Zachary Wright, and Amir Syed, 1–24. Cairo: American University of Cairo Press, 2018.

Yang, Philip. *Ethnic Studies: Issues and Approaches*. New York: State University of New York. Press, 2000.

# INDEX

*Note:* Page numbers in italics indicate figures and tables.